JAMES JOYCE AND MEDICINE

J. B. LYONS

JAMES JOYCE
&
MEDICINE

THE DOLMEN PRESS

Set and printed in the Republic of Ireland by the Dolmen Press Limited,
8 Herbert Place, Dublin 2

Designed by Liam Miller

SBN 85105 229 0

*Distributed outside Ireland, except in
Canada and in the United States of America
by Oxford University Press*

CONTENTS

LIST OF ILLUSTRATIONS

Between pages 112 and 113

You, James Joyce, lonely to-night in Zürich listening to the roar of the lions and hoping perhaps for the sound of children in boats off Killiney strand or for the call of seagulls around the head of Howth in the early morning. You, artist-father, lonely to-night because you went too early for our love, turning away from us before we could say, Yes, YES!

James Liddy—*Esau My Kingdom for a Drink.*

PREFACE

Anyone who proposes to add to the existing library of Joyceana should recall Patrick Kavanagh's minatory question, with its revealing answer:

Who killed James Joyce?
I, said the commentator,
I killed James Joyce for my graduation.

In the present instance graduation is not my purpose; the book takes its origin from the conviction that a clinical examination of the author's life will add to our comprehension of his writings and to a more compassionate understanding of his angularities of personality.

One of the earliest commentaries on *Ulysses* was written by Joseph Collins, an American medical practitioner, but Dr. Collins did not refer to the wealth of medical allusion in Joyce's writings. C. G. Jung compared the famous novel to a tape-worm in an uncomplimentary analysis in 1932. Joyce's ocular disorder has been briefly discussed by Dr. W. J. Ford and by Dr. Carl Sasse. A more detailed account is to be found in Dr. N. Fabricant's *Thirteen Famous Patients*. A South American doctor has written an article James Joyce Y La Medicina.[1]

Apart from these publications, a mere handful in comparison with the number of books and articles on Joyce which have been written since his death, I have been unable to find any clinical studies of Joyce despite the fact that his adult life was one protracted illness. The terms of reference of the present study of Joyce and medicine include the author's illhealth, physical and emotional (the latter necessitating a detailed account of his family history and early traumatic environment); his ineffectual attempt to study medicine; the raffish companions of that period, particularly Oliver St. John Gogarty who influenced him so strongly; the use of medical jargon and the depiction of illnesses and anatomy in Joyce's writings.

Joyce's ambivalence towards his father is understandable; his disagreement with his mother over religion caused him great unhappiness and in due course he was himself a most devoted father who suffered endlessly because of his daughter's mental illness.

He described himself as 'inclined to alcoholism' and the degree of this tendency (which fortunately he managed to keep within reasonable control) as well as his strong vein of sexuality—it is not fanciful to suggest that the Penelope episode is the expression of Joyce's sex fantasy—and penchant for obscenity are dealt with in later chapters. Finally, the stomach disorder which plagued him and baffled his doctors and eventually killed him is considered in appropriate detail.

Perhaps I should explain that in a study of this kind—as in any diagnostic work-up—abnormal reactions receive paramount attention. An endeavour is made in the last chapter, 'Post Mortem', to offset this possibly lopsided approach.

1. The focus of interest in the articles of Hazel Samilowitz, M.D., Yves Gandon, and Vintila Horia (published in *Psychiatric Communications*, *Hippocrate*, and *Tribuna Medica* respectively) is literary rather than medical.

Edward Brandabur's pyschoanalytical study, *A Scrupulous Meanness*, did not reach me until my book had gone to press.

CHAPTER I

A DISAFFECTED YOUTH

James Augustine Joyce, son of John Stanislaus Joyce formerly of Cork and his wife Mary Jane, née Murray, was born in 41, Brighton Square,[1] Rathgar, Dublin on 2 February 1882. Before long the family moved from the well-to-do suburb to a pleasant coastal town some miles from Dublin and his first memories may have been of their new home, 1, Martello Terrace, Bray. 'It was cold and dark under the seawall beside his father's house. But the kettle would be on the hob to make punch.'

As a toddler he had more than the usual share of self-assurance. When relatives turned up unexpectedly on a day when his father and mother were away he entertained them, singing and vamping on the piano. Naturally he felt himself to be the very centre of his world and as a very tiny tot, coming downstairs from the nursery a step at a time, clutching a nursemaid's hand, to join his parents at dessert, he would call out step by step until he reached the dining-room door, 'Here's me! Here's me!'

Richard Ellmann, the author of the definitive biography of Joyce, describes him in his early childhood as 'a well-behaved, slim little boy ... with a pale face and eyes of the palest blue to lend, when he was not laughing, an impenetrable coolness, an odd self-sufficiency, to otherwise regular and predictable features'.

He had his first lessons from Mrs. 'Dante' Hearn Conway, a pious and bigoted lady who lived with the Joyces and for a time he attended a kindergarten in Bray run by a Miss Raynor. His disposition in those early days won him the sobriquet 'Sunny Jim'; he had a beautiful voice and sang at a concert at Bray Boat Club on 26 June 1888.

The household also included William O'Connell, a grand-uncle, and temporarily John Kelly of Tralee who feature in *A Portrait of the Artist as a Young Man* as Uncle Charles and Mr. Casey respectively. A child's eye is quick to notice a deformity:

> And when he had tried to open Mr. Casey's hand to see if the purse of silver was hidden there he had seen that the fingers could not be straightened out: and Mr. Casey had told him that he had got those three cramped fingers making a birthday present for Queen Victoria.

John Kelly, a political agitator, attributed his cramped fingers to a prison sentence and young Joyce readily accepted this mistaken explanation but many who have never picked oakum develop an identical deformity due to contracture of fibrous tissue in the palm of the hand and this common disorder is known in medical parlance as 'Dupuytren's contracture'.[2]

When six and a half years old he was sent to boarding-school at Clongowes Wood. To such a little boy (nicknamed 'half-past six') the experience was traumatic. His loneliness is recalled in *A Portrait*: 'He longed to be at home and lay his head on his mother's lap. But he could not: and so he longed for the play and study and prayers to be over and to be in bed.' He was the youngest boy in the school: 'He felt his body small and weak amid the throng of players and his eyes were weak and watery.'

For the first time he sensed the absurd importance attached to social position and may have felt a pang of insecurity as he faced his interrogator.

> . . . Nasty Roche had asked:
> —What is your father?
> Stephen had answered:
> —A gentleman.

In his misery morbid thoughts entered his mind. He might die. He might die before his mother could come. And there would be a dead mass for him in the chapel like there had been for Stan Little who had died from pneumonia in five days.

At the end of term all griefs were forgotten in the excitement of his return to Bray.

> There were lanterns in the hall of his father's house and ropes of green branches. There were holly and ivy round the pierglass and holly and ivy, green and red, twined round the chandeliers. There were red holly and green ivy round the old portraits on the walls. Holly and ivy for him and for Christmas.

The Rev. George Byrne, S.J., James Joyce's contemporary at Clongowes, remembered him as 'a kid among kids' and thought him unhappy and too young for a boarding-school. But the well-filled school day is an antidote to melancholy. In his class, *Elements*, Joyce was among the first six or eight. He took the part of an imp in a play, sang in a third-line concert, wrote a hymn to the Blessed Virgin Mary, and was caught raiding an orchard with a boy named Furlong, causing a wit to remark, 'Furlong and Joyce will not for long rejoice.'

He did not return to Clongowes after the summer term of 1891. Early in the following year the family moved to Leoville, Carysfort Avenue, Blackrock, Co. Dublin and in collaboration with a boy who lived next door Joyce started to write a novel. He was then ten years old and had already written *Et Tu Healy!* a lament for Parnell.

The Joyces' move to Dublin's North side was necessitated by financial improvidence, the outcome of John S. Joyce's insobriety. Evicted by a succession of landlords they grew accustomed to the evasions and humiliations enforced by poverty but the generosity of the Jesuits enabled James and his brother Stannie to attend Belvedere College as non-paying pupils.

The only essay surviving from James Joyce's schooldays, written when he was fourteen years old, contains the following observation: 'The man who has no ambition, no wealth no luxury save contentment cannot hide the joy of happiness that flows from a clear conscience and an easy mind.' Outwardly, at least, he was still an industrious, good-living, and more than ordinarily pious student—a prefect of the sodality of the Blessed Virgin Mary—but he must already have suspected that lack of wealth can be more unsettling than its possession, and very soon his own serenity was to be disturbed by a driving ambition, an uneasy mind, and an unquiet conscience.

The first of these—determination to achieve literary fame—the outcome of his nascent genius, was entirely predictable and remaining long unfulfilled continued to be a reason for unrest for a considerable period. The other causes for disquiet stemmed from religious conflict and post-pubertal maladjustment, the latter making confession a shameful ordeal,[3] the annual retreat an agony of accusation with guilt an inevitable consequence. 'Who made it to be like that, a bestial part of the body able to understand bestially and desire bestially? Was that then he or an inhuman thing moved by a lower soul?'

The manner of his carnal gratification is a matter for conjecture. Is it likely at that age to have been other than a solitary release of sexual tension, a physiological need in male adolescence? Ellmann appears to have accepted at face-value Stanislaus Joyce's account of his brother's sordid encounter with a whore on the canal bank. If true, it was indeed a precocious beginning and might well have caused him to shift uneasily in his seat in the College chapel during Fr. Cullen's sermon. But even prostitutes have professional pride and most of them would jeer at a boy of fourteen.

13

Bernard Shaw has said that Aubrey Beardsley was 'boyish enough to pose as a diabolic reveller in vices of which he was innocent.' Males of all ages boast of imaginary experiences, especially to younger brothers, and James may have been telling Stannie a whopper. According to Michael Schoefield's *The Sexual Behaviour of Young People* only 0.9 per cent of boys have had sexual intercourse before the age of fourteen and less than 3 per cent before fifteen.

Did he really visit Night-town sporadically in his schooldays, as Ellmann suggests? His timidity in certain respects should be recalled: When obliged to kiss the Queen in a game he asked, 'Is there any alternative?' administering only a perfunctory peck; he was a stiff, shy dancer and when he found himself tête à tête with a girl his courage ebbed. The brothel scene in *A Portrait* (incidentally a not altogether convincing representation of how a youngster might react, 'Tears of joy and relief shone in his delighted eyes . . .') may have been projected from memories acquired a few years later when, fortified by alcohol, he certainly did patronise the Dublin stews.

While at Belvedere he began to display a contempt for authority which increased during his years at University College. Stannie in *My Brother's Keeper* has mentioned his 'cheerful and amiable disposition in boyhood and youth' but although he remained prone to spontaneous and even immoderate laughter the happy nature which earned the name 'Sunny Jim' appears to have suffered a change. Eugene Sheehy who found him 'aloof, icy and imperturbable' with an 'impassive poker face', thought his abrupt manner a cloak for shyness. John Eglinton thought him proud, impecunious, and very unhappy:

> As I think of Joyce a haunting figure rises up in my memory. A pair of burning dark-blue eyes, serious and questioning, is fixed on me from under the peak of a nautical cap; the face is long, with a slight flush suggestive of dissipation, and an incipient beard is permitted to straggle over a very pronounced chin, under which the open-shirt collar leaves bare a full womanish throat. The figure is fairly tall and very erect, and gives a general impression of a kind of seedy hauteur; and every passer-by glances with a smile at the white tennis shoes (borrowed, as I understand from a mention of them in *Ulysses*).

It is interesting that Joyce in his own more idealised description of himself (*Stephen Hero*) at the same period referred to the epicene but dissipated appearance which impressed the librarian.

His stiff coarse brownish hair was combed high off his forehead but there was little order in its arrangement. A girl might or might not have called him handsome: the face was regular in feature and its pose was almost softened into beauty by a small feminine mouth. In the general survey of the face the eyes were not prominent: they were small light blue eyes which checked advances. They were quite fresh and fearless but in spite of this the face was to a certain extent the face of a debauchee.

Gerald Griffin recalled him tall and gaunt, leaning against the counter in the National Library, chatting with Sheehy Skeffington, anathematizing the Irish National Theatre movement, his language vivid and vitriolic. Mary Colum was impressed at that time by his aloof and arrogant air, and the late Mrs. J. N. Meenan, a contemporary at University College, remembered him as a young man who picked his nose and told dirty stories.

His humour was impish, his intellect brilliant, his enmity formidable, his behaviour unpredictable. 'He was an enigmatic figure in the midst of his shivering society where he enjoyed a reputation.' His fellow-students called him 'the Mad Hatter', 'Jocax', 'Dreamy Jimmy', the last of these well-chosen nicknames indicating that his finer qualities were not entirely concealed from them but his natural courtesy, for the most part, was reserved for private occasions.

At home, being the eldest, he had things very much his own way:

—Fill out the place for me to wash, said Stephen.
—Katey, fill out the place for Stephen to wash.
—Boody, fill out the place for Stephen to wash.
—I can't, I'm going for blue. Fill it out, you, Maggy.
When the enamelled basin had been fitted into the well of the sink and the old washing glove flung on the side of it, he allowed his mother to scrub his neck and root into the folds of his ears and into the interstices at the wings of his nose.
—Well, it's a poor case, she said, when a university student is so dirty that his mother has to wash him.
—But it gives you pleasure, said Stephen calmly.

His article 'Ibsen's New Drama' was published by the *Fortnightly Review* in April 1900. Some weeks later William Archer wrote to him on behalf of the Norwegian playwright and Joyce's reply, artless and sincere, reflected an almost ingenuous simplicity that his friends at University College would never have suspected.

28 April 1900   13 Richmond Avenue, Fairview,
                                    Dublin.
Dear Sir I wish to thank you for your kindness in writing to me.
I am a young Irishman, eighteen years old, and the words of
Ibsen I shall keep in my heart all my life.
                            Faithfully yours Jas A. Joyce.

How different from his usual manner! What a contrast to the mood
of *The Day of the Rabblement*! In a pamphlet published in 1901 the
young man who was so profoundly grateful for a few words of praise
excoriated Ireland and the Abbey Theatre: '. . . the Irish Literary
Theatre must now be considered the property of the rabblement of the
most belated race in Europe.'

With these publications Joyce was already set on the threshold of a
literary career and methodically he sought the acquaintance of the
leading literary figures. They showed him exceptional kindness and
good-will to which he responded by rudeness as surprising as it was
gratuitous. George Russell (AE) who was impressed by Joyce's talent
thought him as proud as Lucifer and said to a friend, 'I wouldn't be
his Messiah for a thousand million pounds. He would always be
criticising the bad taste of his deity.' His attitude towards Yeats caused
the latter to remark, 'Never have I seen so much pretension with so
little to show for it.' Lady Gregory recommended him as a reviewer
to the editor of the *Daily Express* but when in due course he dealt
with her *Poets and Dreamers* the critique was disparaging. And in
Ulysses he referred to her as 'that old hake Gregory.'

The instances of disaffection could be multiplied but since this
chapter on James Joyce's youth is not intended as an essay in denigration it is as well to say without delay that within a few years the acerbity
caused by what Proust refers to as 'the ill-balanced mentality of early
manhood' lessened. George Moore remarked in a letter to Edward
Marsh, 'Joyce left a disagreeable reputation behind him in Dublin, but
he came back after some years a different man and everything I have
heard of is to his credit.'

Proust would have it that 'once youth is outgrown, it is seldom that
anyone remains hidebound by insolence.' Fortunately, insolence and
disaffection, however common, are not invariable accompaniments of
youth. Ideally, their occurrence demands an explanation so that sympathetic correction may be applied.

The hitherto unrealized frequency of psychological disorders among
university students has become evident since the development of

16

student-health clinics. A review of a three year period at Oxford showed a suicide rate eleven times that of a similar age group in the general population and seventeen times that of young men in the armed services. A nervous breakdown was responsible in more than fifty per cent of 145 students absent because of illness for a term or longer. The medical records of 797 students who entered University College, London in 1950 indicate that four per cent developed severe psychiatric disturbances and that an additional ten per cent had lesser psychiatric problems.

Contributory factors, apart from those personal problems concerning sex, family life, and religion, shared by all adolescents, include difficulties with studies and integration. The concept of identity—i.e. our images of ourselves as persons, what we are and what we are not—is of particular importance in understanding the attitudes of the young and Dr. N. Malleson points out that, 'Adolescence is essentially a time of changing identities . . . In general, one can say a person is likely to be happy and to be efficient when his subjective notion of identity corresponds with his objective occupational rôle.' Understandably it is not always easy to draw a line between the extremes of normal sensibility and the abnormal; perhaps for this reason diagnostic labels are imprecise when psychogenic disorders ensue—'emotionally disturbed', 'affective disorders', 'anxiety-depressive states'.

By most present-day student-health clinic standards James Joyce would have been regarded as 'emotionally disturbed'. Environmental factors, religious conflict, problems of identity and of a creative personality, may explain the disaffection, one consequence of which was his failure to settle into an appropriate occupation after taking the B.A. in 1903. Instead he decided to study medicine.[4]

CHAPTER 2

AN UNSUCCESSFUL MEDICAL STUDENT

'Then he went to Cecilia's treat on his solo to pick up Galen': thus, in *Finnegans Wake* James Joyce refers to a brief and inglorious period as a Dublin medical student, an apparently futile episode somewhat neglected by Joycean commentators; a puzzling episode and yet, together with the tentative attempt to espouse a medical career in Paris, an episode stamped indelibly on the pages of Joyce's books. Why did Joyce want to be a doctor? What were his capacities for the medical profession? Why did he fail in his ambition? Answers to the first question are speculative; the evidence suggests that he was actually well-suited to the practice of medicine; lack of funds may have determined his failure, but preoccupation with literature and a dislike for chemistry may have been equally important.

In the absence of a particular bent any youth's decision to follow one profession rather than another rests on obscure influences of which the more palpable are parental example, the direction which friends are taking, and the promise of affluence and social cachet.

That Joyce held the medical profession in some esteem, although not unaware of the limitations of many of its members, is suggested by his choice of a doctor as the hero of *A Brilliant Career* the unpublished play he wrote in 1900, and by Gerty McDowell's musings over Reggy Wylie.

> Only now his father kept him in the evenings studying hard to get an exhibition in the intermediate that was on and he was going to Trinity college to study for a doctor when he left the high school like his brother W. E. Wylie who was racing in the bicycle races in Trinity college university.

Gerty's thoughts, a pastiche of the sentiments expressed by the heroines of romantic novelettes, do not necessarily indicate that Joyce himself was in any way impressed by the medical students of his day but Stephen Dedalus is aware that they have an aura of dedication and accomplishment for simple folk and when the old crone who brings milk to the Martello Tower shows respect for Buck Mulligan he resents it.

—Taste it, sir, she said.
He drank at her bidding.
—If we could only live on good food like that, he said to her
somewhat loudly, we wouldn't have the country full of rotten
teeth and rotten guts. Living in a bogswamp, eating cheap food
and the streets paved with dust, horsedung and consumptives'
spits.
—Are you a medical student, sir? the old woman asked.
—I am, ma'am, Buck Mulligan answered.
Stephen listened in scornful silence. She bows her old head to a
voice that speaks to her loudly, her bonesetter, her medicineman;
me she slights.

James Joyce's father had studied medicine in Cork, or rather, as
Stanislaus Joyce remarked, 'one should say he was enrolled in the
school of medicine for three years, since he studied as little as possible,
and instead made a big name in sport and dramatics, and by his wild
life while a student.' According to Richard Ellmann, Joyce *père*, who
entered Queen's College, Cork in 1867 'began his studies seriously
enough, winning, by his own account, several exhibitions', but in June
1868 he was ploughed. Having repeated the year he was again unsuccessful and to quote the unfilial words of Stanislaus, 'many human
lives were saved by his giving up the study of medicine'.

Subsequently Joyce *père*, the last man to be disturbed by failure,
would have viewed this period as something to boast about and James
Joyce and his surrogate Stephen Dedalus must have heard of it time
and time again.

When John S. Joyce went to Cork in 1894 to sell his properties he
took James with him and the journey is recalled coldly in *A Portrait
of the Artist as a Young Man.*
On the night mail Stephen Dedalus

> listened without sympathy to his father's evocation of Cork and
> of scenes of his youth—a tale broken by sighs or draughts from
> his pocket flask whenever the image of some dead friend appeared
> in it, or whenever the evoker remembered suddenly the purpose
> of his actual visit. Stephen heard, but could feel no pity. The
> images of the dead were all strangers to him save that of uncle
> Charles, an image which had lately been fading out of memory.

Next morning, breakfasting off drisheens in the Victoria Hotel, Mr.
Dedalus twisted the points of his moustache and interrogated the

waiter who supplied local news as best he could.—Well, I hope they haven't moved the Queen's College, anyhow, said Mr Dedalus, for I want to show it to this youngster of mine.

The young impressionable boy and the feckless, improvident father sauntered through the sunny city.

> Along the Mardyke the trees were in bloom. They entered the grounds of the college and were led by the garrulous porter across the quadrangle. But their progress across the gravel was brought to a halt after every dozen or so paces by some reply of the porter's.

Eventually they entered the college.

> They passed into the anatomy theatre where Mr Dedalus, the porter aiding him, searched the desks for his initials. Stephen remained in the background, depressed more than ever by the darkness and silence of the theatre and by the air it wore of jaded and formal study. On the desk he read the word *Foetus* cut several times in the dark stained wood. The sudden legend startled his blood: he seemed to feel the absent students of the college about him and to shrink from their company. A vision of their life, which his father's words had been powerless to evoke, sprang up before him out of the word cut in the desk.

Finally Mr. Dedalus located the initials cut in his salad days. He showed them to his son and they departed; the father was well pleased with himself, the introspective boy so susceptible to the power of words was still troubled by the graven letters: 'the word and the vision capered before his eyes as he walked back across the quadrangle towards the college gate.'

Some years later towards the completion of his Arts course at University College James Joyce was urged by his father to seek a clerkship at Guinness's Brewery. Joyce *père* may have been mindful of his own early days at the Distillery at Chapelizod but when James opted instead for medicine the father offered no objection, possibly seeing the hand of fate in the choice and leaving it to fate to supply the wherewithal to fulfil its vagaries.

Stanislaus, who worshipped his elder brother, noted in his diary in 1904, 'Jim has a face like a scientist. Not an old fumbler like Huxley or Tyndall, but like one of those young foreigners—like Finsen or Marconi'. Appearances, however, are notoriously deceptive; the record shows no factual basis for Stannie's assertion.

An analysis of James Joyce's examination marks at Belvedere, where he won three exhibitions as well as prizes for Latin and English composition, is provided in Kevin Sullivan's *Joyce among the Jesuits*. Presumably he worked hardest, as is the way of boys, at subjects which he liked. His performance in arithmetic was excellent, in algebra and geometry good, but his bent was for languages. His highest average was for French; he did well in Latin and Italian and took first place in Ireland for English composition in two successive years.

The science-master at Belvedere at the time was Mr. P. Bertram Foy, a brother-in-law of Mr. Dempsey—Mr. Tate in *A Portrait*—the English-master. Foy was the best teacher in the school according to Joyce's friend F. J. Byrne, but Joyce did not shine in his subjects. In the junior grade he was awarded twenty per cent for chemistry and seems to have given it up; for physics in the junior grade and middle grades respectively his percentages were twenty and thirty-five but in the senior grade he was awarded a derisory two per cent.

During his matriculation year and for First Arts mathematics and natural philosophy—the elementary principles of mechanics, pneumatics and hydrostatics—were obligatory. His percentages for natural philosophy at University College were 36.6 and 46.6 (Ellmann).

'Thursday. Ten to eleven, English; eleven to twelve, French; twelve to one, Physics . . .' The Professor of Natural Philosophy at University College was Preston and a physics lecture is depicted in *A Portrait*.

> The formula which he wrote obediently on the sheet of paper, the coiling and uncoiling calculations of the professor, the spectre-like symbols of force and velocity fascinated and jaded Stephen's mind. He had heard some say that the old professor was an atheist freemason. O the grey dull day! It seemed a limbo of painless patient consciousness through which souls of mathematicians might wander, projecting long slender fabrics from plane to plane of ever rarer and paler twilight, radiating swift eddies to the last verges of a universe ever vaster, farther and more impalpable.
> —So we must distinguish between elliptical and ellipsoidal. Perhaps some of you gentlemen may be familiar with the works of Mr W. S. Gilbert. In one of his songs he speaks of the billiard sharp who is condemned to play:
>
> > On a cloth untrue
> > With a twisted cue
> > And elliptical billiard balls.

He means a ball having the form of the ellipsoid of the principal axes of which I spoke a moment ago.

The evocative image led to a vulgar comment from a student behind Stephen whose anarchical spirit at once conceived a 'sabbath of misrule' in which his grave teachers danced in inappropriate abandon.

The professor had gone to the glass cases on the sidewall, from a shelf of which he took down a set of coils, blew away the dust from many points and, bearing it carefully to the table, held a finger on it while he proceeded with his lecture. He explained that the wires in modern coils were of a compound called platinoid lately discovered by F. W. Martino.

He spoke clearly the initials and surname of the discoverer. Moynihan whispered from behind:

—Good old Fresh Water Martin!

—Ask him, Stephen whispered back with weary humour, if he wants a subject for electrocution. He can have me.

Moynihan, seeing the professor bend over the coils, rose in his bench and, clacking noiselessly the fingers of his right hand, began to call with the voice of a slobbering urchin: Please, teacher! This boy is after saying a bad word, teacher.

—Platinoid, the professor said solemnly, is preferred to German silver because it has a lower coefficient of resistance by changes of temperature. The platinoid wire is insulated and the covering of silk that insulates it is wound on the ebonite bobbins just where my finger is. If it were wound single an extra current would be induced in the coils. The bobbins are saturated in hot paraffin-wax . . .

Stephen listened, less interested in the substance of the lecture than in the manner of the lecturer, distracted by the behaviour of the audience, resenting the uncouthness of his fellow-students, unmindful of his own defects.

The droning voice of the professor continued to wind itself slowly round and round the coils it spoke of, doubling, trebling, quadrupling its somnolent energy as the coil multiplied its ohms of resistance.

Whatever scraps of physics Joyce picked up in Belvedere and University College were put to advantage in *Ulysses* re-echoing in Leopold Bloom's mind.

Where was the chap I saw in that picture somewhere? Ah, in the dead sea, floating on his back, reading a book with a parasol open. Couldn't sink if you tried: so thick with salt. Because the weight of the water, no, the weight of the body in the water is equal to the weight of the. Or is it the volume is equal of the weight? It's a law something like that. Vance in High school cracking his fingerjoints, teaching. The college curriculum. Cracking curriculum. What is weight really when you say the weight? Thirtytwo feet per second, per second. Law of falling bodies: per second, per second. They all fall to the ground. The earth. It's the force of gravity of the earth is the weight.

Passing the Ballast Office Bloom mused:

Fascinating little book that is of Sir Robert Ball's. Parallax. I never exactly understood. There's a priest. Could ask him. Par it's Greek: parallel, parallax. Met him pikehoses she called it till I told her about the transmigration. O rocks!

From Sandymount Strand he watched the Bailey light winking and recalled, 'Red rays are longest. Roygbiv Vance taught us: red, orange, yellow, green, blue, indigo, violet.'

Joyce's marks at University College are not, of course, a valid re-flection of his actual ability or knowledge. He was in doubt, according to Stannie 'as to whether university studies were, after all, worth the trouble'. He read widely and Gogarty said that 'he was packed with erudition and with unfamiliar scholarship'. His percentages for French, English, and Italian respectively at the B.A. examination in 1902 were 58.1, 43, and 52.1, by no means a resounding success.

His decision to study medicine caused raised eyebrows. A contem-porary, Constantine Curran, told the present author that he first heard Joyce's intention of becoming a medical student in the autumn of 1902, when they were walking, as they often did, on the North Bull Wall. Not concealing his surprise Curran dismissed the idea as fan-tasy. Joyce demurred saying that as a doctor he could make enough money in a matter of years to allow him to devote the rest of his life to literature.

There is a relevant passage in *A Portrait* where 'in a listless peace' Stephen Dedalus stands on the steps of the National Library listening to the chatter.

He heard the students talking among themselves. They spoke of two friends who had passed the final medical examination, of the chances of getting places on ocean liners, of poor and rich practices.

—That's all a bubble. An Irish country practice is better.

—Hynes was two years in Liverpool and he says the same. A frightful hole he said it was. Nothing but midwifery cases.

—Do you mean to say it is better to have a job here in the country than in a rich city like that? I know a fellow . . .

—Hynes has no brains. He got through by stewing, pure stewing.

—Don't mind him. There's plenty of money to be made in a big commercial city.

—Depends on the practice.

The degree of B.A. in modern languages was conferred on 31 October 1902 and Stanislaus has recounted a subsequent conversation between his brother and the Dean, Fr. Darlington, who enquired about the young man's plans for the future. When Joyce declared his determination to pursue a literary career Fr. Darlington asked, 'Isn't there some danger of perishing of inanition in the meantime?'

'That is by tradition', Joyce replied, 'one of the ever-pressing perils of the career, but it has its prizes, too'. Father Darlington instanced a successful Dublin barrister who while studying law had supported himself by journalism but Joyce retorted with a sarcasm which was lost on the Dean, 'I may not have that gentleman's talents'.

But Jim was not wholly deaf to the dean's advice [Stanislaus wrote in *My Brother's Keeper*] and after some hesitation he chose medicine as an interim career and was inscribed in that faculty. I can hardly believe that he did more than dally with the idea, though he took some real interest in medicine and attended lectures for a while . . . and, moreover, the choice of medicine rather than letters seemed to betoken a nascent sense of practical values.

Stannie's account is not altogether reliable. His brother's decision to study medicine was taken much earlier in 1902 but may, indeed, have been influenced by Fr. Darlington who was made dean of the medical school in Cecilia Street at the beginning of that year.

In November 1902 a note in *St. Stephen's* over the initials of James N. Meenan,[1] later Professor of Medicine at University College, stated:

Much pleasure was occasioned at the school when it became known (for how could it have been unknown when it was a secret?) that Messrs. J. F. Byrne, Seamus O'Kelly and Joyce intend to join the ranks of Cecilia Street. The veterans who are now in the last lap of their course, look forward to their keeping the old flag flying during their time at the school.

The Catholic University Medical School, forerunner of the present medical faculty at University College, Dublin—the largest medical faculty in Ireland—was then an obscure and struggling school overshadowed by older rivals, the College of Surgeons and Trinity College. Established in 1855 under the Rectorship of John Henry Newman, part of a university without a charter, 'an Institution of Hope, founded in Faith on the basis of Charity', it occupied premises in Cecilia Street previously owned by the Apothecaries' Hall which had started a medical school there in 1837.

That school had flourished for a time but when Benjamin Alcock—remembered to-day by all medical students for 'Alcock's canal'—was appointed to a chair in Queen's College, Cork, its classes dwindled. The Catholic University purchased the building and refitted it. Sir Dominic Corrigan the foremost Catholic physician could not be prevailed upon to become professor of medicine to the new school which was formally opened on 2 November 1855 with thirty-six enrolled students. Richard Lyons, a young Cork man who had seen service in the Crimea, was given this chair and Mr. Ellis was Dean and Professor of Surgery.

The lack of a charter, a serious obstacle, was overcome when the College of Surgeons 'recognised' its lectures enabling the Cecilia Street students to take the conjoint diplomas of the Colleges of Physicians and Surgeons.

The Catholic University changed its name to University College in 1882 and became part of the newly established Royal University. The medical school in Cecilia Street appears to have had an almost independent existence for a time attended by two groups of students, those intending to take the conjoint diplomas and those taking the medical degree of the Royal University. The latter required an Arts degree and took their preliminary scientific subjects at University College.

The National University of Ireland replaced the Royal University in 1909 and the Catholic University Medical School—which gloried in having maintained the direct link with Newman's University—was reunited with University College and in due course the Cecilia Street buildings were vacated, the faculty moving to Earlsfort Terrace.

The late William Doolin, F.R.C.S.I., a former editor of the *Irish Journal of Medical Science* and sometime Professor of Medical History at University College, Dublin, who had himself attended 'Cecilia Street'—the School was familiarly known by the name of the street in which it stood—has referred to 'the cramped, near-slum atmosphere of the School's surroundings' and the contrast when 'emerging in the late afternoon from the noisy, crowded hall of the School, to turn down Dame Street, one was faced by the magnificent pile of Trinity College, rising at the very hub of the city's life, every line of its rich Georgian structure vocative of security, of affluence, of prestige.'

At the turn of the century Ambrose Birmingham,[2] Registrar and Professor of Anatomy was the driving force of the School. 'Ambie' was the author of a dissecting manual illustrated by himself, and contributed a chapter to Cunningham's celebrated *Textbook of Anatomy*. He was an inspired teacher and illustrated his lectures by black-board sketches. Blue chalk was used to depict veins, red for arteries—sometimes the chalks got mixed and a newcomer to the class would be puzzled when Ambie held up a chalk and asked 'What colour is this?' until he realized that the Professor was colour-blind.

James Joyce's first visit to Cecilia Street is described in *Silent Years* by F. J. Byrne ('Cranly' in *A Portrait*) who through his enthusiasm for handball had become acquainted with many of the professors at Cecilia Street where he often called when arranging handball tournaments.

In March, 1902, I told Dr. Birmingham that there were three acquaintances of mine in University College who were toying with the idea of going for medicine, and who had asked me to make general enquiries about it, chiefly about the matter of maximum expenses. Dr. Birmingham said immediately, 'Bring them here some afternoon to see me—come any time before six o'clock'. One late afternoon early in April I accompanied the three men to the Medical School. They were John Bassett, Vincent Cosgrave, and James Augustine Joyce.

I introduced the three to Dr. Birmingham and acted most of the time as spokesman for them. They appeared well satisfied with what they learned, and two of them, Cosgrave and Joyce, applied there and then for registration as medical students. When this had been done, Ambrose Birmingham said to me, 'What about you—would you think of going for medicine?' And I replied flippantly, but laughingly, 'I might consider that, if you'd pay my fees.'

When Cosgrave and Bassett left, Byrne and Joyce stayed on chatting with Professor Birmingham who said, 'It isn't a big place; in fact we're hampered for lack of room, but I'd like you to see what there is of it.' First he showed them into a small room behind the lecture-theatre where Nolan, the anatomy porter stored the apparatus for injecting preserving solution into the femoral arteries of the corpses.

It will be recalled that the opening words of *The Day of the Rabblement*, 'No man, said the Nolan, can be a lover of the true or the good unless he abhors the multitudes . . .' caused some mystification. Joyce was referring to Giordano Bruno of Nola but many of his fellow students thought immediately of Nolan the anatomy porter. F. J. Byrne described this worthy as 'a mild-mannered, falsetto-voiced, elderly, white-haired man. He always wore a cap, and his general appearance, particularly his face, faintly suggested Bismarck.'

Birmingham showed them the dissecting-room where students were grouped about the 'stiffs'. He introduced them to Mr. P. J. Fagan,[3] Assistant Surgeon to St. Vincent's Hospital, an anatomy demonstrator whom at first sight Byrne had taken to be the porter's assistant—'a grey-eyed, rough-looking, middle-aged man.'

Birmingham left them and went to speak with a florid, athletic-looking, balding man possibly in his early thirties who was examining an open abdomen with great concentration. Evidently a man of substance and importance. Beneath his apron striped trousers and expensive, highly-polished shoes were visible and a frock coat and shiny topper hung nearby.

The two older men conversed for a full ten minutes while Joyce and Byrne waited 'intensely interested in, but intensely ignorant of what had been going on.' Later Birmingham explained that this was Mr. Alexander Blayney,[4] Surgeon to the Mater Hospital, and that he was dissecting in connection with a very critical operation which he was to do next day.

According to Ellmann James Joyce's name was inscribed on the Register of the Medical School on 2 October 1902. He may have attended Professor Sigerson's biology class and some lectures in physics and chemistry but unassiduously.

Temple, a character in *A Portrait*, says, 'The most profound sentence ever written is the sentence at the end of the zoology. Reproduction is the beginning of death.' *Ulysses* contains a reference to Sigerson—'Our national epic has yet to be written, Dr Sigerson says' —but Constantine Curran who for years was a close friend of Sigerson never heard anything from the latter to indicate a recollection of

Joyce as a student in his class. Incidentally, it is surprising in view of the frequency with which Joyce took his 'fictional' characters from the living that he did not find a place in *A Portrait* for George Sigerson, a savant who would have graced any campus with distinction. Born in Strabane in 1836 a descendant of the Norse invaders of Ireland ('Sigur's son') he spent some years in a French school and took a medical degree at Queen's College, Cork. He was appointed lecturer in Botany at the Catholic University in 1865 and became Professor of Biology holding similar posts at the Royal University and the National University of Ireland, retiring from the latter in 1923 two years before his death at an advanced age. Meanwhile, in addition to a translation of Charcot's *Dieases of the Nervous System,* his publications included *Modern Ireland, Bards of the Gael and Gall, The last Independent Parliament of Ireland,* and *The Easter Song of Sedulius;* his historical works were praised by Lord Acton and Darwin proposed his election to the Linnean Society. Sigerson had a long flaxen beard and so magnificent was his appearance that when Augustine Birrell, the Chief Secretary, who was then working on his University Bill, saw him in the College, he asked who this was and said, 'Such a monument must certainly have a university to hold it.'

Joyce never ventured beyond the threshold of medical education in Dublin. Would he have shown clinical aptitude had he continued? Words were Joyce's medium and obsession ('He read Skeat's Etymological Dictionary by the hour and his mind, which had from the first been only too submissive to the infant sense of wonder, was often hypnotised by the most commonplace conversation.') but he had considerable powers of observation which instinctively adopted the habit of incessant exercise which teachers of clinical medicine exhort their students to develop.

> He got down off the tram at Amiens St Station instead of going on to the Pillar because he wished to partake in the morning life of the city. This morning walk was pleasant for him and there was no face that passed him on its way to its commercial prison but he strove to pierce to the motive centre of its ugliness . . . As he walked thus through the ways of the city he had his ears and eyes ever prompt to receive impressions . . .

His interpretation of what he saw bears the impress of a flawed psychological make-up. Not for him to hear with Francis Thompson, another hapless medical student, 'the drift of pinions'; not for him biased by the sordid to discern 'the many-splendoured thing'. Young

Stephen Hero's brutal dismissal of peasant life as 'a life of dull routine
—the calculation of coppers, the weekly debauch and the weekly piety
—a life lived in cunning and fear between the shadows of the parish
chapel and the asylum!' overlooks other values, tenacity, courage,
love; values that Joyce learned about as he grew older.

On the faces and the bodies of the crowd Joyce read the lineaments
of disease as accurately as any medical student: 'Father Conmee at the
altar rails placed the host with difficulty in the mouth of the awkward
old man who had the shaky head'. And in the Ormond Hotel

> Ben Dollard bulkily cachuchad towards the bar, mightily praise
> fed and all big roseate, on heavyfooted feet, his gouty fingers
> nakkering castagnettes in the air . . .
> —Ben Machree, said Mr Dedalus, clapping Ben's fat back
> shoulderblade. Fit as a fiddle, only he has a lot of adipose tissue
> concealed about his person.—Fat of death, Simon, Ben Dollard
> growled.

There is a superb vignette in *A Portrait*.

> Stephen often glanced at his trainer's flabby, stubblecovered
> face, as it bent over the long stained fingers through which he
> rolled his cigarette, and with pity at the mild lustreless blue eyes
> which would look up suddenly from the task and gaze vaguely
> into the blue distance while the long swollen fingers ceased their
> rolling and grains and fibres of tobacco fell back into the pouch.

That is the face of a sick man and a page or two further on we read
with no surprise, 'the practice in the park came to an end when Mike
Flynn went to hospital'.

Joyce could be as flippant, too, as the most cynical student.
—Circumcised! says Joe
—Ay, says I. A bit off the top.

*   *   *

In the Michaelmas term of 1902 medical lectures at both University
College and Cecilia Street commenced on Monday, November 2. Sixteen days later Joyce wrote to the Ecole de Médecine in Paris seeking
admission and received a reply from the Secretary of the Faculty.

Monsieur, Ce n'est point la Faculté de médecine, mais le
Ministère de l'Instruction publique qui statue dans chaque cas
particulier, sur les demandes formées par les étrangers, dans le
but d'obtenir des facilités pour la recherche du diplôme univer-
sitaire français de docteur en médecine.

Je ne puis que vous conseiller de vous mettre en instance auprès
de M. le Ministre de l'Instruction publique, en vous conformant
aux indications contenues dans la note ci-jointe.

La décision de M. le Ministre dont vous recevrez avis, vous
fixera sur les conditions qui vous sont faites.

Recevez, Monsieur, l'assurance de ma considération très dis-
tinguée.

Pr Le Doyen:
Le Secrétaire de la Faculté.

His sudden preference for the Sorbonne is puzzling. J. F. Byrne
refers cryptically to 'two reasons, the less impelling of which was
financial . . .' underlying his friend's decision to go abroad. Ambrose
Birmingham had informed Byrne that he could make enough money
to pay his fees by 'grinding' candidates for the College of Surgeons'
entrance examination—'most of these young men have more money
than brains, and they are willing to pay well for grinding'—and presumably Joyce could have raised funds in the same way. Writing to
Lady Gregory, however, he represented himself as a victim of prejudice which is difficult to credit; in Dublin grinding is largely a matter
of individual enterprise. Furthermore, it appears (*My Brother's
Keeper*) that he actually declined evening classes in French at University College, disclaiming a competence to teach the language although
the Dean told him he would merely be tutoring 'little bits of clerks';
and we have seen that he was offended by Fr. Darlington's suggestion
that he could pay his way by journalism. Yet he proposed to exist in
Paris by teaching English and writing articles and reviews.

Having made up his mind he set about canvassing anybody who
might be useful to him with a thoroughness which surprised Stanislaus
who remarked, 'In my brother business lost to poetry a "go-getter"
on the American model'.

His plea to Lady Gregory is suffused with self-pity and persecutory
feelings.

7 St. Peter's Terrace, Cabra, Dublin.

Dear Lady Gregory: I have broken off my medical studies here and am going to trouble you with a history. I have a degree of B.A. from the Royal University, and I had made plans to study medicine here. But the college authorities are determined I shall not do so, wishing I dare say to prevent me from securing any position of ease from which I might speak out my heart. To be quite frank I am without means to pay my medical fees and they refuse to get me any grinding or tuitions or examining—alleging inability—although they have done and are doing so for men who were stuck in the exams I passed. I want to get a degree in medicine, for then I can build up my work securely. I want to achieve myself—little or great as I may be—for I know that there is no heresy or no philosophy which is so abhorrent to my church as a human being, and accordingly I am going to Paris. I intend to study medicine at the University of Paris supporting myself there by teaching English. I am going alone and friendless—I know of a man who used to live somewhere near Montmartre but I have never met him—into another country, and I am writing to you to know can you help me in any way. I do not know what will happen to me in Paris but my case can hardly be worse than it is here. I am leaving Dublin by the night boat on Monday 1st December and my train leaves Victoria Station for Newhaven the same night. I am not despondent however because I know that even if I fail to make my way such failure proves very little. I shall try myself against the powers of the world. All things are inconstant except the faith of the soul, which changes all things and fills their inconstancy with light. And though I seem to have been driven out of my country here as a misbeliever I have found no man yet with a faith like mine.

Lady Gregory promised to help if possible but doubted her ability to do so, 'as my only real friend in Paris is a very devout Catholic Churchman'. She asked 'was there not an idea of your entering Trinity?' and suggested that he should do so. She wrote on Joyce's behalf to John Millington Synge—'who has lived for a good many years in Paris on very small means and could probably give you practical advice'—and to a Dr. Thomas J. Maclagan[5] of London who sent Joyce a letter of introduction to Dr. Rivière.

George Russell (AE) solicited aid from George Moore without success: 'George Moore is useless. I saw him today and he was in one of his bad moods, irritable about everything, and as I expected before I went, he said his friends in Paris would wonder why the devil he sent anybody to see them who was not in their craft. I think Miss Gonne is more hopeful as an acquaintance there.'

William Archer discouraged the venture in uncompromising terms.

25 November 1902.   71 Alleyn Park, West Dulwich, S.E.

Dear Mr. Joyce I am going to Italy on Friday, so cannot see you as you pass through London. If you carry out your intention of going to Paris, and care to call upon Miss Blanche Taylor at 28 Avenue Friedland, I will write to her asking her to give you any information she can. But I am sure she will only tell you that you are in a hopeless quest. Indeed I cannot dissuade you too strongly from making this attempt, if you are really dependent on earning money by teaching English. The market for such teaching is, I believe, extravagantly overstocked in Paris, and even if you did ultimately get a little teaching, you could not possibly combine it with medical studies. It is hard enough by giving lessons all day to keep body and soul together in Paris; and how you can expect to do that, and at the same time qualify as a doctor, passes my comprehension.

Forgive my frankness. It is, of course, no business of mine; but I am sure you are making a mistake. Yours faithfully WILLIAM ARCHER

From London towards the end of November W. B. Yeats offered practical assistance:

. . . I hope you will breakfast with me on Tuesday morning. I shall set my alarm clock and be ready for you as soon as the train gets in. You can lie down on my sofa afterwards and sleep off the fatigue of the journey. You can dine with me and catch your Paris train afterwards . . . I think you should let me give you one or two literary introductions here in London as you will find it much easier to get on in Paris (where perhaps a great many people do not want to learn English) if you do some writing, book reviews, poems etc. for the papers here.

From the Mansion House on November 29 the Lord Mayor of Dublin, with the ready generosity of public men, addressed 'to whom it may concern' an unstinting letter of recommendation.

I know the bearer Mr. Joyce since his childhood, and I am also well acquainted with his family. He is a young man of excellent character and whose career as a student has been distinguished by industry and talent.

He goes abroad to have an opportunity of further pursuing his studies and I look forward with very great hopes to his having the same brilliant success that he has had at home.

T. C. HARRINGTON
Lord Mayor.

Joyce took the steamer from Kingstown to Holyhead on the night of 1 December 1902. Next morning W. B. Yeats met the boat-train at Euston. He introduced Joyce to the editor of the *Academy* and later they called on Arthur Symons who talked about Verlaine, Dowson, Beardsley, and Lionel Johnson, and played the Good Friday music from *Parsifal*. Standing up from the piano Symons said, 'When I play Wagner I am in another world', which amused Joyce always alive to the affections of others. He was tickled, too, by Yeats's sally, 'Symons has always had a longing to commit great sin but he has never been able to get beyond ballet girls.'

That evening Joyce went on via Newhaven and Dieppe to Paris where he put up at the Hôtel Corneille, 5 rue Corneille. Still business-like he presented his letter of introduction to Dr. Rivière who lived in the rue des Mathurins.

Alexander Joseph Rivière (1859-1946) who graduated in Paris in 1884 had been influenced as a student by Jacques-Arsene d'Arsonval, a pioneer in the use of electricity in medicine, who said of his pupil, 'Rivière was the first to enter into my house of science and he made it better for having come in.' A specialist in physical medicine, author of *Outline of Clinical Physical Therapy*, editor of the *Journal of Physiotherapy* he was the first to advocate the use of diathermy in tuberculosis and malignant disease; the first to employ X-ray therapy for cancer and the first in France to treat it with radium. By 1902 he was a leading exponent in his field and his kindness to an impecunious Irish student is eloquent testimony of an amity which was not reserved for individuals but strove to overcome the self-interest of nationalism. He became the founder and President of the International Medical Association against War.

Rivière, who subsequently corresponded on and off with Joyce, gave him a lavish lunch temporarily assuaging the pangs of hunger. 'So much saved!' Joyce wrote in a letter home. He had been fed well, too, in

33

London by Yeats who paid for hansom-cabs and buses. But now the business-like young man was face-to-face with reality.

I have certain definite information about the medical course. The first thing is to have a French baccalauréat but those who have foreign degrees may be dispensed therefrom by the Minister of Public Instruction. I have written to the Minister and this morning called at the Ministry and was told there that the dispensation would probably be accorded me in a few days. Thereupon I went to the Secretary of the Faculty of Science at the Sorbonne and he gave me a provisional card of admission to the course for the certificate in physics, chemistry and biology (the whole year's work). There are no fees to pay for lectures but the lectures begin at 9 in the morning continuing for an hour or two hours and practical work begins in the afternoon at 1.30 and goes on for two or three hours. There are no written exams: all exams are oral and last about a quarter of a[n] hour. My exam for the certificate will come off July next. I am somewhat late as the last day for demands to the Minister was 1 Dec, but I daresay, as I am a foreigner, I will be excused. I can therefore have a fortnight or so to work between this and Christmas.

The rigours of winter had settled upon Paris. Breakfast cost three-pence, lunch ninepence, dinner a shilling, and there were other expenses: 'I have to get an apron and sleeves and a dissecting case at once if I begin work on Monday . . .' He wrote reviews which would bring in a few pounds; he turned down a post at the Berlitz School because it would interfere with his studies but took on a pupil for two or three lessons a week; and within twelve days of his arrival in Paris he asked his hard-up parents if he should go home for Christmas hinting that he would prefer to travel by the more expensive short sea-route, Calais-Dover.

Naturally, motherly concern determined that 'home you *must come if only for a week*' and his father took out another mortgage.

Fabulous artificer, the hawklike man. You flew. Whereto? Newhaven-Dieppe, steerage passenger. Paris and back. Lapwing. Icarus. *Pater, ait.* Seabedabbled, fallen, weltering. Lapwing you are. Lapwing he.

He arrived in Dublin on 23 December and although lectures at the Sorbonne recommenced early in the New Year the would-be physician did not set foot in Paris again until 23 January. And then his studies at the Bibliothèque Nationale and the Bibliothèque Ste. Geneviève were literary and philosophical rather than medical.

Aristotle's phrase formed itself within the gabbled verses and floated out into the studious silence of the library of Saint Geneviève where he had read, sheltered from the sin of Paris, night by night. By his elbow a delicate Siamese conned a hand-book of strategy. Fed and feeding brains about me: under glow-lamps, impaled, with faintly beating feelers: and in my mind's darkness a sloth of the underworld, reluctant, shy of brightness, shifting her dragon scaly folds.

We can picture him descending the hill along the rue Valette—behind him the towering dome of the Pantheon and below, just visible above the house-tops of the Boulevard St. Germain, the roof of Notre Dame—crossing the rue d'Ecole to reach the Boulevard and passing sombrely through one or other of the narrow streets that lead to the icy river.

The grey winds, the cold winds are blowing
    Where I go;
I hear the noise of many waters
    Far below,
All day, all night I hear them flowing
    To and fro.

But that was just one mood and in the city of Villon and Verlaine a romantic young man—for what else but the romanticism of im-maturity, underlying a carapace of arrogance, could have motivated this extraordinary episode?—a romantic young man had a part to play.

My Latin quarter hat. God, we simply must dress the charac-ter. I want puce gloves. You were a student, weren't you? Of what in the other devil's name? Paysayenn. P.C.N., you know: *physiques, chimiques et naturelles*. Aha. Eating your groatsworth of *mou en civet*, fleshpots of Egypt, elbowed by belching cabmen. Just say in the most natural tone: when I was in Paris, *boul' Mich'*, I used to.

If his affairs prospered he would have from various journals, he calculated, something over £200 a year. Meanwhile like Villon's wolves all too often he had to 'live off the wind'. He found it a useful strata-gem to call on acquaintances around lunchtime. He borrowed small sums wherever he could, one of his creditors being Joseph Casey an

35

Irish expatriate printer included under another name in *Ulysses*: 'They have forgotten Kevin Egan, not he them. Remembering thee, O Sion.' He importuned his indigent family repeatedly for assistance and even if it entailed selling a carpet his pleas were not ignored. But once at least the relief arrived too late to ease that day's privations.

With mother's money order, eight shillings, the banging door of the post office slammed in your face by the usher. Hunger toothache. *Encore deux minutes.* Look clock. Must get. *Ferme.* Hired dog! Shoot him to bloody bits with a bang shotgun, bits man spattered walls all brass buttons.

By now medicine seems to have been forgotten. Ellmann suggested that Joyce's French may not have been up to coping with technical lectures. On the whole this seems unlikely. Scientists with an inadequate command of a language can usually comprehend technical matters more easily than generalities; Joyce, a competent linguist, would have had no great difficulty in following elementary science lectures.

Perhaps he was unable to pay his fees. His first impression, as we have seen above, was that he would have to pay no fees. More mature investigation may have revealed that this was incorrect. According to Herbert Gorman whose biography of Joyce was written under the latter's supervision, 'He attended class in the rue Cuvier once and never went there again . . . he discovered fees must be paid in cash and without delay.'

Perhaps he was too sanguine in his expectations that his application sent in several days after the closing date would be accepted, or it may have been his dislike for chemistry. On 25 February 1920 he wrote to Harriet Shaw Weaver: 'Perhaps I should have continued in spite of certain very adverse circumstances but for the fact that both in Ireland and in France chemistry is in the first year's course. I never could learn it or understand in the least what it is about.' Whatever the reason the would-be doctor had deserted Aesculapius permanently for letters, his earlier steadfast purpose, but the interlude provided some of the ineradicable memories that permeate his books.

Spring was approaching; sunlight transformed 'the slender trees, the lemon houses' of the Latin quarter.

Paris rawly waking, crude sunlight on her lemon streets. Moist pith of farls of bread, the froggreen wormwood, her matin incense, court air . . . In Rodot's Yvonne and Madeline newmake their tumbled beauties, shattering with gold teeth *chaussons* of pastry, their mouths yellowed with the *pus* of *flan breton*. Faces of Paris men go by, their wellpleased pleasers, curled conquistadores.

Noon sumbers. Kevin Egan rolls gunpowder cigarettes through fingers smeared with printer's ink, sipping his green fairy as Patrice his white. About us gobblers fork spiced beans down their gullets. *Un demi setier!* A jet of coffee steams from the burnished caldron. She serves me at his beck. *Il est irlandais. Hollandais? Non fromage. Deux irlandais, nous, Irlande, vous savez. Ah oui!* She thought you wanted a cheese *hollandais*.

Then a telegram from Dublin shattered him and the dream ended.

You were going to do wonders, what? Missionary to Europe after fiery Columbanus. Fiacre and Scotus on their creepystools in heaven split from their pintpots, loudlatinlaughing: *Euge! Euge!* Pretending to speak broken English as you dragged your valise, porter threepence, across the slimy pier at Newhaven. *Comment?* Rich booty you brought back; *Le Tutu,* five tattered numbers of *Pantalon Blanc et Culotte Rouge,* a blue French telegram, curiosity to show:
—Mother dying come home father.

And so at Easter 1903 he came home; no longer a medical student, his next rôle was to be a medical student's pal.

CHAPTER 3

A MEDICAL STUDENTS' PAL

Oliver St. John Gogarty used the singular in *Tumbling in the Hay*—
'he was only a medical student's pal, not a medical by any means'—
but Joyce had many friends in the medical schools. A former University College professor would have it, indeed, that he spent dis-
proportionate time in the company of 'the medicals'. Commenting
on the 'exceptionally high moral standard' prevailing in the College
that author remarks (*A Page of Irish History*): 'Readers of Mr James
Joyce will get a different impression . . . Joyce is true as far as he
goes, but confining himself to a small knot of medical students he
gives a wrong impression of the whole.'

The group with which Joyce associated included J. F. Byrne,
Vincent Cosgrave, John Rudolf Elwood, Simon Broderick, and of
course, Gogarty, whose books and verses vividly recreate those
roistering times.

> O there goes Mrs. Mack;
> She keeps a house of imprudence,
> She keeps an old back parlour
> For us poxy medical students,
> To show, to show
> That we are medical students,
> To show, to show,
> That we are medical students,
> To show, to show
> That we medical students don't give a damn.

Possibly the devil-may-care attitude is exaggerated for even if
concupiscence occasionally won the day the medicals, above all,
were in a position to fear the physical dangers abounding in the
diseased brothels of Night-town.[1]

> Tyrone Street of the crowded doors
> And Faithful Place so infidel . . .
> There's nothing left but ruin now
> Where once the crazy cabfuls roared;
> Where new-come sailors turned the prow
> And Love-logged cattle-dealers snored;

The room where old Luke Irwin whored
The stairs on which John Elwood fell . . .

Joyce describes Elwood—Temple, the gypsylike youth in *A Portrait* and *Stephen Hero*—as 'a lean student with olive skin and lank black hair.' He is presented to us as 'an emotional man,' a provincial whose remarks made 'in an indistinct bleating voice' are frequently prefaced by the countryman's 'By hell!' He is something of a butt:—Blast him, curse him! said Cranly broadly. Sure, you might as well be talking, do you know, to a flaming chamber pot as talking to Temple. Go home, Temple, For God's sake, go home.

Evidently Elwood suffered much at the hands of J. F. Byrne (Cranly).

Cranly pointed his long forefinger

—Look at him! he said with scorn to the others.

Look at Ireland's hope!

They laughed at his words and gesture. Temple turned on him bravely, saying:

—Cranly, you're always sneering at me I can see that. But I'm as good as you any day. Do you know what I think about you as compared to myself?

—My dear man, said Cranly urbanely, you are incapable do you know, absolutely incapable of thinking.

—But do you know, Temple went on, what I think of you and of myself compared together?

—Out with it, Temple! the stout student cried from the steps. Get it out in bits . . .

—I'm a ballocks, he said, shaking his head in despair, I am and I know I am. And I admit it that I am.

Dixon patted him lightly on the shoulder and said mildly:

—And it does you every credit, Temple.

—But he, Temple said, pointing to Cranly. He is a ballocks too like me. Only he doesn't know it. And that is the only difference I see.

Elwood was also something of a radical. To all and sundry his mode of address was 'Citizen!' hence his own nick-name 'the Citizen.'[2]

—I'm a believer in universal brotherhood, said Temple glancing about him out of his dark, oval eyes. Marx is only a bloody cod.

Cranly gripped his arm tightly to check his tongue, smiling uneasily and repeated:

—Easy, easy, easy!

Temple struggled to free his arm but continued, his mouth flecked by a thin foam:

—Socialism was founded by an Irishman and the first man in Europe who preached the freedom of thought was Collins. Two hundred years ago. He denounced priestcraft, the philosopher of Middlesex—Three cheers for John Anthony Collins!

Joyce presents him, too, ('By hell I'm a freethinker') as something of a religious sceptic.

—Hell, Temple said. I can respect that invention of the grey spouse of Satan. Hell is Roman, like the walls of the Romans, strong and ugly. But what is Limbo?

Put him back into the perambulator, Cranly, O'Keeffe called out.

Cranly made a swift step towards Temple, halted, stamping his foot, crying as if to a fowl:

—Hoosh!

Temple moved away nimbly.

—Do you know what limbo is? he cried. Do you know what we call a notion like that in Roscommon?

—Hoosh! Blast you! Cranly cried, clapping his hands.

—Neither my arse nor my elbow! Temple cried out scornfully. And that's what I call limbo.

In *Stephen Hero*, Dedalus and Cranly encounter Temple in his cups.

At Noblett's corner where they always halted, they found Temple declaiming to a little ring of young men. The young men were laughing very much at Temple who was very drunk. Stephen kept his eyes fixed on Temple's shapeless mouth which at moments was flecked with a thin foam as it strove to enunciate a difficult word. Cranly stared at the group and said:

—I'll take my dyin' bible Temple has been standing those medicals drinks . . . The bloody fool!

Temple caught sight of them and at once broke off his discourse to come over to them. One or two of the medicals followed him.

—Good evening, said Temple, fumbling at his cap.

—*Druncus es.*

The two medicals laughed while Temple began to search his pockets. During the search his mouth fell asunder.
—Who has the money? said Cranly.
The two medicals laughed and nodded towards Temple who desisted from his search disconsolately, saying:—Ay, by hell . . . I was going to stand a drink . . . Ah, by hell! . . . Where's the bob I had? . . .
—You changed it in Connery's.
The other medical said:
—He got stuck in his first today. That's why he went on to the beer tonight.
—And where did you raise the money? said Cranly to Temple, who began to search his pockets again.
—He popped his watch for ten bob.
—It mustn't be a bad watch, said Cranly, if he got ten bob for it. Where did he get ten bob?
—Ah no! said the second medical. I popped it for him, I know a chap named Larkin in Granby Row.
The big medical student . . . came over to them and said:
—Well, Temple, are you going to take us down to the kips?
—Ah, blazes, said Temple, all my money's gone . . .
As, by hell, I must have a woman . . . By hell, I'll ask for a woman on tick.

Stanislaus Joyce noted in his *Dublin Diary*: 'Elwood has a hectic-coloured, blue-tinted face, with an immature, shambling deportment like a young recruit . . . He is reported to be the best chemist in the medical school.' And later in the *Diary* he observed: 'Not that I don't like Elwood, for instance, or that O'Callaghan isn't a good-natured, thick-headed fellow, but when together they become very boisterous and gross.'
Gogarty saw Elwood in a more affectionate light and spoke of his dancing eyes and beautiful mouth, and of 'his exaltations and exclamations at the wonder of the world and his adventures in it.'
On his departure to Buenos Aires Gogarty wrote:

Oh, send to bring the Springtime back
Your basic old subliming knack—

The verses to Citizen Elwood in South America (published in *Secret Springs of Dublin Song*) are not up to Gogarty's usual standard.

Ah, John
Since you are gone
We've proved you what we knew before
The One and Only
You left us lonely
When to the Southern land you bore
Our mightly loss and sadder sequel
Because we cannot find your equal.

Tumbling in the Hay features Elwood returned from his travels. 'Senor, begob,' shouted the Citizen, exalted by his dream of himself. Heavily moustachioed, clad in sheepskin trousers and bearing silver-mounted pistols he made a mock raid on the dissecting-room in Cecilia Street. But he was confronted unexpectedly by Ambrose Birmingham and the irate professor had the firearms confiscated by the police.

Like many of the Cecilia Street students he joined the Dungannon Club, a republican political group, and became a prominent member. At the time Dan Sheehan was its leader; the wags referred to him as 'god' and Elwood was his prophet. Serious-minded and reserved the 'god' had less to say than the lieutenant who made solemn pronouncements on his behalf in a theatrical way. It was good fun—and excellent propaganda.

Elwood's theatrical flair was put to good purpose, too, on the concert stage and *St. Stephen's* reported that at the Mater Hospital smoking concert held on Shrove Tuesday, 1904, 'Mr. Elwood, 'midst a dead hush, solemnly and slowly chanted that mediaeval Latin poem —'*Ora et labora*'—to the music of muffled bells cleverly and impressively tolled by Mr. Andy Cullen. The most pachydermatous of the audience were moved to tears at this most unearthly display of musical solemnity.'

Gogarty's kinder version of Elwood is almost certainly more accurate than that of the Joyces, for Stanislaus Joyce had a prejudice against medical students and James, due to malice rather than the dictates of symbolism, used acid liberally when depicting his friends. But even the well-disposed Gogarty agreed that it was impossible to spend a companionable hour with Elwood, such was his eccentricity, 'not to mention a continuous or even coherent conversation. He appears to think in flashes from some deep, uncommunicable life.'

It was his habit to begin, half inaudibly, in the middle of a sentence.

"In a bad way, begob. The Citizens are in a bad way." "Where are they?" I inquired. I knew that he was referring to Weary and Barney and the four-combine that consisted of Dolan, Hegarty, McCluskey and Roowan. "All but Hegarty," the Citizen added.

From that I deduced that the results of the exam in the Royal were unfavourable to my friends. "Were they all stuck?" I asked, to confirm my suspicions.

The Citizen smiled brightly and mischievously, though he must have been included in the *débâcle*.

"And where are the boys?"

He looked towards Golly's and joined me who was going there. "I was stuck myself," he volunteered, so cheerfully that it seemed an achievement to have failed in a medical exam . . .

He may have experienced this perverse distinction many times, but Citizen Elwood eventually qualified as a medical practitioner becoming a Licentiate of the Apothecaries' Hall (Dublin) in 1915.

He died of pneumonia in Carrowbehy, Co. Roscommon on 27 March 1934 having meanwhile earned a reputation in the local community for his prowess in land reclamation. A few weeks before his unexpected death, the Roscommon County Council held a special meeting to recommend a state subsidy in support of his research, and some of the County Councillors testified that they had seen proof of Elwood's system on his own property with 'clover and the finest grasses flourishing on the top of wild bog without ever tilling a sod of it.'

According to an obituarist, in politics as in science Jack Elwood went the scientific way. He earned a tribute prized in rural Ireland, a funeral more than a mile long.

On a morning almost 20 years later a white-haired, carelessly-dressed septuagenarian entered the sedate office of the *New York Times*. The uncompromising informality of the man's attire—'unjacketed, his trousers held up by braces that ran over the shoulders of a short-sleeved, open-collar shirt,'—rather startled a sub-editor to whom he spoke and whose interest had already kindled before he realized that here in the flesh was 'Cranly'. Their meeting led to the publication of J. F. Byrne's autobiographical *Silent Years*.

John Francis Byrne was born in Essex Street, Dublin, within a stone-throw of the river Liffey. He attended the Carmelite Seminary in Lower Dominick Street and later Belvedere College where James

Joyce, two years younger, was a pupil. Their acquaintance ripened to friendship when Joyce entered University College in October 1898.

During the academic year 1898-1899 Byrne did not attend classes, acting as tutor to two boys who lived at Elm Green, Castleknock. He does not seem to have proceeded to an Arts degree and although he registered at the medical school in 1902 (and was successful in the first medical examination in 1903) his intention was hardly more serious than Joyce's. 'I filled a formal application to become a medical student knowing well as I did so, that I would never be a medical practitioner.'

A dominating honesty was the quality which impressed itself upon the New York sub-editor when confronted by the elderly Byrne. As a young man this commendable virtue may have been seen as a less praise-worthy directness. He did not put his sceptical intelligence to good purpose. He read in a desultory way in the National Library, indulged in strenuous walks in the Wicklow Hills, and spent a lot of time playing chess and handball.[3] Because of his appearance and his prowess at chess he was sometimes called 'the White Bishop' and when Joyce read in D'Alton's *Memoirs of the Archbishops of Dublin* that Thomas Cranly, a Carmelite, was appointed Archbishop in 1399 he was attracted by the name and gave it to his friend.

Byrne played regularly in the D.B.C. smokeroom where he introduced Joyce to John Howard Parnell, thereby providing material for *Ulysses*.

> John Howard Parnell translated a white bishop quietly and his grey claw went up again to his forehead whereat it rested.
> An instant after, under its screen, his eyes looked quickly, ghost-bright at his foe.

For a long period Byrne and Joyce were inseparable.

> Stephen repaired to the Library where he was supposed to be engaged in serious work. As a matter of fact he read little or nothing in the Library. He talked with Cranly by the hour either at a table, or, if removed by the librarian or by the indignant glances of students, standing at the top of the staircase. At ten-o-clock when the library closed the two returned together through the central streets exchanging banalities with other students . . .

44

Byrne would have it that at this period Joyce resented anyone who came between them—'He was jealous of the few to whom I gave my time or attention'—but Stanislaus, too, was jealous of the interloper who monopolized his brother's company, a sentiment which no doubt influenced him in the *Dublin Diary*.

Byrne has the features of the Middle Ages. A pale, square, large-boned face; an aquiline nose with wide nostrils, rather low on his face; a tight-shut, lipless mouth, full of prejudice; brown eyes set wide apart under short thick eye-brows; and a long narrow forehead surmounted by short, coarse hair brushed up off it like an iron crown. His forehead is lined, and he has a steady look. He is low-sized, square, and powerful looking, and has a strong walk. He dresses in light grey and wears square-toed boots. Jim calls him the Grand Byrne; he has the grand manner, the manner of a Grand Inquisitor.

Stanislaus's biased account dismisses Byrne, whom he called 'Thomas Square-toes,' as an unthinking man who deliberated 'Behind an inpenetrable mask like a Cistercian bishop's face, and one is given to understand great mental activity. Having spoken he pretends to infallibility. The more subtle the conversation becomes, the more brutally he speaks. He is fond of the words "bloody" and "flamin".'

It might be expected that Byrne who loved the lonely Wicklow hills would find the stews of Night-town uncongenial and its denizens repulsive and this is borne out in *Stephen Hero*.

The big medical student roared laughing and turning to Cranly against whom he had a grudge on account of the affair in the *Adelphi,* he said:
—Will you have a woman too if I stand?
Cranly's chastity was famous . . . .
—Well I'll stand women all round if Cranly has one, said the big student . . . .

We have already seen that it was Byrne who introduced Joyce to Cecilia Street in 1902. From Paris in December he sent a post-card to Byrne and another to Vincent Cosgrave on which were written respectively a poem and some remarks in dog-latin concerning whores. The scatology was not intended for Byrne's eyes but Cosgrave showed him the post-card and Byrne's distaste for the squalid brought him into conflict with his friend when Joyce returned to Dublin.

45

Vincent Cosgrave, another Dubliner, a 'chronic' who never qualified and the 'Lynch' of Joyce's novels, is described in some detail in *Stephen Hero*.

> . . . a very grave-looking elderly student named Lynch. Lynch was of a very idle disposition and had allowed six or seven years to intervene between (his) leaving school and beginning a course in medicine at the College of Surgeons. He was much esteemed by his colleagues because he had a deep bass voice, never 'stood' any drinks in return for those which he accepted from others,[4] and seldom uttered any remarks in return for those he listened to. He always kept both his hands in his trousers' pockets when he walked and jutted out his chest in a manner which was intended as a criticism of life. He spoke, however, to Cranly principally about women and for this reason Cranly had nicknamed him Nero. It was possible to accuse his mouth of a Neronic tendency but he destroyed the illusion of imperialism by wearing his cap very far back from a shock forehead.

Where most students used 'bloody' or shorter expletives Lynch 'execrated in yellow'; he called the female genital tract *oracle* 'and all within the frontiers he called *oracular*'.

In *A Portrait* Lynch and Stephen Dedalus engage in a banal occupation.

> MARCH 22nd. In company with Lynch followed a sizeable hospital nurse. Lynch's idea. Dislike it. Two lean hungry greyhounds walking after a heifer.

But if Cosgrave was a lecher he also had artistic susceptibilities and it is in Lynch's company that Stephen defines art as the 'human disposition of sensible or intellectual matter for an aesthetic end.' Cosgrave shared Joyce's love of vocal music and whenever the Palestrina Choir, conducted by Vincent O'Brien, sang the music of Palestrina or Victoria they went together to the Pro-Cathedral.

'Lynch had almost taken the final vows in the order of the discontented . . .' and he expressed this discontent to Stephen Dedalus after meeting another student, Donovan.

> Lynch gazed after him, his lip curling in slow scorn till his face resembled a devil's mask:
>
> —To think that that yellow pancake-eating excrement can get a good job, he said at length, and I have to smoke cheap cigarettes!

46

Vincent Cosgrove (sic) is encountered again in that comic master-piece *Tumbling in the Hay*. Gogarty refers to 'Vincent's Mephisto-phelean countenance' but just as he portrays Elwood more sympatheti-cally than did Joyce, so is his Cosgrave an altogether more likeable person than Joyce's Lynch.

'Vincent, who was resident in the Coombe, had fifty conductions to his credit, so he knew what he was talking about. Vincent was one of these medicals who find residence in hospitals so enjoy-able that they deliberately leave one exam of the Final unpassed so as to continue in residence.'

We hear him remarking 'shifts that pass in the night,' when a half-a-dozen half-dressed women run past him down the stairs in Mrs. Mack's; we see him extract a foreign body most ingeniously ('a bit of glass in the cornea. I took it out with my tongue') from Fresh Nelly's eye; we leave him in the Coombe Hospital by the fireside of the students' room, a turkey, a ham ('It was fresh and there was but a slight concavity in its side revealing the fine pink meat and the soft white fat.') and a magnum on the sideboard and we understand why he will not bestir himself to qualify.

Dillon Cosgrave, his elder brother, joined the Carmelite Order and took a B.A. degree at the Royal University. Although extremely know-ledgeable in music and literature, this man appears to have been im-practical and unworldly to the point of eccentricity. Never able to resist following a street-band, he was so simple that his fellow-novices pre-vailed upon him to ask an apple-woman, 'How much are your penny apples?'

Vincent Cosgrave, who eventually committed suicide, may have had some similar character flaw. He maintained his friendship with Joyce after the latter had left Ireland and writing in 1905 brought him up-to-date re Dublin affairs: 'News is plethoric so expect a short letter. Rumour engages Byrne to a Miss Hayden—Mrs. Skeffington's antero-posterior diameter is unaltered—Gogarty has his M.B. at last and is now up for the Fellowship of the Surgeons . . .'

Their association ended during one of Joyce's rare visits to Dublin when Cosgrave caused him intense distress by a false claim that he, too, had courted Nora Barnacle. Long before this ultimate betrayal Joyce had selected Lynch (echoing the memory of a stern upholder of justice, Mayor Lynch of Galway, who hanged his own son from his own window with his own hands) as the fictional name for Cosgrave who had betrayed him by standing by with his hands in his pockets while Joyce was being knocked about in a street fight.

Cosgrave may have been maliciously motivated when he showed Joyce's lewd postcard to Byrne. Fortunately the latter's coolness was temporary and in 1909 it was Byrne who persuaded his friend that Cosgrave's alleged conquest of Nora was unfounded. J. F. Byrne was then living at 7 Eccles Street, later the fictional residence of Leopold Bloom. In the following year he emigrated to America where he remained, apart from brief visits to Europe, until his death in 1960. He lived by journalism and was the inventor of a cipher which he claimed could not be broken.

He wrote to Joyce in October 1923,

> Dear Joyce: If you care to write me I shall be glad to hear from you. You may take up the thread as with the Byrne you last met in Dublin in 1909.
>
> J. F. Byrne.

and he visited him in Paris in November 1927.

Their reunion was so cordial that Joyce sent a note to Mrs. Byrne insisting that her husband must remain with him for some days. With his old directness Byrne took Joyce to task for using in altered form in *A Portrait* an anecdote he had told him about Father Darlington. He should have taken it as he had heard it, or not at all, chided Byrne, recalling a Dublin fish-woman's rebuke to a customer who was fingering the fish: 'If you want the cod ma'am, take it, but if ye don't want the cod, don't maul it.'

Joyce showed him the latest chapters of *Work In Progress* which Byrne read aloud in a rich Dublin accent. The latter recalled his visit to Paris enthusiastically in *Silent Years* but Joyce referred to it superciliously (displaying no concern at all over Cosgrave's fate) when writing to Miss Shaw Weaver.

> The latest Irishman to ring my bell is 'Cranly' of the *Portrait* etc! The 'Lynch' he tells me, of the *Portrait* and *Ulysses* was fished up out of the Thames some months ago. He seems to have come from Ireland to see me, has never been on the continent before, can't speak any French, has seen nothing in Paris and returned to Ireland after a stay of three days.

Byrne and Joyce met for the last time in 1933 in Paris and discussed among other things Gorman's projected biography. In February 1940 Joyce mentioned to Constantine Curran that J. F. Byrne's wife had sought his influence in securing a publisher for a book Byrne had written. Yet in April 1940 Joyce commented thus to Mary Colum:

> It was news to me that Byrne had written a book. I should have been surprised to hear he had read one. Nevertheless it might be a quite remarkable book and in any case he is a very old friend of mine. If you see him let me know how you find him. I did not think he was very well when I last saw him.

To return to the beginning of the century . . . Stanislaus Joyce's *Dublin Diary* refers to another medical student, MacDonald, who according to Cosgrave had the thirstiest face he ever saw. 'It seems to me that his mind needs a pint'. Stanislaus adds that in fact MacDonald rarely drank.

Simon Broderick,[5] too, was abstemious. At the Cecilia Street Debating Society he proposed that for the regeneration of the country it was necessary to steer as clear of 'John Barleycorn' as of 'John Bull'.

Then there was Sarsfield Patrick Kerrigan[6] (M.B., N.U.I. 1910 later medical officer to Castlefin Dispensary District, Co. Donegal, and Honorary Anaesthetist to the County Infirmary, Lifford) who recalled his 'barmedical days' with Joyce; but of all those hedonistic medicals with whom Joyce associated and who influenced his work so strongly, none was gayer or more outrageous than the brilliant, outspoken Oliver St. John Gogarty whom Joyce depicted as Puck Mulligan in *Ulysses*.

CHAPTER 4

BUCK MULLIGAN

Seldom used today except in disparagement, the term 'Buck' was formerly applied to gallants of the eighteenth century and after, in which sense Joyce selected it for his fictional version of Gogarty, well aware that when linked to a surname so unmistakably proletarian as Mulligan, the result would be derisory.

The eldest son of Dr. Henry Gogarty and his wife Margaret Oliver, daughter of a prosperous Galway miller, Oliver St. John Gogarty was born on 1 August 1878. Good fortune appears to have presided at his birth, bringing the priceless gifts of robust health and a cheerful temperament.

'It is better to be born lucky than rich,' he wrote later, but in those early days his parents, if not actually wealthy, were at least quite well-to-do. In addition to the 'spacious and commodious house' in fashionable Rutland Square, they owned Fairfield, a mansion on the outskirts of the city. Here young Gogarty could lie under the elms watching linnets and finches and black-birds; there was a pond on which he floated a raft of pine logs; and a willow-bordered stream down which in a tin bath the boy could drift into the Tolka. Here in Fairfield's lovely garden his lyric sense developed.

In those halcyon days, he attended the Christian Brothers' School, North Richmond Street,[1] where James and Stanislaus Joyce were pupils for a few months in 1893. 'They were the best educators in the country' he wrote in *It Isn't that Time of Year at All!* 'and that is why my father sent me there.' This parent's death from appendicitis in 1891 brought 'a change to misery and servitude.' He was sent first to Mungret College near Limerick, which he disliked intensely, then to Stonyhurst in England—where it hardly lessened his discontent to find that 'the food was somewhat better and the school was cleaner'—and finally he spent a year at Clongowes Wood College.

Medicine being, he said, 'more or less congenital in our family'—his father, his grandfather and his great-grandfather had been doctors—he hardly bothered to consider any other career. He entered the Royal University ('that bodiless examination booth') in 1897 but left in the following autumn, going instead to Trinity College where his father had graduated.

Yeats's remark that Gogarty 'came drunk from his mother's womb' probably did not refer solely to the young man's natural exuberance and *joie de vivre* but this was remarkable. While still a schoolboy he had played soccer for Preston and for Bohemians; he was a strong swimmer and a champion cyclist. His intellectual vigour kept pace with the physical but more selectively. His astonishing facility for memorizing verse was not paralleled by an equal ability to retain anatomy. 'The very thought of it makes me stupid,' he complained.

His intellectual force expressed itself as wit, effervescent, mocking, ribald, and his own verses in the student-period tended towards the obscene.

> There was a young man from St. John's
> Who wanted to Roger the swans
> 'Oh no!' said the porter,
> 'Oblige with my daughter,
> But the birds are reserved for the dons.'

Many of the dons were captivated by this young man of remarkable parts and invited him into their company. At the other extreme he consorted with the least-industrious undergraduates whose constant purpose was inebriation. Once they sold one of their number as a corpse sewed up in sacking to the College of Surgeons. After nightfall this worthy crawled out of the sack and rejoined his friends only to find that they had drunk all the money. 'It's the last time I'll die for yous, yez ungrateful hoors,' he said.

Perhaps Gogarty's most celebrated prank was his arrival at Trinity in a cab with drawn blinds which trundled over the cobbles to stop before the Examination Hall; Gogarty emerged with a hood over his head and the cabby led him into the building. He explained his bizarre conduct in due course saying that he was determined to avoid seeing a red-haired student who brought him bad luck and was the cause of his repeated failures.

Eventually he mastered anatomy and commenced his clinical studies at the Richmond Hospital. On Friday mornings he was a regular and often a solitary attender at the Ear, Nose and Throat dispensary where Sir Robert Woods worked under wretched conditions in a small dark room. The subject was unpopular but Woods was an outstanding teacher '. . . and there was a liberal education going in his speciality if anyone had the sense to avail himself of it.'

The Rotunda Hospital, a famous midwifery centre, was only a stone-throw from 5 Rutland Square, far too close to home for his liking. He preferred to keep his pious mother unaware of his escapades. On an unfortunate occasion, arriving home in his cups in the small hours, he had stumbled on the stairs arousing her. Confronted by Mrs. Gogarty on the landing he exclaimed, 'Oliver meets his afflicted mother!' And so he did midwifery at the National Maternity Hospital, where Alexander Horne was Master.

During his final examination, Gogarty was examined in midwifery by a former Rotunda Master, Dr. Purefoy who had known Dr. Henry Gogarty.

'Are you a son of my friend, the late owner of those magnificent red setters?' 'Yes, sir,' replied the examinee. 'Tell me now, was Rufus a get of Garryowen? Had not your father a share in Garryowen with Giltrap, or did he send his bitches to be served by that great dog?' 'That I cannot say. He and Giltrap were great friends and they used to go off shooting together.'

Apart from illustrating an examiner's ruse to put a candidate at his ease, the conversation brings to mind the curious parallel of Gerty MacDowell in *Ulysses* musing over 'grandpapa Giltrap's lovely dog Garryowen that almost talked it was so human.'

In the dismal ENT dispensary at the Richmond, Gogarty had made a 'fast and reliable friend.' After taking the M.B., B.Ch. in 1907 he decided to specialize in ear, nose and throat surgery and he went to study under Chiari, Hajek, and Bárány at the famous Allegemines Krankenhaus in Vienna. Meanwhile he had married Miss Martha Duane of Moyard, Co. Galway.

By contrast with the ten years he spent qualifying, Gogarty's subsequent advancement was rapid. He became M.D. in 1909, F.R.C.S.I. in 1910; he was appointed ENT Surgeon to the Richmond Hospital in 1908 and obtained a similar post at the Meath Hospital in 1911. He purchased a house in Ely Place where his neighbours included Sir Thornley Stoker and George Moore. Soon he had a remunerative practice, the ingredients of his success including technical ability, a flamboyant personality, and a showy motor-car. His contributions to clinical science were meagre; he read a paper 'Latent Empyemeta of the Nasal Accessory Sinuses' at a B.M.A. meeting in Aberdeen[2] in 1914. He was undoubtedly a deft surgeon but his reputation eventually may have owed something to legendary inflation. An anaesthetist who worked with him declared, 'He's the King of all antrum operations.' But a more critical junior colleague demurred: 'The King? Hardly! Maybe the Old Pretender!'

He was a popular teacher, offering an irresistible combination: instruction and entertainment, but his jocular remarks were often at the expense of other ENT surgeons. He claimed to be able to recognise their 'signatures' on the mutilated throats of their former patients. Mr. P. J. Keogh, ENT Surgeon to Jervis Street Hospital was his particular butt. Gazing into a throat where a tonsil-bed was awry or an uvula missing, he would comment, 'Oh! Keogh!' And his remark to Frank O'Connor, 'There are doctors in this town who don't know the difference between cancer and a sore toe,' showed a scant respect for the ethics of his profession.

His badinage could be light-hearted and amusing, for instance his lines on MacArdle—

Let Surgeon MacArdle confirm you in Hope
A jockey fell off and his neck it was broke
He lifted him up like a fine honest man
And he said, 'He is dead; but I'll do all I can.'

—but it was sometimes inexcusably scurrilous.[3] Driving past a rival ENT surgeon's house when the owner emerged, he said to his companion, 'Just look at the snot doctor!' As Gogarty was friendly and generous this ugly trait is difficult to understand. One of his own friends said of him that he had 'the kindest heart in Dublin and the dirtiest tongue.'

Ulick O'Connor in his biography of Gogarty gives us the following description of his subject's physical appearance:

. . . he is of average height, five feet nine, but appears taller because of his athletic figure. There is a slight effect of broadness about the face, but this is an illusion, as a sculptor's callipers have shown that it is a long narrow head of the northern type. The eyes are striking, vivid blue, so deep in colour that his daughter actually remembers their being a shade of violet at times. His hair is brown, but sometimes streaked with gold from the bleaching of the sun, and inclined to stand upright when brushed sideways. There is a fine sweep to the forehead, broad without being over-intellectual; his features are regular, but the nose is slightly large, a characteristic of the Irish face.

He also cites Padraic Colum's remarks concerning Gogarty's conversational powers: 'Its sudden shifts and inexplicable transitions, its copious quotations of poetry, along with frequent plain statements of practical issues.'

Gogarty supported the Sinn Féin movement. He was a close friend of Arthur Griffith, a friend and admirer of Michael Collins. When the Irish Free State was established he was made a Senator but his outspokenness inevitably created enemies. The Republicans thought him an arrogant, right-wing reactionary and threatened to kill him.

On a cold January night in 1923 he was bundled into a car at pistol-point and driven to a house at Islandbridge on the Liffey. 'Shall I tip the driver?' he asked to the annoyance of his captors. Then he managed to elude them. He dived into the ice-cold water and escaped, swimming the river and gaining the sanctuary of a police-station. The ballad-mongers celebrated the adventure in 'The Lay of Oliver Gogarty,' the last verse of which runs:

> Cried Oliver St. John Gogarty 'A Senator am I
> The rebels I've tricked, the Liffey I've swum,
>   and sorra the word's a lie.'
> As they clad and fed the hero bold, said the
>   sergeant with a wink
> 'Faith, thin, Oliver St. John Gogarty ye've
>   too much bounce to sink.'

Some years later, Renvyle House, an old mansion in Connemara, formerly the seat of the Blakes, which he had purchased and used as a holiday house, was burned to the ground and with it valuable books and pictures.

Middle age found Gogarty with an assured position in Irish life, with many influential friends, but with the same antic disposition. When he accompanied a pilgrimage to Rome led by President Cosgrave and Dr. Fogarty, Bishop of Killaloe, his letter home read: 'His Holiness the Pope yesterday received the Most Reverend Dr. Fogarty and the most irreverent Dr. Gogarty.'

His friends included churchmen, politicians and wealthy landowners but he was probably happiest in the company of men of letters or with the wits in the Bailey Restaurant.

His own flashes of wit were brilliant.[4] When a Dr. Ashe passed him in the street he murmured, 'Poor Ashe fancies he's the whole cigar.' When a young man, G. E. E. Story, a visitor to Ireland, was introduced to him, Gogarty failed to catch his name and said so. 'Story is the name, Dr. Gogarty, Story.' 'Welcome to our rough island, Story.'

His literary output was considerable. In 1907 he contributed to *The Shanachie* under a pseudonym, Oliver Gay. *Secret Springs of Dublin Song* (1918) contains a number of his anonymous poems. *Hyper-*

thuleana (1916), privately published, bore his own name but only twenty-five copies were printed. *An Offering of Swans* appeared in the bookshops in 1923 and was awarded the Tailteann medal for poetry. Later collections of Gogarty's poetry include *Others to Adorn* (1938), *Perennial* (1946), *Collected Poems* (1954). W. B. Yeats published seventeen of his lyrics in *The Oxford Book of Modern Verse* (1936). *As I was Going Down Sackville Street* (1937), a book of memoirs, was succeeded by *I Follow St. Patrick* (1938), *Tumbling in the Hay* (1939), *Rolling Down the Lea* (1950), *It Isn't that Time of Year at All!* (1954) and by some volumes of essays.

Gogarty sued the publisher and printer of Patrick Kavanagh's *The Green Fool* in 1936. Kavanagh had written, 'I mistook Gogarty's white-robed maid for his wife or his mistress. I expected every poet to have a spare wife.' The plaintiff was awarded £100 damages but in 1937 he was obliged to defend an action for libel taken by Henry Morris Sinclair who objected to a passage in *As I was Going Down Sackville Street*. Among those who gave evidence for the plaintiff was Samuel Beckett of Foxrock, then twenty-two years of age and living in France, whom Gogarty's counsel referred to as 'the bawd and blasphemer from Paris.' £900 damages and costs were awarded to Sinclair.

Soon after that Gogarty left Dublin and took consulting rooms in Wimpole Street. It was his second venture at practice in London where he lived for a period when his life was under threat. He volunteered for service at the outbreak of war in 1939, but was rejected because of his age. He then went on a lecture tour in America where he remained, writing and lecturing, apart from occasional visits to Dublin.

He had a heart attack on September 19th, 1957, and was admitted to the Beth David Hospital in New York where he died three days later. His body was flown back to Ireland for burial in Connemara which he loved so dearly.

Gogarty was at C.B.S., North Richmond Street when little Joyce went to Clongowes; he had gone on to Stonyhurst before Joyce's brief sojourn at the Christian Brothers' school. By the time he returned to Ireland, to Clongowes, Joyce was in Belvedere and he was still there during Gogarty's year at the Royal University. Although their paths had crossed so often they probably did not meet until 1901 when a mutual friend introduced the student of the Royal to the Trinity student.

Meeting again on a tram, for their homes lay in the same direction, Gogarty found Joyce's 'shyness as great as the diffidence of a lay brother in a monastery,' but they had a bond in poetry and walking together on the North Side pavements and talking beneath the apple-blossom at Fairfield their friendship kindled. Physically dissimilar and in very different economic circumstances—Gogarty more robust and comparatively affluent—they had in common a deep feeling for beauty and a reverence for art oddly balanced by Rabelaisian humour and an effortless talent for blasphemy.

Fascinated by Joyce's mocking gravity Gogarty bestowed on him nicknames reflecting his multi-faceted personality—'Dante,' 'the virginal kip-ranger,' 'Kinch.' He celebrated his friend's waywardness in a Limerick:

> There is a young fellow named Joyce
> Who possesseth a sweet tenor voice.
> He goes to the Kips
> With a psalm on his lips
> And biddeth the harlots rejoice.

Equally captivated by Gogarty's mirth and 'primrosevested' elegance Joyce portrayed him 'blithe in motley' in *Ulysses*: 'Buck Mulligan, panamahelmeted, went step by step, iambing, trolling.' That he was indebted to Gogarty, as to so many others, for small sums of money is confirmed by a letter from the donor.

Grove,
Fethard,
Co. Tipperary.

Dear Joyce,

Be not distressed at my sudden disappearance subsequent to my presenting you with that cheque. It is on *my* head. You would be foolish not to cash it as I know I have yet 20 £ or 15 £ or 5 £ in the Bank.

Inform me how thou liltest:—Yokoko! Yokoko! Yokoko!

An the Fates be propitious, the Editor of 'Ireland' will send me on Friday 2 £ for the versicles at the beginning of his paper. Kindly lend me your opinion of some of Yeats' work and your attitude thereto. I am subsidised to article the post ere a moon be waned. At present I wind the pastoral pipe.

Write to
thine O. G.

In another letter Gogarty demanded a 'full account of the nuptials of McBride' (who, to the distress of W. B. Yeats, had married Maude Gonne in Paris) and continued in Kiltartan English:

It is myself that write to answer the letter you kindly sent me and I waiting to speak to you and tell you what I was thinking about you. Yourself it is that must have had the strange thoughts about me not writing to you and you so long gone from the old place where you were born and reared. There are fine poets in your country who have been making songs in the tongue in which the sons of Usna were betrayed Naisi outraged as likely enough your grandmother's gran'aunt must have been telling you and you a child at Phibsboro'. I am sending you a song the same it is that a poet made for you about a strange man entirely who was old before his time, and weak, and wizened, and winshy, with a long growth from his upper lip like the 'ould sort' who never shaved the upper lip, and Talbot in the pale. This old man was very strange I'd be for saying he was 'touched', for he lived all alone beyond Rathangan, where the bog is, and never did any work. When the boys would be plowing it's not plowing he'd be, but sitting silent above by a bog hole and it is the bog wind that'd be rambling through his whiskers and waving them about for all the world as if the 'good people' were curling them for him. Curling them they were and no mistake when the poet found him and clapped eyes on him and heard him singing the fairy song I send you, such a sad strange song there never was—the words the new poet put to the air are these:—

William Dara thinks of the sin of his
        childhood and is Sorrowful
If you wait till the winds be blown and
        blown
    And the last grey cloud unclose
If you wait till the mystic heron be flown
    With the one eye and three toes
I shall sit and sigh till the mouse-grey
        moss

57

Obscures the old oak stump
For I a child by the market cross,
Thought of a rabbit's rump.

Recalled at Easter 1903 by his father's telegram, Joyce remained in Dublin until September 1904. After his mother's death he began to drink heavily. His friendship with J. F. Byrne had cooled and Gogarty was now his constant companion. According to Stanislaus Joyce, his brother was encouraged to insobriety by Gogarty who confided to Elwood that he wanted 'to make Joyce drink in order to break his spirit.'

This assertion is difficult to credit and it should be remembered that Stannie had an instinctive dislike of Gogarty who called him 'Thug' and lampooned him in verse.

Poet Kinch had a brother called Thug
His imitator, and jackal, and mug
    His stride like a lord's is
    His pretension absurd is
In fact, he's an awful thick-lug.

From the pubs to the flourishing red-light district was a more or less inevitable step, particularly for aspirant authors anxious to study unrestrained humanity at first-hand. 'I could sit listening to you all night, Kiddie,' Fresh Nelly said to Joyce, whose voice she admired, and their relationship remained on this non-carnal level.

Gogarty's flair for recalling the comic and bizarre veils to some extent the drab scene, but eventually he discloses the unmitigated horror of 'the long rancid hell, the frowsy pores of whose awful denizens tainted even its polluted air.' Joyce, too, was aware of the peril and in *Stephen Hero* Lynch admonished Dedalus: 'But that costs money; and besides it's dangerous. You may get a dose that will last you your life. I wonder you have not got it before this.'

Hoping to win the Newdigate Prize for verse as Oscar Wilde had done, Gogarty went to Oxford early in 1904 from whence he apostrophied Joyce: 'O preposterous Poet! write to thine impossible friend.' During the two terms that Gogarty was away they corresponded and Joyce was missed by his friend who urged him to pay a visit to Oxford.

Be Jaysus Joyce! You must come over here for a day or two
next fortnight. I want your advice and criticism on something
literary. The fare single to Oxford from Dublin is 27/-. Boat
leaves N. Wall at 11 a.m. 1st Class. 3rd cl train gets here 11.30
pm and I shall send you your travelling expenses. (I couldn't trust
you with more.) I ought to send you the ticket perhaps. Let me
know if you will come Thurs. I want to get Drunk! Dhrunk!
Also I'd do with—Come!

Say February 26th. Write by return. Stamp enclosed. You
must bring at least one shirt and a pair of sound boots otherwise
the flags are apt to chill you at night. If I could trust any of these
fellows here we'd have the bluest time out. We may go to London
for a day or two. I'm reading for a Litt.D. which I don't intend
to take out but it enables me to read with the lady students.

This is an excellent place to seek refuge from Ireland. We'll
go round a bit. I can't be an aristocrat for more than ten days at
a time. Don't say you are coming over here or it might do harm
to me in town.

Of course I'll defray you exps. Let me know by return if you
can raise 3£ (1997£ less than you wish.) It would keep you here
two days and I'll send ye back 'arse over tip' process. Madden
would oblige you with £2 and get the other elsewhere. Quid de
feminis injudicius quid.

I forgot to return your poems. They're safe enough. The
brother will send them on to you.

Kindly do not mention any local topic as I am an English
Catholic.

What about a blind! I feel like a Siberian monastic!

Lack of funds may have prevented Joyce from travelling or the
symptoms to which Gogarty jokingly alluded may have made it impossible for him to leave Dublin.

My dear Joyce,
I am indeed sorry to have forsaken you in whom I am well
pleased. Congratulations that our holy mother has judged you
worthy of the stigmata. Pray fervently O my brother that you
may gain increase of grace to remain worthy of them and bear the
favour with becoming humility. As it would be absurd and per-
nicious for me to prescribe for a penis in a poke so to speak I

enclose a letter for you to hand to my old friend Dr. Walsh one of the best. He will see you all right for me and if you can be repaired repair you. How is the novel progressing. I have written a poem and am on a play.

If I would venture an opinion—you have got a slight gleet from a recurrence of original sin. But you'll be all right. When next writing be careful not to wish eternal blasting as the process is intermittent. Won't you write and tell me all the news. I have planted a whore and a lamp-post in the back garden here and things are now quite homely. Don't let any laziness prevent you from presenting the letter as it may become incurable if neglected or if you drink.

Write 'de moechis'

I am writing against the Gnostics.

Adieu!

Staboo!

Yrs.

O.G.

Good luck to the bountiful token.
I have lost two letters begun to you. Congratulations on the Yokoko Inspired Giant!

Worcester College

Friday 10 III

My dear Mick,

A friend of mine has been seeking employment as a water-clock and as he has not met with much success would be glad if he could re-convert his urethra to periodic and voluntary functions. I take the liberty of asking you to advise him from this note as I cannot introduce him myself; being busy teaching the language to the natives here. Mr. Joyce is the name of the tissues surrounding the infected part if you will cure him you will delight me. He may have waited too long and got gleet.

'Rusticus expectat'

With every pleasant thought
of you I remain
archaeologically yours
Oliver Gogarty

The unpleasant disorder is not mentioned again. Gogarty's first term at Oxford terminated towards the end of March.

23. III. '04

Dear Joyce,

I shall be in the overwhelmed city to-morrow, Wednesday. If I rise in time I shall call up to the fortress of *all* the Joyces about 7.45. We must solve the importunate particle—reason, together.

You will be glad to see me again and I reciprocate your feelings.

Yours
Caddie Rouselle

When Joyce competed in the Feis Ceoil in May, Gogarty sent an optimistic letter headed, The Bard Gogarty to the Wandering Aengus.

Sunday 3rd in May, '04

My dear Joyce:

May'st gain Eurydice from the infernal ones on your descent to-day!

I hope you will keep clear of the 'rout' that makes the hideous roar, in other words, that the so long neglected ladies will not overcome you afterwards. Wire immediately the result is heard and raise on the victory calling on you 5£ and come here for a week. 27/- will bring you over. Of course you saw that I haven't the money this term that the sisters three sent me last term. The only explanation of my tardiness in forwarding funds to you is my difficulty of obtaining them. The 10/- reach'd you? Fairview is not an office for issuing orders of cash. However I guessed you would be directed to the General from Fairview P.O.

Chamber music immediately springs into my mind from the appearance of the above abbreviation. I am delighted to hear of your printing the poem. By the way I hope you have copies of them as I forgot to return you the original Ms. Go and see the holy woman—disguised if you like as the gardener—then send me a detailed account of the position of my lady of love. I fear she has no money—is unwilling to ask me. Poor Jennie's a good soul.

This Danaan Druid, O wandering Aengus, obtained but 2nd place in the Newdigate! further cause for impecuniosity. My Alexandrines I think are not traditional—hence these tears. Damn tradition, and the impenetrability of Professors' souls but perhaps

to damn tradition is to wreck Rome and England, and we must
have the one as we must have lingerie on ladies—and we require
the other as the ladies themselves. However, goodluck O Aengus
of the Birds. Sing sweetly so that the stones may move and build
a causeway to Oxford . . .

If Joyce had not refused a sight-reading test he would have been
awarded the gold medal, instead, like Gogarty in the Newdigate, he
was placed second. He wrote seeking the latter's aid on June 3rd.

> 60, Shelbourne Rd.
> Dear Gogarty: I sent you back the budget. I am still alive. Here
> is a more reasonably request. I am singing at a garden fête on
> Friday and if you have a decent suit to spare or a cricket shirt
> send it or them. I am trying to get an engagement in the Kings-
> town Pavilion. Do you know anyone there? My idea for July
> and August is this—to get Dolmetsch to make me a lute and
> to coast the South of England from Falmouth to Margate singing
> old English songs. When are you leaving Oxford? I wish I could
> see it . . .

Gogarty wrote again to 'the wandering Aengus' some days before
the end of his final term at Oxford.

> I thought, beloved, to have brought to you
> A gift of quietness, and ten and six;
> Cooling your brow and your landlady too,
> With ready spondulicks.
> Homeward I go not yet, because of those
> Who will not let me leave lest they repine:
> For from the Bank the 'stream of quiet' flows
> Through hands that are not mine.
> But, O my Knight! I send to you the stars
> That light my very creditable gains.
> And out of Oxford—though 'on my arse'—
> My scorn of all its praise.

He explained his difficult position—'Since I came back I have not
had a ½d from home'—and his numerous debts. 'O'Leary Curtis is
intangible? If not "touch" him. By the Christ crust I'm sorry that I
cannot "make haste to help you." ' He did not anticipate a prodigal's
welcome when he returned home. 'I am cut off from my domicile by
the Mater. So keep room in that dust bin of yours.'

Joyce's financial problems, to which Gogarty alluded in a letter to his friend G. K. A. Bell (later Bishop of Chichester) in July 1904, were more urgent than his own.

. . . Joyce said, when I told him you wept for him—he that moment was discussing with me (alas!) how to raise £3 or rather 3 guineas, 'I never borrow anything but *guineas* now' and when I mentioned the fact that you were weeping he brightened up & said 'We'll make him shed golden tears'. Then suddenly, to me, Write the following to Bell from me: 'Dear Sir; My friend Mr. Gogarty informs me that my conduct is to you a source of amusement. As I cannot continue to amuse you without supporting my corporal estate I take the liberty to ask you to forward three guineas' etc. But we got the money somehow.

During the summer of 1904 Gogarty took the tenancy of the Martello Tower, Sandycove, which he held for several years at an annual rent of £8. Today the Tower is inseparably linked with Joyce but the duration of his stay there is somewhat controversial. Gogarty mentioned his plan of sharing the Tower with Joyce ('He must have a year in which to finish his novel') to Bell, and on July 22 he told Bell that he and Joyce were to go into the Tower in a week's time. From the version given in Gogarty's *Mourning Became Mrs. Spendlove* it would appear that he and Joyce lived in Sandycove for a lengthy period but his statement in *It Isn't that Time of Year at All* 'We lived there for two years' is obviously incorrect.

Gogarty's eldest son, Mr. Oliver Gogarty, S.C. states that a deed of Covenant was made on 17, August, 1904 between 'His Majesty's Principal Secretary of State for the War Department, hereinafter called the Secretary of War, acting for his Majesty of the one part and the above named Oliver Gogarty of the other part, hereinafter designated the tenant.' He thinks it unlikely that his father, Joyce, and Samuel Chenevix Trench (Haines in *Ulysses*) can have lived in the Tower before mid-August. But Joyce's letters from April to August 30, 1904 are headed 60, Shelbourne Road and not until September 10 do we find a letter written from the Tower.

According to Stanislaus Joyce his brother had to leave Shelbourne Road on August 31 when his landlord shut up house to go on holidays. He slept here and there for some nights and then, perhaps on September 7, he joined Gogarty at the Tower. An entry in Stannie's *Diary* (Sept. 14) reads: 'At present he is staying on sufferance with Gogarty in the Tower at Sandycove. Gogarty wants to put Jim out, but he is afraid that if Jim made a name someday it would be re-membered against him that though he pretended to be a Bohemian friend of Jim's, he put him out.'

On September 15, 1904, Joyce wrote from his father's house in Cabra to J. S. Starkey:[6] 'My trunk will be called for at the Tower tomorrow (Saturday) between 9 and 12. Kindly put into it—a pair of black boots, a pair of brown boots, a blue peaked cap, a black cloth cap, a black felt hat, a raincoat and the Ms of my verses which are in a roll on the shelf to the right as you enter. Also see that your host has not abstracted the twelfth chapter of my novel from my trunk. May I ask you to see that any letters coming to the Tower for me are re-directed to my address at once?'

The ostensible reason for his abrupt departure was a shooting in-cident: waking in a nightmare Trench shot wildly at a phantom panther; Gogarty removed the gun but later took a pot-shot at some tin cans which came clattering down on Joyce, who, fearful of dogs and thunder and now of gun-shots, dressed and left.

Some months previously he had fallen in love with Nora Barnacle ('dear pouting little Nora') who accompanied him when he sailed from the North Wall on 8 October 1904 into what was apparently a self-imposed exile. Gogarty's comments were characteristically cruel: 'The Bard Joyce has fled to Pola, on the Adriatic. A slavey shared his flight. Considering the Poet's preaching and propensity the town he has chosen for the scene of his future living is not inappropriately named.'

The remark, a good example of what Padraic Colum called Gogarty's 'incontinence of speech', was not intended as other than verbal fire-works, for amusement and display. Indeed, in some odd way, he thought he could claim credit for the success of 'the ménage à Trieste the Town of the Man of Sorrows.'

'Gogarty, I believe, even waxes sentimental over you,' Stannie told him in July 1905. Vincent Cosgrave writing to Joyce in October 1905 informed him: 'Gogarty desires reconciliation. He desires you back in Dublin.' But Joyce was not to be so easily charmed into amity again.

Gogarty wrote to him from the United States on 14 June 1906.

The Waldorf-Astoria
New York

Dear Joyce: I hope to be able to accept your kind invitation which you gave me as an alternative; I am making a tour of the world and I hope to be on the continent of Europe in the Autumn.

I would much like to see Tokio—Yokogyo, Yokogyo, Yokogyo

—but it is 17 days from San Francisco and the accommodation is not luxurious in that town just now. If I fail to afford to go far West to East you may see me in August, as I will be journeying to Italy then. I suppose I will be gladder to see you than you to see me: but I miss the touch of a vanished hand and the sound of a voice that is still. When I mention voice, I may say that a journey to New York on your part would not be a risk, that is: you would not fail to make money rapidly: there is much money here.

You may have heard that I got the Fellowship[5] R.C.S.I. If you can forget, write to this place: I shall have left: but they will send it after me. I will not be long here. Already I am beaten to the 12th floor; there are 16 floors in all—accommodation for 2000 people. I shall use the top floor for an Olivet and leave. The American edition of 'Sinbad' is out. It runs to 230 stanzas . . . but we may meet in three months time. Yours as ever,

Oliver Gogarty

They did not meet in three months and Joyce referred slightingly to a card which Gogarty sent him from Paris later in 1906: 'Of Gogarty's card I can make nothing. I don't understand why he desires that we should exchange short notes at long distances and at different angles to the equator.' Nevertheless they resumed correspondence. Gogarty wrote several letters to him from Vienna and seemed genuinely anxious to help him.

26-X-'07   IX. Spitalgasse, I,
                                                      St. II, 19.
                                                       Vienna

Dear Joyce: I am glad to hear from you. I was not the author of the letters you speak of: but if they enabled you to get anything out of the reluctant Trieste Post-office they were not without a little value. Some of them, probably, came from Cosgrave who, as Keeper of the Quid, was beginning to fear your uncle's suspicion, and to suspect the clerks of Trieste.

I heard you were stricken with a grievous distemper, and that you were paralysed. You can understand that the sight of your handwriting rejoiced me, as it disproved the statement that your right arm was paralysed. I was not a little surprised as well though the aetiology of a disease which your uncle insisted was altogether ethical should have prepared me for your being miraculously made whole again.

65

Please let me have one word of how you are getting on. Write here and, if I do not answer in due time, drop a line to the Café Klinik (same street) for there is some strange uncertainty about my letters which affects me here.

We have been deploring you in Dublin—your regretful uncle included. Cosgrave longed for you to meet 'The Master' (of both faculties) whose vinous villanelles so constrained McNeill . . .

Let me know about your illness—if I can be of any help.

Yrs ever,
Oliver Gogarty.

10-XII-'07   IX. Spitalgasse, I,
                                                    Vienna

Dear Joyce: Could you come here about the middle of January? It might be worth your while to come for a week in which you might estimate the value of the place to you. I would willingly give 38 Kr a week to have German while here: but—what would be of more importance to you—I could give you an introduction to the Medical Society which would put you in the way of getting as many tuitions as you could take, if you cared. There is only one old fellow at it here. His fee is 20 Kr for 8 lessons; and he has an overflowing monopoly. Regards the medical terms, they would be no obstacle. If you could make such arrangements as might free you from your engagements for a week towards the end of January, let me know, and I will send you a return ticket to Vienna from Trieste. Most of the work would be done between 5 and 9 oc. All the mornings would be at your own disposal. The monopolist here does not speak English! And the place is never without a hundred doctors. At present there are over 300 in the various branches. I have become attached to the University; this will necessitate my remaining here 3 months longer than I expected. Do give the place a week's trial or even five days!

The reasons for suggesting to forward MS are that I don't know enough German to steer it through the press; the English is quainter than your Holy Office; the MS is not confined altogether to verses.

Later I shall make arrangements for whatever tour time will permit me to make.

Sincerely yours,
Oliver Gogarty

16-XII-'07   IX. Spitalgasse, I,
                                    Vienna
Dear Joyce: I am glad you will be able to get the MS printed.
Thanks for your note.

Could you get away for a week in January—the latter half—
to come up here? You would be my guest, and not out of pocket
by the journey or stay.

Things here are not more haphazard than they generally are.
A week would let you see for yourself. Of course, I don't know
more about your affairs than you have told me: but I would
like to see you before I leave; and, since I have become attached
to the University here, I may be kept experimenting so late
(March) that I might not have time to go down south, as I had
originally thought. 38 Kr was the minimum assured whether you
got work or not while I remain.

                                         Ever yrs, O.G.

They did not meet then or in the following year but when Joyce
returned to Ireland on 29 July 1909 the first person he saw was
Gogarty (his uncomplimentary description in a postcard to Stannie
was 'Gogarty's fat back') who happened to be on Kingstown pier. He
avoided a meeting and when he encountered him again some days
later in Merrion Square he cut him. Gogarty ran after him, took him
by the arm and persuaded Joyce to call to Ely Place.

He had already sent Joyce an invitation to lunch at the Dolphin
Hotel—

31-VII-'09   15 Ely Place
                                    Dublin
Dear Joyce: Curiosis Cosgrave tells me you are in Dublin.
Before trying to get you to come to lunch at Dolphin on Monday
next at 1.0'c I would like to have a word with you. My man will
drive you across (if you are in). I leave town at 5 each evening;
but there can be changes if you turn up.

He will call about 3.20. Do come if you can or will. I am
looking forward to seeing you with pleasure. There are many
things I would like to discuss and a plan or two to divert you.
You have not yet plumbed all the depths of poetry; there is
Broderick the Bard! of whom more anon.

                         Yours
                         O.G.

—but had been obliged because of a professional engagement to send a further note postponing the lunch.

When Joyce went along to Ely Place he stiffly refused his host's offer of 'grog, wine, coffee, tea' and declined an invitation to lunch with the Gogartys in Enniskerry. 'You have your life,' he said, 'Leave me to mine.'

Finally Gogarty exploded: 'Well, do you really want me to go to hell and be damned?'

'I bear you no ill-will,' Joyce replied. I believe you have some points of good nature. You and I of six years ago are both dead. But I must write as I have felt.'

'I don't care a damn what you say of me so long as it is literature.'

'Do you mean that?' Joyce asked.

'I do. Honest to Jaysus! Now will you shake hands with me at least?'

'I will on that understanding.'

Their reluctant handshake was a farewell gesture. It was their last meeting but after Joyce's death two books were found on his desk, a Greek dictionary and Gogarty's *I Follow St. Patrick*.

*

In the intervening years they had lost no opportunity to revile each other. 'James Joyce was not a gentleman,' Gogarty told an English literary critic; and to an Irish visitor who had spoken of Gogarty's success in surgery Joyce said, 'God help anyone who gets into the hands of that fellow.'

Gogarty's scathing criticism of *Ulysses*—'That bloody Joyce whom I kept in my youth has written a book you can read on all the lavatory walls of Dublin'—culminated in a savage essay, 'They Think They Know Joyce' (*Saturday Review of Literature*) disparaging 'the cracked mirror of *Ulysses* with its preposterous and factitious parallel to Homer's fairy tale,' and denigrating its author—'this contradictory character, who in his early days knew beauty so well, became chief of the apostles of confusion and ugliness, the leader of the decadents.' And this at a time when the apotheosis of Joyce in the English Literature Departments of American universities was already accomplished! It was—as Denis Johnston has remarked—as if Gogarty had deliberately belched at Mass.

It was no more than the *Pink 'Un*, Bernard Shaw, and the majority of his generation had said already but such a diatribe was unexpected in 1950. It is not fanciful to suggest that it has delayed recognition of Gogarty's own literary achievements and it may have caused Joyce's admirers to see Gogarty as the disruptor of the friendship.

If blame is to be apportioned—and are not sundering years, diverging interests, and varying fortunes responsible for the withering of many friendships?—Joyce's unquestionable susceptibility to persecutory feelings, and Stannie's jealous railings should be remembered. Gogarty's material success would not have enhanced him in Joyce's eyes and his unbridled tongue made many enemies. But Joyce who was by no means honey-tongued in those days, caring not at all for the susceptibilities of others (to his Aunt Josephine, a fervent Catholic: 'I spit upon the image of the Tenth Pius') might have been expected to be correspondingly insensitive to verbal insults.

Certainly it should be remembered to Gogarty's credit that he aided Joyce materially; that his gaiety warmed their friendship for a time; and that he probably introduced him to the National Maternity Hospital, Holles Street, the background to the Oxen of the Sun episode.

CHAPTER 5

THE OXEN OF THE SUN

When James Joyce was two years old a small lying-in hospital was opened in Holles Street by Dr. William Roe.[1] The available funds were meagre and even though the annual expenditure (£316:18:6d in 1886) was infinitesimal compared with the cost of running the National Maternity Hospital to-day, the out-goings exceeded the receipts. The hospital closed in 1893 but on St. Patrick's Day 1894 it re-opened with a new Committee of Management, under the patronage of His Grace the Most Rev. Dr. William Walsh, Archbishop of Dublin ('Billy with the lip', as John S. Joyce disrespectfully called him) who performed the opening ceremony.

Two adjoining houses were purchased for £700 in 1901 and a Royal charter was granted in the following year. Plans for a new wing had to be deferred for economic reasons but in 1928 it was finally decided that the hospital must be re-built and this was successfully accomplished after a public appeal for £50,000.

At first the Mastership was held jointly by Dr. Patrick J. Barry (who retired in 1907) and Dr. Andrew Horne. The latter, who is featured in *Ulysses* ('Of that house A. Horne is lord') was born in Ballinasloe, Co. Galway in 1856 and educated at Clongowes and the Royal College of Surgeons in Ireland—graduating in 1877. He did post-graduate work in Vienna and was Assistant Master at the Rotunda Hospital from 1880-1883. He was President of the Royal College of Physicians of Ireland[2] from 1908-10 and received a knighthood in his last year of office. He died on 5 September 1924 after a long illness.

Under Horne's tutelage generations of students were instructed in the art of midwifery in the hospital and then sent out to apply it hesitantly 'on the district.' Usually 'the doctors' were well received in the homes of the poor but they sometimes encountered hostility. *St. Stephen's* the University College magazine, reported an occasion when two students of Jewish appearance were sent out to deal with a call from the district.

'Yous are Jewmen lookin' for money,' shouted the local gamins. 'Yous aren't from Holles Street at all.'

And such—according to *St. Stephen's,* echoing Joyce—such was the aggressiveness of 'the Juvenile Rabblement' that the student-doctors had to depart.

In most teaching-hospitals a state of conflict, or at best an uneasy peace, exists between the students and the administration and it was so in Holles Street. *St. Stephen's* spoke for the Catholic University students in February 1903: 'There is considerable friction between the Resident Medical Staff and the pupils. There is a code of rules for both; we believe that these rules are never kept. The resident pupils' rooms are in a scandalous condition, and compare very unfavourably with the luxurious apartments of the Matron and Assistant Master . . . the Matron informed one of the resident students that supper was going to be done away with. We hope not. It is a well-known fact in the School that the Hospital has been boycotted by a good section of the students this year, and as residents pay nearly twice what is paid in the Coombe Hospital, they expect to get at least proper attention.'

The next issue of *St. Stephen's* reported that the Committee had done a good deal to improve the condition of the students' rooms and that further improvements were promised. Meanwhile it is more than likely that the students would have overlooked their own faults, and in any case rowdy parties are in the tradition of Dublin Maternity hospitals. The Coombe Hospital was especially noted for abandoned festivity—'From the days when the Roman emperors conciliated the masses with "bread and circuses" down through the mad revelry of the Lords of misrule in the middle ages, and so on to the pre-lenten orgies of less far off times, I doubt if anything quite so barbarous has been experienced in Europe:' thus, with nostalgic exaggeration a former Coombe student[3] recalled the gaiety of youth—but even if the Coombe led, the Rotunda and Holles Street kept up a high standard of competition.

This is the house of full and plenty
You come in full, and you go out empty.

The wit who scribbled a motto appropriate for maternity hospitals may have had in mind both the patients on the labour couches and the crates of stout which were carried into the students' residencies at night-fall.

When Leopold Bloom visited Holles Street Hospital a rowdy drinking session was in progress. Joyce drew on personal recollections of similar carousals when writing the Oxen of the Sun episode and it is tempting to identify the evening of Bloomsday with a bacchanalian evening in Holles Street described by Gogarty in *Tumbling in the Hay,* a wonderfully funny evening enlivened by Kinch, Vincent Cosgrave, and John Rudolf Elwood. Gogarty's chronology, however, is unreliable. It is unlikely that he was in residence in the hospital until after 1905 (when he passed his examination in anatomy); his reminiscence is clearly aided by fiction, for by then Joyce was in Trieste.

That is not to say that the two wayward young men had not visited the hospital together at an earlier date. That they had done so is confirmed by a letter from Gogarty to Joyce in 1904.

> Worcester College,
> Oxford.
>
> Greeting—To those at Holles Street say—"a little time and they shall not see me"—to those at Tyrone Street "again a little time and you shall see me," and—"it is known for a surety that there is fornication among you."

Medical-student visitors come and go without ceremony in hospital residencies; all others need introduction but Gogarty would have vouched for Joyce who with his magpie instinct picked up obstetrical lore as well as the general medical-student bawdiness which is richest in maternity hospitals.

Stuart Gilbert's exegesis of *Ulysses* divides the multi-dimensional novel into several episodes, each focusing on a different art, colour, and organ. The art in the Oxen of the Sun episode is medicine; the colour (appropriate to the robes and dressings of a hospital) white; the organ, the womb.

It is of interest, then, to consider the extent and accuracy of the medical knowledge in this episode and in *Ulysses* in general and the validity of the embryological symbols.

❋

The discussion which Leopold Bloom listened to in Holles Street Hospital touched on favourite topics of a students' commonroom, birth-control ('But, gramercy, what of those God possibled souls that we nightly impossibilise . . .') sterility, abortion ('Lilith, patron of abortions') and the hazards of parturition. The Catholic Church decrees that in an extreme situation the survival of the infant must have prior consideration. Fortunately this ethical dilemma is nowadays so rare as to be of theoretical rather than practical interest and in any case the students 'all cried with one acclaim nay, by our Virgin Mother, the wife should live and the babe to die.' Later they talk about Caesarean section (a relatively uncommon operation in the 1900s) posthumous births, infanticide, anaesthesia, twilight sleep, artificial insemination, the menopause, premature rupture of membranes, monsters, congenital deformity, determination of sex, and the forgotten sponge in the peritoneal cavity.

The very audible 'terrorcausing shrieking of shrill women in their labour' disturbed Bloom who fell silent 'women's woe with wonder pondering.' The students, on the other hand, burst into song (Joyce borrowing from Gogarty): *'The first three months she was not well, Staboo.'*

Bloom was shocked that 'the puerperal dormitory and the dissecting theatre should be the seminaries of such frivolity,' and puzzled by the realization that 'the mere acquisition of academic titles should suffice to transform in a pinch of time these votaries of levity into exemplary practitioners of an art which most men any wise eminent have esteemed the noblest.' The noise and laughter brought the night-sister along; she 'stood by the door and begged them at the reverence of Jesu our alther liege lord to leave their wassailing for there was above one quick with child a gentle dame, whose time hied fast.'

Joyce's numerous correspondences to Homer's sacred oxen need not be recapitulated; he makes explicit reference to 'the art of medicine' and 'the art of physic'; he introduces ('I know a lady what's got a white swelling', 'a little fume of a fellow, blond as tow') appropriate chromatic references. By causing Dixon to ask if Buck Mulligan's increasing girth 'betokened an ovoblastic gestation in the prostatic utricle or male womb', he utilizes a recondite but singularly appropriate item of embryological knowledge. The tiny prostatic utricle is a vestigial remnant of the Müllerian duct from which in the female foetus the uterus and vagina develop.

This minute and impractical detail is a typical example of the useless fragments of information which, to the despair of their teachers, some students of quite limited capacity retain without difficulty. We may be sure that Joyce picked up this intriguing titbit in Holles Street but his reference to Stephen Dedalus as a 'morbid-minded aesthetic and embryophilosopher who for all his overweening bumptiousness in things scientific can scarcely distinguish an acid from an alkali' may be a tacit admission of his own lack of competence in medical matters. Characteristically this did not deter him from ambitious symbolism in the Oxen of the Sun episode where, as he explained to Frank Budgen,

73

Nurse Callan represents the ovum, Bloom the spermatozoon, Stephen the embryo, and the Lying-in Hospital the womb. The slayers of the sacred oxen are those folk who indulge in 'Copulation without population . . . Herod's slaughter of the innocents were the truer name.'

He illustrates 'the crime against fecundity,' referring now to 'a stout shield of oxengut' a shield named 'Killchild', and again hardly more subtly, 'Would to God that foresight had remembered me to take my cloak along! . . . I know of a *marchand de capotes*, Monsieur Poyntz, from whom I can have for a *livre* as snug a cloak of the French fashion as ever kept a lady from wetting.' And there is unmeasured praise and encouragement for a middle-aged Bank accountant who, with a 'modicum of man's work,' has fathered a ninth child. 'Toil on, labour like a very bandog and let scholarment and all Malthusiasts go hang. Thou art all their daddies, Theodore.'

Joyce explained to his friend that the episode contains 'the natural stages of development in the embryo and the periods of faunal evolution in general.' To achieve this object he employed a literary device : commencing in the anglo-saxon style (after an amorphous passage to represent the unfertilized ovum) he continues in the manner of Mandeville, Mallory, Milton, Sir Thomas Browne, and so on imitating successive prose styles until the full richness of the nineteenth century masters, Walter Pater and John Henry Newman, is reached; there follows a disintegration into slang and pidgin English, the after-birth. He was well endowed for this particular method, but, not content with a literary tour de force, he undertook a task for which he was singularly ill-equipped, the anatomical portrayal of foetal development.

Joyce's personal library contained no medical books[4] and we have seen that his contact with formal medical education was tangential. The 'medical notes' (1902) in the Cornell Joyce Collection are mere lists of anatomical terms. During his wife's first pregnancy he asked Stannie 'to study by yourself or with Cosgrave some midwifery and embryology and to send me the results of your study' but is it likely that he could have obtained other than the sketchiest of information from that source?

When writing the Oxen of the Sun episode in 1920, however, he drew a chart depicting an oval of increasing dimensions—the fertilized ovum—appending notes of foetal length in centimetres, and weight in grammes, and points of progressive development. All he needed for this rough plan could have been found in an encyclopaedia but it is clear from the *Ulysses* note-sheets[5] in the British Museum that he studied a text-book of embryology.

74

The notes for the gestation chart in the Cornell Joyce Collection start at the second month:[6]

2. 1–3 cm; 2–6 gr; boat-shape; big head; short limbs; web fingers; eyeless; noseless; earless; mouthless, sexless; 1st bone.
3. 9 cm. 30 gr; lips; ear; sex; finger; jaw bone.
5. Nails; iris membrane; 1st hair; 25 cm. 250 gr.; cheekbones; finger bones.
6. 30–40 cm; 1,000 gr; scrotum empty; skin red; smaller head; pubis; fontanelles.
7. 40 cm. 1,500 grs; heelbone; breast bone; old face; testicles in groin; fore-fontanelles smaller.
8. 45 cm. 2,000 gr; face younger; cheeks fuller; outer ears; nails longer; testicles lower, loose; clitoris; ? nymphs; sacral bones; fontanelles almost shut; caseus gloss in joints.
9. 50 cm. 3,500 gr; tooth sockets; sex full; nails long; hair 3 cm. dark; thigh bone nucleus.

Reading the episode with Joyce's plan in mind it is certainly possible to uncover laboriously within the literary gestation many references appropriate to fertilization and foetal growth. Stephen Dedalus, pondering the haphazard but inexorable process of reproduction, remarks, 'We are means to those small creatures within us and nature has other ends than we,' but it is Bloom, we are told, who represents the spermatozoon which unites with the nurse-ovum 'That man her will worthful went into Horne's house . . .' and, as we know, lending credulity to a system where the part is greater than the whole, the hospital represents the womb. What a pity, incidentally, that Joyce relegates 'Fallopian tube' to use as a whore's expletive in the Circe episode! It should have been utilized here, for fertilization occurs in the tube.[7]

'Before born babe bliss had. Within womb won he worship . . .' But death is inherent in birth, every naked corpse has come naked from the womb. At first, however, we resemble 'strange fishes withouten heads.'

The growing embryo takes on shape and 'at the end of a second month a human soul was infused.' The gesture of 'laying hand to jaw' may mark the development of the fingers and jaw and it is shortly after this that the students sing their bawdy catch, 'The first three months she was not well, Staboo'.

Stephen's reference to the 'university of Oxtail' recalls an early stage when in the 'tenebrosity of the interior' the embryo has a tail.

'The storm that hist the heart' and 'his heart shook within the cage of his breast' are indications of the increasing function of the foetal heart. The individual whose visual organs '. . . were . . . commencing to exhibit symptoms of animation' refers to the development of the eyes; 'whispering in my ears' and 'the outer chamber of my ear' refer to the separate development of auditory function and the pinna. Meaning may be found, too, in 'the chick's nails' and 'slicked his hair' but to attempt to pursue the subject exhaustively would be tedious.

Eventually 'the skill and patience of the physician has brought about a happy *accouchement.*' The new-born infant—'Outflings my lord Stephen'—is born when Stephen Dedalus and the medical students rush helter skelter from the hospital-womb, and immediately takes its first breath: 'The air without is impregnated with raindew moisture, life essence celestial, glistering on Dublin stone there under starshiny *coelum.* God's air, the Allfather's air, scintillant circumambient cessile air. Breathe it deep into thee.'

Just as 17th century Dutch artists when painting interiors revelled in adding to their walls mirrors reflecting miniatures of their creations. Joyce has woven miniatures of life in the world within the main design of embryological development. 'The aged sisters draw us into life: we wail, batten, sport, clip, clasp, sunder, dwindle, die: over us dead they bend.' And like Omar Khayyám—'*What, without asking, hither hurried whence?*'— he ponders the mystery of existence, the future ('whether to Tophet or to Edenville') and the past equally obscure. For all is hidden 'when we would backward see from what region of remoteness the whatness of our whoness hath fetched his whenceness.'

A study of ontogenetic development affords phylogenetic insights and to-day, thanks to 'the late ingenious Mr. Darwin' behind erect and thoughtful *homo sapiens* we see the shadow of 'a cropeared creature of mishapen gibbosity' and behind 'that missing link of creation's chain' man's remote tree-living ancestors.

The past conceals 'cycles of cycles of generations that have lived.' Look back to prehistoric times:

Agendath is a waste land, a home of screechowls and the sand-blind upupa. Netaim, the golden, is no more. And on the high-way of the clouds they come, muttering thunder of rebellion, the ghosts of beasts. Huuh! Hark! Huuh! . . . Elk and yak, the bulls of Bashan and of Babylon, mammoth and mastodon, they come trooping to the sunken sea, *Lacus Mortis.* Ominous, revengeful zodiacal host! They moan, passing upon the clouds, horned and capricorned, the trumpeted with the tusked, the lionmaned the giant-antlered, snouter and crawler, rodent, ruminant and pachyderm, all their moving moaning multitude, murderers of the sun.

The evocation of 'faunal evolution in general' promised by Joyce to Budgen is brilliantly fulfilled. The delightful literary parallel of ontogenesis is a complete success. And the symbolism of sperm and ovum? . . . The depiction of foetal parts? . . . Readers untrained in embryology may find it clever; those with knowledge of the subject are likely to be disappointed. Any physician who has studied the sub-divisions of the zygote, marvelling at the relentless cellular re-duplication, and differentiation which transforms a speck of protoplasm into unbelievably intricate aggregations of cells, numberless as the grains of sand on a seashore, forming tissues and organs, blood and bone, the woof and warp of the mewling puking human infant, will remain dissatisfied.

It may be argued, however, that a medical practitioner stands too close to the subject to appreciate Joyce's intentions; that because of his daily preoccupation with a thicket of human organs he cannot see the wood for the trees; that any uncommitted non-medical reader stands at a better critical vantage point. Conceding this possibility it is interesting to refer to 'The Oxen of the Sun' by A. M. Klein.

In his extraordinarily detailed analysis Klein sees Sir Alexander Horne as 'an inlet of the sea (cf. Golden Horn), that is, the cervix,' the inlet to the womb, rather than the more obvious phallic symbol; he remarks that the monosyllabic alliterative language of the anglo-saxon passage 'is to be considered, in biological terms, as unicellular, amoeboid;' he discerns in Joyce's employment of the word 'cup' an intention of showing 'that invagination preliminary to the fashioning of the gastrula has taken place.'

Anticipating that hostile critics would find in his exegesis 'a forced ingenuity on the part of the commentator,' Klein adduces proofs, 'imprimis, secundo, tertio' to support his argument. But, almost with a shock, one realizes that he was using a faulty transcript of Joyce's letter to Budgen and has misread 'faunal' as 'formal'. His quest of Joyce's representation of 'formal evolution in general' meets no hindrance, however, and we are guided forward through the episode to present-day civilization from the Azoic Rocks. Almost involuntarily one murmurs with Molly Bloom, 'ah, rocks!'

It is difficult to avoid a suspicion that Klein's apparent inventiveness in the sphere of geological evolution may vitiate his conclusions regarding Joyce and embryology. It was Klein's treatise which roused Gogarty to such a pitch that he dashed off the notorious piece for the *Saturday Review of Literature*. Denis Johnston has related how the Irish poet swept into a New York chophouse, threw a quarterly containing the offending article on the counter, and pointed to it indignantly. 'That's what we've come to!' he exclaimed. 'The fellow once spent an evening with me in Holles Street Hospital. And now some character in Canada is probably getting a Ph.D. for analysing his profound knowledge of midwifery.'

Gogarty would, of course, have been astounded to learn that Klein's conclusions are in a certain measure justified by the evidence of the *Ulysses* note-sheets, where, jotted criss-cross in a script difficult to decipher, are innumerable references to embryology which, as Philip F. Herring has pointed out, indicates that Joyce consulted an Italian textbook.

On one sheet we encounter: 'Meetpoint, ovary, tube, womb; nemasperm head on; one winsrace; different appearance of Nurse Callan; male pronucleus and female do fuse; Best time 2nd half after menstr.; when egg not fecundated menstr. angry; regression of follicola, wrinkles, corpo luteo, yellow.' Numerous birth-control methods are cited: 'coito interroto, mezzoritiro, coit interret, 8 days before and aft. not, pessario, spugna, assorbente, capuchon, ovuline, irrigate, powder.' And again details of foetal development: '2nd M. notocorda, formation of cartilage knobs in membrane; 4th M. closure of verteb. col. . . . 2nd M. reduc. no of verteb. tail piece; welding of atlas and epistrophs; 2nd M. formation of thoracic ribs . . . blood islands: comdoni; 4th M.—all red corpuscles; heart descends fr. brain; tube, middle swell, curve L . . .'

Joyce approached his impossible task methodically until, as Robert Janusko has said, 'after sketching out a nine-month framework to his satisfaction, he proceeded to write a chapter of a novel, refusing to subordinate artistic concerns to extra-literary devices.'

*   *   *   *

Mrs. Purefoy's labour was slow—'never was none so hard as was that woman's birth'—but normal; Joyce also alludes to abnormal births including the Virgin birth, 'a birth without pangs;' evisceration (a traumatic expedient resorted to in extreme situations) and 'the distressing manner of delivery called by the Brandenburghers *Sturzgeburt.*'

After Mina Purefoy's delivery (the placenta weighing 'a full pound if a milligram') Bloom enjoins the *regimen sanitas* of Salerno, the first modern medical school, 'Doctor Diet and Doctor Quiet.' Then he follows the students to a rowdy pub and during a disjointed conversation someone exclaims, 'The Leith police dismisseth us.'

Joyce explained to the German translator of *Ulysses* that this is a police-station test for inebriation but it is also a hospital test for dysarthria and he probably picked it up from his medical-student friends from whom he appropriated so much including

> *First he tickled her*
> *Then he patted her*
> *Then he passed the female catheter*

so typical of the effortless bawdy of maternity hospitals.

Stephen Dedalus's question to Lynch 'Which side is your knowledge bump?' relates to Gall and Spurzheim's discarded system of phrenology. Bloom, like Joyce, is a physician *manqué*, and even Molly Bloom would like to know more about physiology: '. . . still he knows a lot of mixed up things about the body and the insides I often wanted to study up that myself what we have inside us in that family physician . . .'

Laryngeal function was of particular interest to Joyce—'The human voice, two tiny silky cords. Wonderful, more than all the others'—but even the banal act of washing is analysed by Leopold Bloom, 'the parts of the human anatomy most sentitive to cold being the nape, stomach, and thenar or sole of the foot.' Another of Bloom's interests, titillated by a suggestion of sadism, is the circulation of the blood, 'A warm tingling glow without effusion. Refined birching to stimulate the circulation.'

An encounter with a blind stripling in Dawson Street directs his thoughts to sensation.

> Sense of smell must be stronger too. Smells on all sides bunched together. Each person too. Then the spring, the summer: smells. Tastes. They say you can't taste wines with your eyes shut or a cold in the head. Also smoke in the dark they say get not pleasure.

Tactile sensation can be improved by training. 'Read with their fingers, Tune pianos.' But there are limits to perception. 'His hands on her hair for instance. Say it was black for instance. Good. We call it black. Then passing over her white skin. Different feel perhaps.

Feeling of white.' And like John Hunter he tries the experiment, fingering a slack fold of his belly. 'But I know it's whiteyellow. Want to try in the dark to see.'

Eventually Bloom meditates upon what Klein anticipated in an earlier episode, 'eons of geological periods recorded in the stratifications of the earth'; upon microbes, germs, bacteria, bacilli, spermatozoa; upon 'the universe of human serum constellated with red and white bodies, themselves universes of void space constellated with other bodies, each, in continuity, its universe of divisible component bodies of which each was again divisible in divisions of redivisible component bodies, dividends and divisors ever diminishing without actual division till, if the progress were carried far enough, nought nowhere was never reached.'

It is as if Joyce, aware of the simple magnifying glass and the compound microscope, had anticipated the more recent revelations of the electron microscope.

X-rays were a comparative novelty in 1904 and naturally interested Bloom. 'Then with those Röntgen rays searchlight you could . . . watch it all the way down, swallow a pin sometimes come out of the ribs years after, tour around the body, changing biliary duct, spleen squirting liver, gastric juice coils of intestines like pipes. But the poor buffer would have to stand all the time with his insides entrails on show. Science.'

Bloom's hand possessed 'the operative surgical quality but that he was reluctant to shed human blood even when the end justified the means, preferring in their natural order, heliotherapy, psychophysicotherapeutics, osteopathic surgery.'

A chemist's shop evokes reflections on pharmacology with added undertones of alchemy:

The chemist turned back page after page. Sandy shrivelled smell he seems to have. Shrunken skull. And old. Quest for the philosopher's stone. The alchemists. Drugs age you after mental excitement. Lethargy then. Why? Reaction. A lifetime in a night. Gradually changes your character. Living all the day among herbs, ointments, disinfectants. All his alabaster lilypots. Mortar and pestle. Aq. Dist. Fol. Laur. Te virid. Smell almost cure you like the dentist's doorbell. Doctor whack. He ought to physic himself a bit. Electuary or emulsion. The first fellow that picked an herb to cure himself had a bit of pluck. Simples. Want to be careful. Enough stuff here to chloroform you. Test: turns blue litmus paper red. Chloroform. Overdose of Laudanum. Sleeping draughts. Love-philtres. Paragoric poppysyrup bad for cough. Clogs the pores or the phlegm. Poisons the only cure. Remedy where you least expect it. Clever of nature.

Homely lotions and liniments are invested with poignancy by Bloom's associations. The application which imparted a wax-like delicacy to his wife's skin contained sweet almond oil, tincture of benzoin, orangeflower water and, of course, white wax. The remedy for neuralgia which Rudolf Virag used to kill himself was 'composed of 2 parts of aconite liniment to 1 of chloroform liniment.' And 'Up the fundament' as an enema Bloom had administered 'one third of a pint of quassia, to which add a tablespoonful of rock salt.'

When it came to prescribing for the appropriately-named Pisser Burke's bladder trouble Bloom ordered

Acid. nit. hydrochlor. dil., 20 minims.
Tinct. nux. vom., 4 minims.
Extr. taraxel. lig., 30 minims.
Aq. dis. ter in die.

but Joyce's printer perpetrated an error which remains uncorrected in successive editions of *Ulysses* where the second ingredient is Tinct. mix. vom.

For sunburn the golden haired Miss Kennedy advocated 'borax with the cherry laurel water.' Bloom, too, favours traditional recipes: 'strawberries for the teeth: nettles and rainwater': oatmeal steeped in buttermilk and old Virag's cure for warts, 'Wheatenmeal with honey and nutmeg' which Bloom alters playfully to 'Wheatenmeal with lycopodium and syllabax.'

Pharmacology merges with dietetics. Bloom 'relished a glass of choice old wine in season as both nourishing and blood-making' and remembered that hot fresh blood was prescribed for the decline. Still more bizarre his reflections in Glasnevin cemetery—'A corpse is meat gone bad. Well and what's cheese! Corpse of milk'—and his dietary analysis in Eccles Street:

concerning the respective percentage of protein and caloric energy in bacon, salt ling and butter, the absence of the former in the lastnamed and the abundance of the latter in the firstnamed.

The illnesses mentioned in *Ulysses* include asthma, anaemia, eczema, the common cold, concussion, St. Vitus's dance, typhoid fever, gastritis, diarrhoea, jaundice, Derbyshire neck, quinsy, gout, acute pneumonia, small-pox, spinal curvature, sciatica, piles, and cobbler's weak chest.

Many remedies have been advocated for the lingering symptoms of pertussis.

> Gasworks. Whooping cough they say it cures. Good job Milly never got it. Poor children! Doubles them up black and blue in convulsions. Shame really. Got off lightly with illness compared. Only measles. Flaxseed tea. Scarlatina, influenza epidemics.

Gerty McDowell suffers from some of the minor disorders common among female adolescents.

> Her figure was slight and graceful, inclining even to fragility but those iron jelloids she had been taking of late had done her a world of good much better than the Widow Welch's female pills and she was much better of those discharges she used to get and that tired feeling.

The handy-woman Anne Kearns uses Lourdes water for her lumbago. Richie Goulding, similarly afflicted, employs a different therapy: 'Wife ironing his back. Thinks he'll cure it with pills. All bread crumbs they are. About six hundred per cent profit.'

Paddy Dignam, 'the wall of the heart hypertrophied' died suddenly: 'Breakdown, Martin Cunningham said. Heart. He tapped his chest sadly.' A death like Parnell's.

J. J. O'Molloy has tuberculosis: 'Cleverest fellow at the junior bar he used to be. Decline poor chap. That hectic flush spells finis for a man. Touch and go with him.'

Haemoptysis, a common complication of that disease is well described—'He applies his handkerchief to his mouth and scrutinizes the galloping tide of rose-pink blood'—and an old-fashioned theory of causation, appropriate in the context, is mentioned: 'And the beds of the Barrow and the Shannon they won't deepen with millions of acres of marsh and bog to make us all die of consumption.' But poverty is a contributing factor: 'In a room lit by a candle stuck in a bottleneck a slut combs out the tatts from the hair of a scrofulous child.'

Dans ce bordel où tenons nostre état (Circe) a hard chancre, albuminoid urine, and a depressed patellar reflex would be commonplace and hypospadia might be encountered. 'Bronzed with infamy' indicates a syphilitic rash and 'a dark mercurialised face' side-effects of treatment for syphilis. 'Some chap with a dose burning him' is an obvious allusion to gonorrhoea; both infections would have been frequent in 'an army rotten with venereal diseases.'

Bloom's reference to colonial civilization evokes the remark, 'Their syphilization you mean,' from the Citizen implying that the invaders introduce the disease to an uninfected populace, but Joyce may be referring, too, to Kraft-Ebing's dictum that G.P.I. is a product of syphilization and civilization.

Joyce incorrectly calls the epileptic cry 'piercing' and displays the lay-man's general prejudice against persons with epilepsy: 'profuse yellow spawn foaming over his bony epileptic lips.' Paralysis is exemplified by Commendatore Bacibaci Beninobenone and by the face of William Shakespeare 'rigid in facial paralysis.' The latter's, 'Weda seca whokilla farst' represents dysphasia.

Leopold Bloom has transvestist tendencies: 'I tried her things on only once, a small prank, in Holles Street.' His father afflicted by involutional melancholia took a suicidal dose of aconite, 'resorted to by increasing doses of grains and scruples as a palliative of recrudescent neuralgia.' Myles Crawford has 'incipient jigs'; Mr. Breen dreamt he saw the ace of spades walking up the stairs; Simon Dedalus's drinking has brought his family to ruin; and had Gerty McDowell's father 'only avoided the clutches of the demon drink, by taking the pledge or those powders the drink habit cured in Pearson's Weekly, she might now be rolling in her carriage, second to none.'

Certainly a 'pandemonium of ills' is skilfully deployed in *Ulysses* and Joyce is at his best in describing symptoms—

> A cough ball of laughter leaped from his throat dragging after it a rattling chain of phlegm—

or in a literary evocation of mania:

> A hater of his kind ran from them to the wood of madness, his mane foaming in the moon, his eyeballs stars. Houyhnhnm, horse-nostrilled.

The texture of the novel, entertwining skein after skein of meaning and purpose, may explain why he so seldom goes beyond merely naming a disease. His ability to delineate suffering in clinical detail is more easily seen in the less complex pages of *Dubliners*.

CHAPTER 6

DUBLINERS

Serious illness has several aspects. A frightening disaster to the patient and to his dear ones, it is a diagnostic and therapeutic challenge to the doctor and a cause for endless speculation to the uninvolved onlooker, who frequently manages to extract a vicarious thrill from the sinister sickroom drama. Children, especially, are affected in this way; the possibility of death, an event so remote and improbable for themselves, when seen as an approaching reality for another plays upon their fertile imaginations.

The narrator of the first story in *Dubliners*, a youngster, knowing that the Rev. James Flynn lies dying from a third stroke passes the house night after night studying the lighted square of the bedroom window.

> He had often said to me: 'I am not long for this world,' and I had thought his words idle. Now I knew they were true. Every night as I gazed up at the window I said softly to myself the world paralysis. It had always sounded strangely in my ears, like the word gnomon in the Euclid and the word simony in the Catechism. But now it sounded to me like the name of some maleficent and sinful being. It filled me with fear, and yet I longed to be nearer to it and to look upon its deadly work.

Joyce expands his perceptive description of a boy's reactions in this sombre situation by indicating his hesitation next day in the corpse-house competing with his wish to view the corpse: 'There he lay, solemn and copious, vested as for the altar . . . His face was very truculent, grey and massive, with black cavernous nostrils and circled by a scanty white fur.'

And yet the elders could say, 'No one would think he'd make such a beautiful corpse.' Contrasting, too, with the callow youth's interest in the mystery of the dead priest's life is the bereaved sister's wish to soften the details of his mental illness, telling how he was found in the dark in his confession-box.

> Wide awake and laughing-like to himself . . . So then, of course when they saw that, that made them think that there was something gone wrong with him . . .

84

Her words are pathetically suited to her wish '. . . that made them *think* that there was something *gone wrong* with him . . .' As if the palpable fact of his insanity was not at once revealed! And, then, her desire to attribute the breakdown to some understandable circumstance: 'It was that chalice he broke . . . That was the beginning of it . . .'

The old woman in 'The Sisters' is skilfully drawn—'[she] proceeded to toil up the narrow staircase before us, her bowed head being scarcely above the level of the bannister-rail'—and there is a graphic picture of decrepit old age in 'Ivy Day in the Committee Room'.

It was an old man's face, very bony and hairy. The moist blue eyes blinked at the fire and the moist mouth fell open at times, munching once or twice mechanically when it closed.

Old Cotter ('The Sisters') sometimes talks of 'faints and worms'[1] but it is Mr. M'Coy ('Grace') who resembles Bloom in liking to air his medical knowledge.

'No,' said Mr Kernan. 'I think I caught cold on the car. There's something keeps coming into my throat; phlegm or . . .'
'Mucus', said Mr M'Coy.
'It keeps coming like from down in my throat; sickening thing.'
'Yes, yes', said Mr M'Coy, 'that's the thorax.'
He looked at Mr Cunningham and Mr Power at the same time with an air of challenge . . .

There is a remarkable description in 'A Painful Case' of *hippus*, ability to constrict the pupils voluntarily.

It was an oval face . . . The eyes were very dark blue and steady. Their gaze began with a defiant note, but was confused by what seemed a deliberate swoon of the pupil in to the iris, revealing for an instant a temperament of great sensibility. The pupil reasserted itself quickly . . .

We encounter 'little Keogh the cripple', epilepsy, a pervert, a lady who assuaged her romantic desires 'by eating a great deal of Turkish delight in secret,' Michael Furey ('I think he died for me') who died of tuberculosis, and Mr. Duffy who 'lived at a little distance from his own body, regarding his own acts with doubtful side-glances', but the disorder which dominates *Dubliners* is alcoholism.

Freddy Malins in 'The Dead' ('they were dreadfully afraid that Freddy Malins might turn up screwed') is the least degenerate of

Joyce's drunkards. A forty year old bachelor, feckless and amusing but still socially acceptable, Malins is a problem to his mother ('And his poor mother made him take the pledge on New Year's Eve') but to no one else, unlike Farrington ('Counterparts') whose household is disturbed by his drunkenness.

Farrington, a clerk in Crosbie and Alleyne's, has 'a hanging face, dark wine-coloured.' Well advanced in alcoholism he finds difficulty in coping with his work. 'The dark damp night was coming and he longed to spend it in the bars, drinking with his friends amid the glare of gas and the clatter of glasses.' After pawning his watch to raise funds the pub-crawler begins with 'tailors of malt, hot' in Davy Byrne's and then went on to the Scotch House and later to Mulligan's of Poolbeg Street.

Mr. Kernan, 'a commercial traveller of the old school which believed in the dignity of its calling,' an older man, gave the lie to the tradition of his profession by falling downstairs in a pub ('Grace').

> Two gentlemen who were in the lavatory at the time tried to lift him up: but he was quite helpless. He lay curled up at the foot of the stairs down which he had fallen. They succeeded in turning him over. His hat had rolled a few yards away and his clothes were smeared with the filth and ooze of the floor on which he had lain, face downwards. His eyes were closed and he breathed with a grunting noise. A thin stream of blood trickled from the corner of his mouth.

When he came round a friend took him home. Mrs. Kernan who accepted her husband's intemperance 'as part of the climate' exclaimed: 'Such a sight! O, he'll do for himself one day and that's the holy alls of it. He's been drinking since Friday.'

The friend is at pains to disclaim responsibility for Kernan's condition and Mrs. Kernan inveighs against other so-called friends: 'O, you needn't tell me that, Mr Power. I know you're a friend of his, not like some of the others he does be with. They're all right so long as he has money in his pocket to keep him out from his wife and family. Nice friends!' And then, despite the object-lesson before them, the poor woman's hospitable instinct is to offer Mr. Power a drink. 'I'm so sorry that I've nothing in the house to offer you. But if you wait a minute I'll send round to Fogarty's at the corner.'

Mr. Cunningham was another of Kernan's real friends, but his sympathy probably lay with Mrs. Kernan for Cunningham 'had married an unpresentable woman who was an incurable drunkard. He had set up house for her six times; and each time she had pawned the furniture on him.'

Female alcoholics are possibly more devious and determined than males. At an inquest ('A Painful Case') on Mrs. Emily Sinico: 'Miss Mary Sinico said that of late her mother had been in the habit of going out at night to buy spirits. She, witness, had often tried to reason with her mother and had induced her to join a League.'

Mrs. Sinico's hidden motive for drinking was unrequited love but the cause of alcoholism is usually more complex. To any parent a drunken offspring is an unfathomable mystery, and the old caretaker in 'Ivy Day in the Committee Room' cannot understand why his son turned out badly. 'Now who'd think he'd turn out like that! I sent him to the Christian Brothers and I done what I could for him, and there he goes boozing about. I tried to make him someway decent . . . "I won't keep you", I says. "You must get a job for yourself." But, sure, it's worse whenever he gets a job; he drinks it all.'

Mrs. Mooney ('The Boarding House') had separated from her husband 'a shabby stooped little drunkard with a white face and a white moustache and white eyebrows, pencilled above his little eyes, which were pink-veined and raw.' The youngster in 'Araby' waited impatiently. 'At nine o'clock I heard my uncle's latchkey in the hall door. I heard him talking to himself and heard the hallstand rocking when it had received the weight of his overcoat. I could interpret these signs.' Maria ('Clay') hoped 'that Joe wouldn't come in drunk. He was so different when he took any drink.'

Nineteen year old Eveline Hill ('Eveline') unspeakably wearied by her drunken father's meanness and afraid of his violence, has an instinctive understanding of a psychosomatic disorder: 'She knew it was that that had given her the palpitations.'

Stephen Dedalus, too, recalls poignantly in *A Portrait* how he was mortified by his father's behaviour.

> They had set out early in the morning from Newcombe's coffee-house, where Mr Dedalus's cup had rattled noisily against its saucer, and Stephen had tried to cover that shameful sign of his father's drinking-bout of the night before by moving his chair and coughing. One humiliation had succeeded another—the false smiles of the market sellers, the curvetings and oglings of the barmaids with whom his father flirted . . .

He had to contend also with his own post-pubertal guilt feelings.

A tremulous chill blew round his heart, no stronger than a little wind, and yet, listening and suffering silently, he seemed to have laid an ear against the muscle of his own heart, feeling it close and quail, listening to the flutter of its ventricles.

Fortunately he could forget both his inner turmoil and the material squalor surrounding him, preoccupied by an analysis of aesthetic pleasure, 'a spiritual state very like to that cardiac condition which the Italian physiologist Luigi Galvani, using a phrase almost as beautiful as Shelley's called the enchantment of the heart.'

It should be realised that at the time of Joyce's literary apprenticeship vivisection was the subject of acrimonious controversy, the anti-vivisection faction being then more vocal than to-day and the emerging benefits of medical science less apparent. Arguing with Cranly in *Stephen Hero* Stephen remarks, 'The modern spirit is vivisective. Vivisection is the most modern process one can conceive.'

In this novel we encounter 'a very shock-headed asthmatic man' and also Glynn, possibly a case of Friedrich's ataxia, who 'was unable to keep his head steady as he suffered from inherited nervousness and his hands trembled very much whenever he tried to do anything with them,' but the fullest clinical description is of Stephen's dying sister.

There could be no doubt now that the girl was in a bad way. Her eyes were piteously enlarged and her voice had become hollow: she sat half propped-up by pillows in the bed all day, her damp-looking hair hanging in wisps about her face . . . She began to whimper when she was told to eat or when anyone left her bedside.

There is a pitiful picture, too, of a suicide.

A pace or two from the brink of the water a thing was lying on the bank partly covered by a brown sack. It was the body of a woman: the face was to the ground and from the thick black hair a pool of water had oozed out. The body was curved upwards with legs abroad . . . someone had drawn down the nightdress. The woman had escaped from the asylum the night before and Stephen heard many criticisms of the nurses.

The reviews and essays collected in *The Critical Writings of James Joyce* touch now and then on medical matters, the harshness of Agamemnon towards Electra being seen by Joyce as the behaviour of a man driven to extremes by the agony of gout and Orestes' vision at Delphi interpreted as an hypnotic trance. Here he sides with the sentimentalists in the vivisection controversy—'Science may improve yet demoralize'—and is taken in by Wilkie Collins's ridiculous account of Dr. Benjulia 'crushed and broken, aloof from sympathy at the door of his laboratory, while the maimed animals flee away terrified between his legs, into the darkness.' He applies the physiological terms *systole* and *diastole* inaccurately but with literary force to the ebb and flow of love and wisdom. To attribute Oscar Wilde's homosexuality to 'the epileptic tendency of his nervous system' and to compare a politician's 'violent outbursts' with epilepsy are examples of more culpable inaccuracy.

He is at fault, too, in equating 'cognition' and 'simple perception' and it is difficult to understand why he should take exception to what he calls a notion popular among advocates of 'science', the modern notion of Aristotle as a biologist. Nor is it easy to see why Joyce (and the ghost of Captain Alving) is puzzled because Alving's children did not both have congenital syphilis.

My spouse bore me a blighted boy,
Our slavey pupped a bouncing bitch.
Paternity, thy name is joy
When the wise sire knows which is which.

Both swear I am that self-same man
By whom their infants were begotten.
Explain, fate, if you care and can
Why one is sound and one is rotten.

Is it not merely that Alving's disease, then in the tertiary stage, was much less infective when he seduced the servant? The latter (and hence her child) was uninfected whereas seven or eight years earlier, the disease in its primary or secondary stage was transmitted readily to Mrs. Alving who infected her son.

What little of science there is in the *Critical Writings* is not well handled but there is an amusing reference to charms and herb-healing —'if the wind changes while you are cutting wild camomile you will lose your mind'—and an arresting allusion to 'what keen pain contact with gross natures inflict on a sensitive boy.'

We have seen that a plethora of gross natures is displayed in *Dubliners,* and, when writing the stories, Joyce told Constantine Curran 'I shall call the series "Dubliners" to betray the soul of that hemiplegia or paralysis which many consider a city.' Literary critics (conveniently overlooking Joyce's eulogy on another occasion,[2] 'Dublin has been a capital for thousands of years . . . it is the "second" city of the British Empire . . . it is nearly three times as big as Venice') have seized upon this idea of paralysis finding in it a lode rich in symbolism. But Curran, in a better position than they to judge the truth of Joyce's assertion, has recently drawn on his own memories of Dublin, a ferment of literary and political activity in the 1900s, and remarks, 'Nothing seemed to me more inept than to qualify the focus of this activity as a hemiplegia or paralysis, however much one might quarrel with its exuberance or fanaticisms. That Joyce thought fit to call it so is the measure of his ardour and youthful impatience.'

Neither ardour nor impatience adequately explain why a young man should paint his native city in sombre colours.[3] Two weeks after the publication of *Dubliners* a discerning critic in 'The New Statesman', judging it to be a work of genius, wrote 'Mr. Joyce seems to regard this objective, dirty and crawling world with the cold detachment of an unamiable god.' More than half a century later when an abundance of biographical material is available, the morbid mood of Joyce's collection of short stories is perfectly understandable and, taken together with his erratic behaviour and persecutory feelings, suggests a diagnosis of psycho-neurosis.

Although less autobiographical than *A Portrait* Joyce's personal environment is reflected from the pages of *Dubliners*. His relatives and his father's friends lent something to the creation of its characters. It was Uncle William's little son who pleaded with his father (Farrington in 'Counterparts') 'Don't beat me, pa! And I'll . . . I'll say a *Hail Mary* for you'; Mr. Kernan was a composite of John Stanislaus Joyce and his friend Richard Thornton.

The fallacy of identifying Joyce too closely with Stephen Dedalus has been pointed out by Maurice Beebe and others and this possible source of error must be kept in mind when compiling a clinical history. The comparable fallacy of identifying Joyce's fictional *Dubliners* with his actual *milieu* could be equally misleading. That is not to say, however, that valid diagnostic information about an author may not be obtained from an objective perusal of his fiction. Ernest Hemingway, discussing the genesis of fiction, said, 'You invent fiction, but what you invent it out of is what counts. True fiction must come from everything you've ever known, ever seen, ever felt, ever learned.'

Everything Joyce knew, everything he had ever learned, ever seen, ever felt contributed to the invention of *Ulysses* where we find, too, on almost every page the glow of his recovered good-humour. But

Dubliners, leaving aside the universal application of its tormented characters, plunges us into the almost unrelieved unhappiness of shabby, lower middle-class homes. The joy, the beauty, the opulence that the ancient city also contained appear to have been wilfully excluded just as the wilful vagaries of fate had excluded the young Joyces from much that they might have enjoyed. Presumably each of them reacted in his or her own way to the privations imposed upon the family by their father's alcoholism—'our father who art not in heaven' murmured one of John S. Joyce's daughters wryly—and Stanislaus, provider of some raw material for *Dubliners,* recalling the drabness of youth said that it would never have occurred to him that by dispassionate writing 'one could raise oneself above all that mean, shiftless, poverty-stricken life and regard it without hatred, even with compassion and humour.'

Joyce himself in the satirical 'Holy Office' introduced purgation as an ugly but effective metaphor. It seems likely that the literary catharsis was involuntary, the symptomatic culmination (so often seen in medical practice) of protracted emotional distress. An item from Joyce's juvenilia referred to by Stanislaus in *My Brother's Keeper* may be quoted in support of this viewpoint.

> *Silhouettes* . . . was written in the first person singular, and describes a row of mean little houses along which the narrator passes after nightfall. His attention is attracted by two figures in violent agitation on a lowered window-blind illuminated from within, the burly figure of a man, staggering and threatening with upraised fist, and the smaller sharp-faced figure of a nagging woman. A blow is struck and the light goes out. The narrator waits to see if anything happens afterwards. Yes, the window-blind is illuminated again dimly . . . and the woman's sharp profile appears, accompanied by two small heads . . . of children wakened by the noise. The woman's finger is pointed and warning. She is saying, 'Don't waken Pa.'

When the vicissitudes of the Joyce ménage at the turn of the century are remembered how can one avoid identifying Joyce *père* with that menacing shadow behind the window-blind? If this interpretation is correct the impress of John Stanislaus Joyce on his son's career is even greater than hitherto appreciated.

CHAPTER 7

A DISTURBED HOUSEHOLD

'*Curse your bloody blatant soul*'. Mr. Dedalus's invective has the authentic ring of speech; no pen could fashion the phrase. The author of *Ulysses* has recorded an example of his father's mastery of vituperation. John Stanislaus Joyce was born in Cork on 4 July 1849 the only son of James Augustine Joyce a handsome man whose business ventures had twice ended in bankruptcy, and his wife Ellen O'Connell the daughter of a prosperous merchant. Despite rheumatic fever and a serious attack of typhoid fever in his schooldays he was a vigorous athlete in early manhood. As we have seen he attended Queen's College, Cork, for some years but his witty, pleasure-loving nature was an obstacle to success. Instead he was destined to be an example of Mahaffy's generalization that young men with good tenor voices go to the devil with remarkable rapidity.

John Joyce's father died of typhoid at an early age but his widow was well-off and perhaps to separate her son ('the only child of an only child, the spoiled son of a spoiled son, the spendthrift son of a spendthrift') from his Cork cronies she moved to Dublin in 1874 or 1875 but the larger city immediately afforded greater scope for the determined playboy whose attributes and activities are listed in *A Portrait*: 'A medical student, an oarsman, a tenor, an amateur actor, a shouting politician, a small landlord, a small investor, a drinker, a good fellow, a storyteller, somebody's secretary, something in a distillery, a tax-gatherer, a bankrupt, and at present a praiser of his own past'. Bowling was another of his accomplishments. He was a member of the Chapelizod Distillery's bowling team and years later, quite unrepentant, he recalled a famous victory over the Dollymount Club.

We beat Dollymount and I made a big score, and by God I was carried around the place and such a time we had. I was made a lot of and was taken around by the boys on their shoulders; and my God the quantity of whiskey that I drank that night! It must have been something terrible for I had to go to bed. I was not very long in bed when half a dozen came up to me and said that they were having a sing-song downstairs, adding: 'Come on Jack, don't have them beat us at the singing.' I told them to go to hell that I couldn't come down. Begor I couldn't walk so I told them to clear out to Blazes.

He had purchased shares in the distillery and had been appointed secretary with a yearly salary of £300. His job had come to an end and his shares were worthless when the managing-director's dishonesty caused insolvency but through political influence he secured a well-paid sinecure in the office of the Collector of Rates. The post brought him £500 per annum to which must be added rents from house property in Cork amounting to about £300 per annum.

He needed every penny and more for his tastes were expensive, his ways expansive. The celebration at the Oval Bar in the small hours of a particular election victory remained vivid in John Joyce's memory.

> By God Almighty, such drinking of champagne I never saw in all my life! We could not wait to draw the corks, we slapped them against the marble-topped counter. The result was we were there drinking for about three hours and when we came out the question was what were we to do with ourselves at that ungodly hour of the morning. Then I thought of the Turkish Baths and there I went after having any God's quantity of champagne. Oh dear, dear God, those were great times.

Great times, indeed! The note of nostalgia is remarkable but on 2 December 1881, John Joyce, now married, took out his first mortgage. The pattern of his life and his family's fortune was already determined. The following passage written by a Dublin psychiatrist in the *Journal of the Irish Medical Association* is very relevant. 'If there is a picture characteristic of Irish culture, this is probably it. The male, doted on by his mother, reared in a monosexual atmosphere in school, who has never learned to form a friendship with the opposite sex of his own age—then marries and takes a "housekeeper" into his home—while he continues his friendship with his male friends —"the lads". She goes on to become the mother of his children, invests her life in these and so carries on the pattern into the next generation.' But as if to compound misfortune for the Joyces their mother died from cancer when many of the children were still young.

May Murray, fair-haired and attractive, the daughter of a commercial traveller for wines and spirits, was ten years younger than her husband when he married her on 5 May 1880. Their first home was 47, Northumberland Avenue, Kingstown, where a son who did not survive was born in 1881. When John Joyce took out the first mortgage on his Cork property his wife was pregnant again. Their second son, named James Augustine after his paternal grandfather, as we have already seen, was born in Rathgar on 2 February 1882.

Margaret ('Poppie') the eldest girl was also born in 41, Brighton Square, West, on 18 January 1884 but Stannie (17 December 1884) and Charles (24 July 1886) were born in 23, Castlewood Avenue, Rathmines. George (4 July 1887), Eileen (22 January 1889), Mary (18 January 1890) and Eva (26 October 1891) were born in 1, Martello Terrace, Bray and the move to Leoville, 23, Carysfort Avenue, Blackrock, a large house where Florence Elizabeth (8 November 1892) was born could have been necessitated by the size of the family.

In 1892 the work of the Collector's Office was taken over by the Dublin Corporation and John Joyce was given an annual pension of £132:2:4. He worked sporadically for a solicitor, canvassed advertisements for the *Freeman's Journal,* and did odd jobs at elections. When they were still living in Blackrock, Stannie, then nine or ten years of age, coming through the town with some other boys caught sight of his father 'quite drunk but still elegant and with his eye-glass fixed, playing a piano-organ in the main street of the town and crooning "The Boys of Wexford". Meanwhile the Italian organ-grinder stood looking at him, with legs crossed, wondering at what he no doubt called mentally *questi matti d'inglesi.*' The boys crept by discreetly and Stannie hurried home to break the bad news.

Soon they were on the move again. 'Two great yellow caravans had halted one morning before the door and men had come tramping into the house to dismantle it. The furniture had been hustled out through the front garden . . .' Stephen Dedalus and 'his red-eyed mother' were taken from Blackrock to a bare cheerless house in Dublin. Mr. Dedalus, railing drunkenly, 'We're not dead yet, sonny. No, by the Lord Jesus (God forgive me) nor half dead.'

The move to the north side of the city represents a watershed in John Joyce's affairs; the days of prosperity lay behind him and the future was to be a progressive descent into squalor. Another daughter (Mabel) was born in November 1893. The family's whereabouts depended upon the indulgence of a succession of unpaid landlords; 'Mr. Dedalus had not an acute sense of the rights of private property; he paid rent very rarely.' But whereas at first they had needed two furniture vans and a float when moving a time came when they needed only the float. A son christened Frederick who died when a few weeks old was born at 2, Millbourne Avenue. The last of Mrs. Joyce's numerous confinements took place at 29, Windsor Avenue,

Fairview. Brought home in his cups the father proclaimed his potency. 'By God, I'm not dead yet!' he boasted. Upstairs the male infant was already dead.

To the world at large John Joyce continued to present an impressive appearance. In *May It Please the Court* Judge Sheehy remembered him as 'a dapper little man, with military moustache, who sported an eyeglass and cane, and wore spats.' Hail fellow well met in the bars he was a 'character', the hero of a hundred stories, one of which the Colums recorded in *Our Friend James Joyce*. Sitting on a jaunting-car on the way to the races John Stanislaus cursed the rain. A pious crony rebuked him: 'Don't you know John, that God could drown the world?' 'He could if He wanted to make a bloody fool of Himself.' At home the street angel was becoming the proverbial devil.

Mr Dedalus hated his wife's maiden name with a medieval intensity: it stunk in his nostrils. His alliance therewith was the only sin of which, in the entire honesty of his cowardice, he could accuse himself. Now that he was making for the final decades of life with the painful consciousness of having diminished comfortable goods and of having accumulated uncomfortable habits he consoled and revenged himself by tirades so prolonged and so often repeated that he was in danger of becoming a monomaniac. The hearth at night was the sacred witness of these revenges, pondered, muttered, growled and execrated.

The diminished comforts of his father's house (Stannie called it 'Bleak House') are described by Stephen Dedalus in more detail in *A Portrait*.

He pushed open the latchless door of the porch and passed through the naked hallway into the kitchen. A group of his brothers and sisters was sitting round the table. Tea was nearly over and only the last of the second watered tea remained in the bottoms of the small glass jars and jampots which did service for teacups. Discarded crusts and lumps of sugared bread, turned brown by the tea which had been poured over them, lay scattered on the table. Little wells of tea lay here and there on the board and a knife with a broken ivory handle was stuck through the pith of a ravaged turnover.

He asked where his parents were and was told, 'Goneboro toboro lookboro atboro aboro houseboro.' But why move again? 'Becauseboro theboro landboro lordboro willboro putboro usboro outboro.'

95

He grew accustomed to the daily background of poverty relieved occasionally by a new mortgage or when he himself won an exhibition.

He drained his third cup of watery tea to the dregs and set to chewing the crusts of fried bread that were scattered near him, staring into the dark pool of the jar. The yellow dripping had been scooped out like a boghole, and the pool under it brought back to his memory the dark turfcoloured water of the bath in Clongowes. The box of pawn tickets at his elbow had just been rifled and he took up idly one after another in his greasy fingers the blue and white dockets, scrawled and sanded and creased and bearing the name of the pledger as Daly or MacEvoy . . .

By now the two older boys were bound to resent their father's behaviour and Stannie (Maurice in *Stephen Hero*) hardly bothered to conceal his bitterness.

. . . they both paused outside to listen for the sounds of wrangling and even when all seemed peaceful Maurice's first question to his mother when he opened the door was 'Is he in?' When the answer was 'No' they both went down to the kitchen together but when the answer was 'Yes' Stephen only went down, Maurice listening over the banisters to judge from his father's tones whether he was sober or not. If his father was drunk Maurice retired to his bedroom but Stephen, who was untroubled, discoursed gaily with his father.

Stannie regarded his father as 'a balking little rat'. He wrote in his diary 'I loathe my father' but amended it another day: 'I am wrong in saying that I loathe Pappie. I have absolutely no liking for him.' The bickering upset Stannie: 'I have grown up with it; it is associated in my mind forever with the sound of Pappie's voice drunkenly haranguing his silent family, that deep, open-vowelled, rasping, blatant voice, listening to which, I at least understand hate . . .' He thought his elder brother was less affected but he misinterpreted James's insouciance and in due course he came to this conclusion himself: 'In spite of his seeming equanimity, he suffered from it more deeply than I did because of his attachment to his father and because his mind was haunted by clear visions of what life might be made to yield.'

Stephen Dedalus, more selective in his memories than Stephen Hero, thought happily of his father in Bray, 'of how he sang songs while his mother played and of how he always gave him a shilling when he asked for sixpence'; grown older he resented his 'equivocal position in Belvedere, a free boy', and any allusion to his father by a schoolfellow 'put his calm to rout' instantly.

Heedless of the havoc he was causing John Joyce ranted and raved at the table grinding his teeth and threatening his wife, 'Better finish it now—' She thought of getting a separation but her confessor treated her enquiry so unsympathetically that she let the matter drop. On at least one occasion his threats went beyond verbal violence. He ran at his wife in a drunken rage catching her by the throat and shouting, 'Now by God is the time to finish it.' The children screamed and tried to separate them but James jumped on his father's back and they fell to the ground permitting Mrs. Joyce to escape with the girls to a neighbour's house. She may have complained to the police, for a police sergeant called to the house a few days later and had a long talk with Mr. and Mrs. Joyce.

There were, of course, less harrowing times when Joyce *père's* relations with his family were cordial; during the holiday in Mullingar, for instance, and the trip to London with his son at the latter's expense.

Furthermore even the barest surroundings can be transformed by music, a constant solace for the Joyces, a delight to Stephen Dedalus.

> The voice of his youngest brother from the farther side of the fireplace began to sing the air 'Oft in the Stilly Night'. One by one the others took up the air until a full choir of voices was singing. They would sing so for hours, melody after melody, glee after glee, till the last pale light died down on the horizon, till the first dark nightclouds came forth and night fell.

James was devoted to his mother who had an excellent voice and was a brilliant pianist. Sometimes she went with him to visit the Sheehy's and played when he sang. Eugene Sheehy recalled her as frail, sad-faced, and gentle and he remembered her son, 'linking her towards the piano with a grave old world courtesy.' Gogarty described Mrs. Joyce as 'a naked nerve'. She had many sorrows to bear not the least being her sons' religious scepticism, an affront to her piety. This was not to be tolerated in silence and she blamed James unjustly for Stannie's defection. But like any mother she attributed his loss of faith to bad companions rather than to some inward uncontrollable turmoil of soul.

> —Stephen, you may use that kind of language with your companions whoever they are but I will not allow you to use it with

97

me. Even your father, bad as he is supposed to be, does not speak such blasphemy as you do. I am afraid that you are a changed boy since you went to that University. I suppose you fell in with some of those students . . .

Another grief was the death at fourteen of Georgie, a handsome clever boy to whom she was deeply attached. 'He was her youngest, and, after her estrangement from Jim, her favourite son.' (*My Brother's Keeper*). When he fell ill she was undecided at first whether to send him to the Mater Hospital ('that's where you're sent when there's something the matter with you' one of the Joyce girls said quite seriously) or to nurse him herself. She decided to keep him at home and the illness is described in *Stephen Hero*, Isabel substituted for Georgie.

> She showed very little animation except when the piano was playing in the room below and then she made them leave the bedroom door open and closed her eyes. Money was still scarce and still the doctor ordered her delicacies. . . .

Stephen, like Dylan Thomas at a later date—'Rage, rage, against the dying of the light'—wished to communicate a message against despair. 'He could not go into his sister and say to her "Live! live!" but he tried to touch her soul in the shrillness of a whistle or the vibration of a note,' but to no avail.

> The doctor came with Mr. Dedalus on a car, examined the girl and asked had she seen a priest. He went away saying that while there was life there was hope but she was very low: he would call in the morning. Isabel died a little after midnight. Her father, who was not quite sober walked about the room on tiptoe, cried in little fits every time his daughter showed a change and kept on saying 'That's right, duckey: take that now' whenever her mother forced her to swallow a little champagne and then nodded his head until he began to cry afresh.

Georgie is said to have died from typhoid fever but a curious feature of the illness noted in Joyce's description—'There's some matter coming away from the hole in Isabel's . . . stomach . . . Did you ever hear of that happening?'—casts doubt on that diagnosis. Evidently Georgie had a sinus discharging pus from the abdominal wall, an unlikely complication in typhoid fever but perfectly understandable in tuberculous peritonitis, death resulting from a miliary spread of the disease.

Charlie Joyce's decision to become a priest may have been a consolation to his mother and for a time she and her daughters had pleasure in seeing him among the contingent from Clonliffe College filing into the Pro-Cathedral for High Mass wearing a soutane and biretta and carrying a missal. But the rector found him 'a parti-cularly stupid boy' a phrase with which his father taunted him when about a year later he returned home realizing that he did not have a vocation.

Mrs. Joyce worried about him and expressed her anxiety about his future when writing to her eldest son in Paris.

> Charlie is a conundrum I can't make him out, he simply refuses to take any appointment and says he will act as he likes and if we wish to put him out we can do so and talks about singing in the streets Stannie sets him sums and exercises in writing and french and marvellous to say is gentle and does his best with him so things are going on in this way for the present (C — is very bitter against your Pappie on different accounts (drink etc.) and seems to forget that anything whatever was ever done for *him* he speaks cruelly of his father. My dear Jim I cannot say I like these dis-positions in Charlie but he may not be happy and this may cause him to act as he does he turns on me sometimes but that does not last but I often wonder how he can do so.

Charlie was tall and good-looking with small features and thick black hair. He wore glasses and had a slight cast. He inherited the family gift for singing and at one time thought of becoming an actor. His verses, such as the following example, would have been too awful for inclusion even in *The Stuffed Owl*:

> *Her milky breast, so full of woe,*
> *Doth rise beneath a fall of lace.*

Stannie thought him 'an absurd creature . . . an amusing clown when boisterous but rough and loud-voiced, being round-shouldered and awkward and naturally very strong,' but Mrs. Joyce reported in another letter to Paris that 'Charlie is changed and is improved in his demeanour he speaks more sensibly and wishes to get something to do I earnestly hope he may succeed as I cannot see how things here are to be managed in the future.' Eventually he got a job in a wine-merchant's office but the bibulous proprietor liked his clerk and took him with him from pub to pub on Saturdays.

Mrs. Joyce worried about her eldest daughter, too. 'Poppie is beginning to cry out about herself she would go to any business or give time to be taught I would like to put her to something by which she would learn and have something for herself. The girl cannot even get shoes or a pair of gloves.' Between one thing and another the poor woman was distraught, and heedless of herself may have ignored the early signs of cancer. By April 1903 her condition was grave and her son was sent for and given the bad news by his father. 'Hurrying to her squalid deathlair from gay Paris on the quayside I touched his hand. The voice, new warmth, speaking. Dr. Bob Kenny is attending her. The eyes that wish me well. But do not know me.'

She improved temporarily and was able to get up in the afternoons but her condition deteriorated again. Dr. Kenny, whom Mrs. Joyce called Sir Peter Teazle, wanted a second opinion and sent for Professor James Little,[1] an uncle of the boy of that name who had died in Clongowes. The term cirrhosis of the liver which they used may have been an euphemism to conceal a death sentence from their patient. The grief-stricken children watched her die slowly and painfully through the long summer days. One dreadful evening her husband reeled home and stood by her bed: 'I'm finished. I can't do any more,' he lamented. 'If you can't get well, die. Die and be damned to you.' Horrified, Stannie shouted 'You swine!' and was about to hit him when he saw his mother struggling to get out of bed. James led his father out of the room and Mrs. Joyce pacified Stannie. 'You mustn't do that. You must promise me never to do that, you know that when he's that way he doesn't know what he's saying.'

She died in coma on 13 August 1903 and her sons' ungracious refusal to obey an uncle's peremptory command to kneel and pray for her may have been a histrionic expression of their bewilderment.

Mother's deathbed. Candle. The sheeted mirror. Who brought me into the world lies there, bronzelidded, under few cheap flowers. *Liliata rutilantium.*
I wept alone.

Later he purged his grief in 'Tilly' contrasting his desolation with a cattle-drover's rude contentment.

Boor, bond of the herd,
Tonight stretch full by the fire!
I bleed by the black stream
For my torn bough!

The most inconsolable of all was the youngest child, Mabel, and James sat with her on the stairs, his arms about her, comforting her, no longer the intransigent agnostic. 'You mustn't cry like that,' he said to the little one. 'There's no reason to cry. Mother's in Heaven. She's far happier now than she's ever been on earth but if she sees you crying it'll spoil her happiness. You must remember that when you feel like crying. You can pray for her, if you wish. Mother would like that. But you musn't cry any more.'

On the funeral evening John Joyce sat weeping in the parlour. Finding him there alone Stannie, overcome by rage, upbraided him bitterly. When his son's tirade finished the bereaved man showed no resentment. 'You don't understand, boy,' he said quietly. Recalling the erstwhile playboy in that moment of abject resignation it is difficult not to have some vestige of sympathy for the broken man whose excellent qualities of conviviality and gregariousness had set him on a Hogarthian road to ruin.

CHAPTER 8

'AN OLD MAN GONE'

Glancing along Bachelor's Walk Leopold Bloom noticed Dilly Dedalus outside an auction room. 'Must be selling off some old furniture. Knew her eyes at once from the father. Lobbing about waiting for him. Home always breaks up when the mother goes.' The household at 7, St. Peter's Terrace, Phibsborough, became chaotic after Mrs. Joyce's death and any sympathy for John Joyce is forfeited because of his behaviour, his failure to provide for his family and his frenzied anger.

He had a scurrilous tongue and addressed his children, boys and girls alike, in an abominable way. To one of his daughters: 'Y' black-looking mulatto. You were black the day y' were born, y' bitch. Y' bloody, gummy toothless bitch, I'll get y' a set of teeth.' To Charlie: 'Y' dirty pissabed, y' bloody-looking squint-eyed son of a bitch. Y' ugly bloody corner-boy, you've a mouth like a bloody nigger.' To Stannie: 'Oh, y' bloody-looking yahoo of hell!' Even his eldest son was threatened: 'Break his arse with a kick, break his bloody arse with three kicks! Oh, yes. Just three kicks.'

They grew accustomed to starvation rations, to cold and darkness and knew that when money was available it made the situation even more intolerable because of their father's drunkenness.

Poppie, the eldest girl, tried to run the house as best she could and Stannie noted, 'She seems to wish if anyone is to suffer that she should be the victim. What an extraordinary sense of duty women have!'

Their privations are recorded in *Ulysses*.

> Katey went to the range and peered with squinting eyes.
> —What's in the pot? she asked.
> —Shirts, Maggy said.
> Boody cried angrily:
> —Crickey, is there nothing for us to eat?
> Katey, lifting the kettlelid in a pad of her stained skirt asked:
> —And what's in this? . . .
> —Peasoup, Maggy said.
> —Where did you get it? Katey asked.
> —Sister Mary Patrick, Maggy said.

They learned how to extract money from their father.

—Did you get any money? Dilly asked.

—Where would I get money? Mr Dedalus said.

There is no-one in Dublin would lend me fourpence.

—You got some, Dilly said, looking in his eyes.

—How do you know that? Mr Dedalus asked, his tongue in his cheek . . .

— I know you did, Dilly answered. Were you in the Scotch house now?

—I was not then, Mr Dedalus said, smiling. Was it the little nuns taught you to be so saucy? Here.

He handed her a shilling.

—See if you can do anything with that, he said.

—I suppose you got five, Dilly said. Give me more than that.

—Wait awhile, Mr Dedalus said threateningly. You're like the rest of them, are you? An insolent pack of little bitches since your poor mother died.

Life drifted hopelessly from day to day but like wild flowers on a wasteland, humour managed sometimes to lighten their despondency. Mr. Kettle called to see John Joyce who was out. He told the girls to tell their father he had called. 'You won't forget, now. Mr. Kettle— what you boil water in.' When Mabel re-told it as a joke Eva said, 'Fortunately he didn't know it's Mr. Teapot we boil the water in. We don't have a kettle.'

James and Charlie were also drinking heavily and Stannie, the only sober male in the house, sometimes had to cope with three drunks at the same time. Commenting on this he said, 'Another, perhaps, might have been able to distil low comedy out of a situation in which a drunken father rails at two drunken sons for being drunk, but I fancy that to do so, one must know the situation only at secondhand.'

Charlie was his father's *bête noire*. When the boy went out in the evening the father shouted, 'Where are y' going, Ch-a-a-arlie? Down to the Murrays? Going to sponge on them for porter, eh? Sucking porter that's all y're good for. You seem to be very fond of them. Y'll get out of this y' bloody waster of hell. Y' can go to stay with the Murrays, then.' He began to consort with his brother's medical friends, slept three nights running with a whore in Tyrone Street and spent four days in jail before a fine for drunkenness was paid. Not surprisingly he found himself before long in the Whitworth Hospital with tuberculous pleurisy.

103

Meanwhile James had left home to stay in a furnished room in Shelbourne Road and later at the Martello Tower. He returned briefly to 7, St. Peter's Terrace in September 1904 before leaving for the Continent with Nora Barnacle. When one considers the home he left behind and the responsibility he evaded his departure can hardly be seen as self-imposed exile. It was flight.

There seems no doubt that he was aware of the responsibility towards his penniless sisters that the eldest son of an improvident father should have shouldered.

> She is drowning. Agenbite. Save her. Agenbite.
> All against us. She will drown me with her eyes and hair. Lank coils of seaweed hair around me, my heart, my soul.
> Salt green death.
> We.
> Agenbite of inwit. Inwit's agenbite.
> Misery! Misery!

He did not choose to drown in the Dublin pool of tears and in due course he inveigled Stannie to join him in Trieste.

A link with Ireland was maintained by correspondence. In February 1907 in a letter to his father he declared, 'I have a great horror lest you should think, that now that I have gained some kind of position for myself, I wish to hear no more of you . . . on the contrary I assure you, if you will show me what I can do or get others to do I shall be glad to give the ball another kick.'

He received the following *cri de coeur*.

> . . . my remaining pension is £6 a month, out of which *I should pay* £2. 12. 4 a month, which leaves £3. 7. 8 to live on and dress on, or 2/3 a day! I need hardly say it could not be done—five girls, one—well Charlie, myself and nigger. If I had some permanent position, however small and if the aforesaid ex-ecclesiastic had the ability and inclination to get some employment to enable him to live, *off my hands,* things would be different. Now, I must break up house, (by the way that won't entail much energy, as everything is broken up quite sufficiently already) and go into lodgings *by myself*. I have been for the past fortnight trying to get the 3 little ones fixed and have so far succeeded that I could get them into a convent (Glasnevin) through the influence of Mr. James Kavanagh for £24 a year. He has asked me to write you both to know what you could do. If you and Stannie can afford

8s/- a week (4s/- each) I will pay the balance. I may tell you I am in hope of getting a small job, £1 a week, and if so I should not need anything from you. Write me by return and such a letter as I can show—Then as to Charlie, you say you can get him a position?—*do*, for I can't stand it any longer, and for many reasons I *must* get rid of *him*. Well, Poppie is so insolent and my life has been made so unendurable by her that *she* must go. I understand she has some arrangement made to get someplace, and if May and Eily wish they may lite in lodgings with me, or if not?—. At present as you see I have barely enough to support and dress myself, after helping to provide for the 3 young children. As I am to be evicted from here within the next week or so, I am looking for lodgings for *myself* but must get the little ones fixed first.

Presumably his sons sent what they could spare but in May 1909 John Stanislaus forwarded another long statement of distress.

My last shilling went on Sunday dinner and since then we are entirely *without food, coal* or *light,* nor do I know any means under Heaven of getting a penny as I have exhausted all my friends, and so we have another fortnights starving to do. My clothes, too, are patchwork. However, there is no use going on farther into this gruesome subject! My object is that you and Stannie should be in possession of all the facts and that whatever happens you now know how matters stand.

Charlie too is on my hands I cannot get him anything to do. Nor do I think he much cares . . .

That summer saw a number of changes in John Joyce's household. Poppie entered the Order of Mercy and went to New Zealand where she died in 1964. Charlie married and emigrated to America where he experienced even greater poverty in Boston than he had already known. Eva accompanied her brother to Trieste after his visit to Dublin in August. Perhaps he was not moved wholly by fraternal generosity in taking her with him for he confided to Stannie, 'Eva will hardly be an extra expense as I should have to get a servant in any case and that would have cost me about 20 crowns a month, with which she can dress herself and take some lessons in typing and shorthand. She has learnt some dressmaking and says (or rather snorts) that she will be able to do something in that line.' The snorting was due to adenoids and with the fortitude of her times she submitted to tonsillectomy two days before leaving Dublin.

During his second visit to Dublin in 1909 James received a telegram from Stannie. 'Wire £4 writ landlord.' He promised to send something immediately and instructed his brother how to supplement it.

> Raise 4.66 [crowns] and pay at once one month and promise double rent on 1st December. I cannot send more. Pappie is in Jervis Street Hospital (eyes) and I am supporting this house . . . A notice to quit has been served on this house for the 1st of December so that, thank God, we will all be on the pavement together for Xmas.

He bought boots and an overcoat for Eileen and took her with him to Trieste intending to have her voice trained. She settled there very happily, unlike Eva who returned to Dublin in July 1911. She took a post as governess and gave English lessons.

Mabel ('Baby') Joyce, then seventeen years old, fell ill in June 1911 and when her father called in Dr. G. F. Macnamara[1] to see her the doctor summoned the 'fever cab' to transfer her to Cork Street Fever Hospital where she died from typhoid fever. James's letter of condolence evoked a reply charged with maudlin self-pity.

> I must thank you, Jim, for your kind and sympathetic letter and remittance and the beautiful wreath. Everything was carried out as it should be and as *you* would wish. So much for the past— now the present has been made so unbearable to me by the callous, unnatural treatment I am receiving from my three daughters, that I am resolved to leave Dublin and them on the 1st prox. Since my poor baby died they have left me alone, and refuse to even take a walk with me. Everyone here, as in the last house we stayed in, crys shame on them for their cruel conduct towards their Father. I will allow Florrie £2 a month out of my cheque, and Eva will have £1 or 25/- from you and May has nearly 10/- per week all found, so that the three can live well until they get some employment—but live with them any longer, after the eight years of misery I have endured, is out of the question.

Charlie Joyce returned from America with his wife and three children and when James paid his final visit to Dublin in the summer of 1912 his condescending comment in a letter to Stannie reads: 'Charles made a good impression on me—a decent poor fellow. Will do what I can for him.' With his characteristic practicality in organising the affairs of others he turned over to Charlie an offer of the post of tenor in Sandymount Church at a salary of £10 a year but also in characterstic vein he continued to rely on Stannie to raise the wind, complaining to Nora, 'Stannie has not sent me what I asked him for. Eileen and Florrie would have nothing to eat but for me. Stannie has sent them nothing and Charlie nothing and me nothing.'

Like all budding authors he could persuade himself that once his book was published the enormous sales would solve all his problems and he toyed with the idea of buying the sheets of *Dubliners* from Maunsell and publishing it himself, setting up Charlie in an office in Jervis Street as distributor. This came to nothing and Charlie mentioned his lack of fortune disarmingly in a letter to Stannie.

> I have not succeeded in getting employment yet. Jim has tried everything he thought likely to open something for me but without success. Jim says I lost the job in the telephone through my own fault . . . Florrie, too, has got nothing to do and Eva is approaching the end of her apprenticeship in Read's. Pappie has left the Iveagh House and is now living in the same house with Jim and Nora. I have had to get out door relief . . . By the way, you must not think that I in any way expect help from you. You have already too many calls and I must try to manage somehow. Jim, of course, has helped me since he came here, but really I would rather not have anyone to turn to, for then something must surely happen.

When Eileen became engaged to Frantisek Schaurek, a Czech bank cashier in Trieste, whom she married in 1915, her father wrote to his eldest son (May 5, 1914) from Beaumont Convalescent Home—'As you see by above, I am located here. I have been two months in hospital and am trying to get well in this convalescent Home, and am feeling somewhat better'—enquiring about the engagement and about his daughter ('She is the only one of my daughters *now alive* who never gave me insolence, or showed contempt for me') and discussing an invitation to visit Trieste.

> . . . and as you *again* ask me to go over, perhaps, as things have turned out here, and the cruel treatment I have received from my daughters here, I may go over to you on a visit for a month. Of course only on the understanding that I would not be any incumbrance to you or Nora and that I should pay my way, as I have to do here. Not having heard from Stannie for some years, I take it my memory is entirely obliterated from his filial mind . . . Let me know exactly *when* you mean I should go, as I will

require to make some preparation. I need not say it would afford me great pleasure to see *you all* before I die . . .

We hear no more about this projected visit which the war may have stopped but correspondence continued and in December 1916 John Joyce wrote using the notepaper of J. G. Lidwell, Solicitor.

> 33 Upper Ormond Quay,
> Dublin.
> 14/12/1916.

My dear Jim,
    I should have replied to your last sooner, but for the fact that I have been *again* in hospital for 3 weeks with my old complaint. I am, however, somewhat better, but as this will be my *last Xmas* I wish to write to *you.* I hope things have turned out better for you? let me know. I am at present rather low (Financially) If you could spare me £1 you would greatly oblige. I will return it next month. You must remember when you were last over *I* was able to help you. How are all at home? Give them my love and also to *yourself.* I would be glad to hear from you by *return* and believe me to be.

> Your Fond Father.
> John Stanislaus Joyce! !

P.S. Censor, I believe, requires full name.
    He has got it.

His state of penury continued and in January 1920 he was still seeking aid: 'I am in a *dreadful state* for clothes and boots. The prices now charged here are *quite prohibitive* as far as *I* am concerned. Do, like a good fellow, write me and let me know if I may expect to see you again before I die. My time is very nearly up. So that there is no time to lose . . . I have made a fresh will, *leaving you all I have,* some £150. Poor Lidwell's death necessitated this, so that what you send me will be returned with thanks.'

Meanwhile other members of the family were faring better. Charlie was re-employed by the Telephone Company and had five children of whom May Joyce (later Mrs. Monaghan) wrote to her eldest brother, 'the little girl Eileen is very delicate, but the others are healthy. George promises to be very clever, the eldest, Jimmy, is Charlie on a small scale.'

The latter wrote to his brother on 17 May 1920.

30 North Gt. Georges St.,
Dublin.

Dear Jim,

Yesterday I visited Pappie who is at present in hospital suffering from impecuniosity. I had not seen him for a long time and as he is the only one who seems to know your correct address I only got it yesterday. The last time I wrote you, as well I remember, you were in Switzerland and I wrote to you there. Then I heard you had left Switzerland for Trieste. I got your address from Aunt Josephine and wrote but apparently you did not get my letter. Mysterious business!

You are writing another book, I hear. I would like to hear about it. I never hear of or meet anyone who seems to have any news of you or anyone over there. News of a general kind here is nil. You may knock up against Gogarty one of these days. He left Dublin for Italy this morning. How is Stannie? I have treated him badly. It is awkwardness more than anything else that keeps me from writing to him. Remember me to him. Remember me also to Nora and Eileen and tell Lucy and Georgie I hope we shall soon meet again.

Let me know if you get this. I would greatly like to have a letter telling of your own doings and how you are all living. Also if you have a group photo I would like a copy.

Best wishes and kind regards from May and Charlie.

Joyce arranged that he be sent a copy of *Ulysses,* second edition, in 1923 and in the following year Charlie, who was then living in London, visited him in Paris. 'Strange to say like Shaun his work is postal night duty,' Joyce informed Miss Weaver with *Finnegans Wake* in mind.

Joyce and Nora Barnacle were legally married at the Registry Office, Kensington on 4 July (John Joyce's birthday) 1931 and during their stay in London they met Charlie, by then a widower and re-married. Young George Joyce who in the best family tradition was unemployed was offered a job by his uncle but the recent registry office marriage had offended religious susceptibilities. 'I had offered my nephew George who is workless £1 a week if he would help me with my notes from 2 to 5 p.m. every day but his stepmother (he is 21) took from him the *Exagmination* I had lent him and we were given to understand that our influence etc. etc.'

Charlie Joyce remained in London where he died on 18 January 1941, five days after the death of his famous brother.

Stannie spent most of the first Great War in internment. Later he obtained a professorship at the University of Trieste. He married Nelly Lichtensteiger in 1927 and their only child, a son whom they named James, was born in 1943. Stannie suffered from kidney stones and had one or more attacks of pyelitis. During a visit to London in 1954 Stannie developed symptoms of heart disease from which he died on Bloomsday, 16 June 1955.

Eva Joyce died on 25 November 1957. Mrs. Eileen Schaurek, who was widowed in 1926, returned to her native city where she died on 27 January 1963. Mrs. May Monaghan died in December 1968. Florence Joyce is the only surviving member of the family.

✳   ✳   ✳   ✳

Returning to the Dublin of the early thirties we find John Stanislaus Joyce after spells in the Iveagh Hostel settled as a lodger with Mr. and Mrs. Albert Medcalf at 25, Claude Road, Glasnevin. Mrs. Schaurek visited him there, perhaps once or twice a year, and seems to have been the only one of his daughters to do so.

Sending birthday greetings to Paris in 1931 he asked, 'do you recollect the old days in Brighton Square, when you were Babie Tuckoo, and I used to take you out in the Square and tell you all about the moo-cow that used to come down from the mountains and take little boys across.' He was probably somewhat bewildered by his son's fame but not displeased by the reflected glory although it added nothing to his material comfort.

He was now eighty-two and found it easier to recall the past, the consequence of his folly erased by the passage of time, the good days remembered, his youth in Cork, his early manhood, his fair pretty wife and his bright youngsters.

> Every night of my life and in the daytime too I think of all these things—they all come back to me and my God when I think of the times I used to have and here I am now—well I had a good time anyway.

Once more the old rascal steals our sympathy if not our respect. His cousin had been Lord Mayor of Dublin; another cousin was M.P. for Cork and Mayor of that City—but here he was ending his days in poverty. When asked what he knew about the quality of the water of the Liffey he replied, 'I don't know a damn thing about it because I never drank it without whiskey in it.' And during one of the rare periods when he was not taking a drink he had protested with absurd vehemence, 'I would not have one for God Almighty if He came down especially from the heavens.'

Now his health was failing. Mrs. Schaurek paid him one of her infrequent visits in July or August 1931 after she returned from a trip to London to see James and Nora. He was taken seriously ill on 22 December and Medcalf summoned doctor and priest. After receiving the Last Sacrament he was removed by ambulance to Drumcondra Hospital.[2]

Medcalf was not able to inform Mrs. Schaurek until later that night. She went to the hospital next day and her father asked for his pipe and tobacco and matches and the book he was reading.

On Christmas Eve the old man seemed in fine fettle and spoke of leaving hospital in a few days. Next day there was a relapse and Mrs. Schaurek could not understand what he was saying. She called to his lodgings and took his valise which contained some letters, and his photographs. Later a letter from James was delivered to 25, Claude Road but Medcalf refrained from giving it to him as he seemed so low.

Albert Medcalf called to the hospital on the morning of Boxing Day and found him improved again. Mrs. Schaurek came to Claude Road at lunch hour and was told about the letter. When Medcalf gave it to her she opened it. There was a postal order for £1 in it which she said she would hold. She had already written to Paris and now decided to wire, 'Pappie failing' but Medcalf insisted that she should wire 'Pappie dying!' He went to the hospital again that evening and told the old man about the letter and the postal order which pleased him greatly.

On the following day a wire was despatched from Paris to Dr. Kerry Reddin.

My father dangerously ill Drumcondra Hospital. Diagnosis uncertain. Will you please arrange he gets best medical specialists. All expenses my charge. My thanks advance. James Joyce 2 avenue St. Philibert, Paris.

The Medcalfs appear to have been devoted to their old lodger and visited the hospital several times daily. Albert Medcalf called after tea on 29 December, and was told that Mrs. Schaurek had been there earlier. The house-surgeon had just seen the patient who was not expected to last the night.

Shortly before eight p.m. it was clear that death was imminent. A nurse lit a candle and held it in John Joyce's limp fingers; the Sister put a crucifix in the other hand. There were no relatives present but Medcalf knelt at the bedside and prayers for the dying were recited. *Mary, Mother of grace, Mother of mercy, protect me from the enemy and receive me at the hour of death.* He died peacefully just then. *Eternal rest give unto him, O Lord. May perpetual light shine upon him.*

Medcalf wired Paris and then went round to Mrs. Schaurek's to tell her, but she was out. The remains were taken to the Church on the following evening and the burial took place in Glasnevin Cemetery —where at Paddy Dignam's funeral Simon Dedalus, remembering his wife's grave, had said, 'I'll soon be stretched beside her. Let Him take me whenever He likes'—on New Year's Eve.

Paul Léon's enquiry from Medcalf on behalf of Joyce was easily answered. The deceased's personal effects were pitifully meagre—'an old suit of clothes, a coat, hat, boots and stick.'

1 Catholic University School of Medicine, Cecilia Street.

2 The National Maternity Hospital, Holles Street in 1904.

3 Sir Andrew Horne, Master of the National Maternity Hospital.

4 Mirus Bazaar Programme cover, 1904.

overleaf

5 Joyce's plan for foetal development.

6 A page from the *Ulysses* note-sheets.

Dall'Amministrazione del civico Ospitale

Viene invitato *Sig. Joyce Giacomo professore di lingua inglese*
reperibile al N.ro *45 – Via Nuova p. III*
d'intervenire *quanto prima* *dalle 9* alle *2* ore
meridiane alla Cancelleria dell'Ospitale dal sottoscritto, porta N.ro *6*
per la rifusione delle occorse spese *per la moglie Nora*
o produzione di analogo certificato di povertà.

Trieste, il dì *6|8* – 190*7*

R. 2

7   Hospital bill for Nora Joyce, 1907.

opposite

8   Professor Vogt's prescription for eye-glasses, 1932.

35

REZEPT für *James Joyce*
Paris

Rechts	Ferne	Links

Rechts		Links

Pupillen-Distanz
.... mm

Rechts	Nähe	Links
gleichzeitig		$+ 17.0 = gl + 2.75$
$+ 17.0 !$		$78°$ *Vat*

Rechts		Links

Pupillen-Distanz
63 mm

ZÜRICH, *14. Sept* 19 32   *sig. Prof. Vogt*

Verre coquille + 6°.00 –

Bitte wenden!

Mrs. Joyce

Pension Delphin
Mühlebachstr. 69   Zürich

D^{r}= med. H. Freysz

Chirurgie

für ärztliche Bemühungen

betr. Mr. Joyce sel.
10.-13.1.41

Fr. 300.--

Zürich, den 31. Jan. 1941

Börsenstrasse 16

Postcheck VIII 4381

Dankend erhalten

p. Dr Freysz

L. Wens

9   Dr Freysz's fee, January 1941.

CHAPTER 9

PATER FAMILIAS

Young men in love show a certain similarity of behaviour; there is, too, a sameness about their epistolary effusions. In the thronged streets of London G. K. Chesterton hoped

> That 'mid those myriad heads one head find place,
> With brown hair curled like breakers of the sea . . .

Joyce on 15 June 1904 wrote: 'I may be blind. I looked for a long time at a head of reddish-brown hair and decided it was not yours. I went home quite dejected.' The object of his affection was Nora Barnacle, a nineteen year old Galway girl, a chambermaid in Finn's Hotel, Dublin. He had met her some days previously. He 'walked out' with her for the first time on 16 June 1904 a day later consecrated as Bloomsday.

Their acquaintance ripened. Soon he was using pet-names in his letters—'My dear little Goodie-Brown-Shoes'—and had taken her glove as a favour.

> Your glove lay beside me all night—unbuttoned—but otherwise conducted itself very properly—like Nora. *Please* leave off that breastplate as I do not like embracing a letter-box.

A week or so later she was, 'My particularly pouting Nora,' and he closed his letters with words which would have charmed any girl : 'Now, adieu, dearest. I kiss the miraculous dimple at thy neck. When you come next leave sulks at home—also stays.'

Her sulks hint of a tempestuous wooing, the pace at first too fast for a provincial girl of conventional Irish upbringing.[1] She was poorly educated and they had little enough in common—'Nora, of course, doesn't care a rambling damn about art,' he informed Stannie at a later date—and as a practising Catholic she must have been disturbed by his blasphemy. 'How I hate God and death! How I like Nora! Of course you are shocked at these words, pious creature that you are.'

Nevertheless his courtship prospered, his passionate attachment bringing him a restless happiness.

> My dear Nora. It has just struck one. I came in at half past eleven. Since then I have been sitting in an easy chair like a fool.

I could do nothing. I hear nothing but your voice. I am like a fool hearing you call me 'Dear'.

A letter written early in September was more joyous.

Sweetheart I am in such high good humour this morning that I insist on writing to you whether you like it or not . . . When I am happy I have an insane wish to tell it to everyone I meet but I would be much happier if you gave me one of those chirruping kisses you are fond of giving me. They remind me of canaries singing.

He may have attempted to resist his feelings and it seems that he thought of joining a group of travelling actors. 'I could put no energy into the plan because you kept pulling me by the elbow.'

His declarations were unreserved—'No human being has ever stood so close to my soul as you stand'—but when it came to an admission of *love* he was prepared to equivocate.

You ask me why I don't love you, but surely you must believe I am very fond of you and if to desire to possess a person wholly, to admire and honour that person deeply, and to seek to secure that person's happiness in every way is to 'love' then perhaps my affection for you is a kind of love. I will tell you this that your soul seems to me to be the most beautiful and simple soul in the world . . .

By now they were planning a future in which their lives were joined. He left her in no doubt about his unorthodoxy—

My mind rejects the whole present social order and Christianity —home, the recognised virtues, classes of life, and religious doctrines. How could I like the idea of home? My life was simply a middle-class affair ruined by spendthrift habits which I have inherited. My mother was slowly killed, I think, by my father's ill-treatment, by years of trouble, and by my cynical frankness of conduct. When I looked on her face as she lay in her coffin—a face grey and wasted with cancer—I understood that I was looking on the face of a victim and I cursed the system which had made her a victim—

And what he proposed to her (failing to see that it is life and not 'systems' which makes victims of us all) was not the customary union blessed by Church and State but that they should live abroad in a natural marriage.

We can imagine with what alarm she may have received his proposal but if there is something more wonderful than the way of a man with a maid it is the unlimited trust of the latter who so lightly pledges her future. 'I hope you are happier in your mind,' Joyce wrote to her, 'now that the boat is really beginning to whistle for us.' And yet Nora Barnacle's feelings on 8 October 1904 must have been not unlike those of Eveline, the heroine who gave her name to a story in *Dubliners*.

> She stood among the swaying crowd in the station at the North Wall. He held her hand and she knew that he was speaking to her, saying something about the passage over and over again . . . Through the wide doors of the sheds she caught a glimpse of the black mass of the boat, lying in beside the quay wall, with illumined portholes. She answered nothing. She felt her cheeks pale and cold and, out of a maze of distress, she prayed to God to direct her, to show her what was her duty. The boat blew a long mournful whistle into the mist.

Unlike Eveline she went aboard and next day they were in London. At one time there had been some question of settling there but finally they went to Zurich where on 11 October, in the Gasthaus Hoffnung, their marriage was consummated. *'Elle n'est pas encore vierge; elle est touchée,'* he confided to Stannie.

Unfortunately there had been a mistake about the post he expected at the Berlitz School and as a last resort he had to go to Pola where during the winter Nora was constantly cold and often tearful. Occasionally they had tiffs, as yet trivial enough to be called 'funny affairs' by Joyce, 'lovers' quarrels' by Nora. Towards the end of December Joyce informed Stannie, 'Nora has conceived, I think, and I wish her to live as healthily as possible.' The idea of being a father did not please him.

Joyce was transferred to the Berlitz School in Trieste in March 1905, a pleasant change. 'Nora sings sometimes when she is dressing . . . At present she is licking jam off a piece of paper. She is very well, wears a veil now and looks very pretty.' But as the year wore on and her pregnancy became noticeable they were turned out of one lodging after another. For Nora the heat was an additional hardship and she lay exhausted on the bed half the day.

Joyce encountered trials of a different kind: Grant Richards the prospective publisher of *Chamber Music* was bankrupt and John Lane returned the poems with a rejection slip. In due course he began to experience the disillusionment that young men feel in the latter months of their wives' first pregnancies. Ungallantly he made Stannie his confidant: 'Nora is almost always complaining. She can eat very few of the sloppy Italian dishes and whatever she eats gives her a pain in her chest. She drinks beer but the least thing is enough to make her sick . . . The Trieste people are great "stylists" in dress, often starving themselves in order to be able to flaunt good dresses on the pier and she with her distorted body (Eheu! peccatum?) and her short four crown skirt and hair done over the ears is always nudged at and sniggered at.'

She was impractical and wept when unable to make clothes for the baby. He came to the conclusion that she was not of robust constitution and was in poor health.

> But more than this I am afraid that she is one of those plants which cannot be safely transplanted. She is continually crying. I do not believe that she wants to have anything more to say to her people but I am quite sure (it is her own statement) that she cannot live this life with me much longer. She has nobody to talk to but me and, heroics left aside, this is not good for a woman. Sometimes when we are out together (with the other English 'professor') she does not speak a word during the whole evening. She seems to me to be in danger of falling into a melancholy mood which would certainly injure her health very much. I do not know what strange morose creature she will bring forth after all her tears. . . .

His prize remark, however, was 'One of the English teachers said that she was not worthy of me and I am sure this would be many people's verdict . . .' He wished to avoid any tragic ending of the love-affair but was also determined to avoid 'that abominable spectre which Aunt Josephine calls "mutual tolerance".'

On 19 July he returned to the same theme.

> Nora seems to me to be in very poor health. All yesterday and the day before she has been laid up with neuralgia and pains and today she seems to be dropping down with weakness. It is very difficult for either of us to enjoy life in these circumstances.

The female's love for her unborn child strengthens during its gestation; the male's feelings are less predictable, resentment as common as any other. Paternal love, late flowering, may be delayed until birth is accomplished, stimulated into existence then by the infant's helplessness, perhaps, or by pride of possession. Nora Joyce's labour pains commenced unexpectedly during the afternoon of Thursday, 27 July—with characteristic incompetence she had miscalculated her dates—and at about nine p.m. Dr. Gilberto Sinigaglia, one of Joyce's pupils, delivered the baby.

Then all at once in his very next letter to Stannie we encounter Joyce in a new rôle, that of a devoted father.

> It was not very pleasant for me—the six hours—but it must have been a damn sight worse for Nora. But Dr. Sinigaglia told me she was brave and hardly uttered a cry, only clapped her hands when she heard it was a boy. She is very well. The child appears to have inherited his grandfather's and father's voices. He has dark blue eyes. He has a great taste for music because while I was nursing him yesterday he eyed me with great fixity as I whistled several operatic airs for him. Nora gives him her own milk.

In September he informed his brother: 'The child has got no name yet, though he will be two months old on Thursday next. He is very fat and very quiet. I don't know who he's like. He's rather like that pudgy person of two years old who frowns at the camera in my first photograph but he has the "companion's" eyes.'[2] And naturally the infant began to feature in the budget. 16 August 1906: 'In my list I forgot to include bonnet for Georgie 3 lire . . .' 25 September 1906: 'My assets are two centesmi as yesterday I had to get shaved and to pay a laundry bill and to buy medicine for Georgie who has a bad cold on his chest.'

The fond father continued to chronicle his son's development.

> Nora has a talent for blowing soap-bubbles. While I was wading through a chapter of *Dorian Gray* a few days ago she and Georgie were blowing bubbles on the floor out of a basin of suds. She can make them as big as a football. Georgie is a great favourite with everyone here. All the people we frequent know his name. He had added to his vocabulary 'O Gesù Mio' 'Brutto, brutto' and cleans out his ear when told to do so.

From Rome on 30 September 1906: 'Georgie, I fear, has an attack of bronchitis. If not better tomorrow I will call in a doctor.' And some days later: 'Georgie seems better at last. His medicine and doses went up to about 5 lire and I bought a bottle of some tonic for

Nora. Georgie . . . can walk across the room by himself now and has two teeth.'

In order to economise they decided to eat in their room rather than in the *trattoria* but Nora spent a fortnight's money in four days. Nevertheless they managed to exist, the baby thriving unaware of the family's difficulties.

> Georgie is very well and fat. He spends his day pulling about papers clothes and shoes. He is cursed frequently by both his parents for mislaying the comb and the sponge or the towel or my hat or shoes: and when asked where it is he points to the ceiling or the window and says 'là!' The other evg I began to talk to Nora about something serious (!!!): but he wouldn't allow it. He made such a noise that we had to stop and talk to *him*.

Eventually they were put out of the room and Joyce had difficulty in finding another. 'The old Bethelemites must have been like these Italian bastards,' he remarked. 'I feel for poor old Joseph.'

Despite their poverty he bought a rocking-horse at Christmas for the little son on whom he doted. 'Certainly Georgie is the most successful thing connected with me. But he's only a small part mine. I think he rather likes me, however. When I come to eat he pulls over the chair and says "Se" (sede).'

His parents took him with them to a comic opera and when the infant crowed a man in front of them turned round crossly and said 'sh!' much to Joyce's annoyance. The latter was more justifiably annoyed when by mischance in the street a carter's whip flicked the infant under the eye causing a long weal across his cheek and nose. 'It puts my teeth on edge to write of it,' he informed Stannie. Fortunately it subsided quickly.

By February 1907 he was longing to be back in Trieste and the *pater familias* returned there early in March with his son and wife who was five months pregnant. Joyce was in hospital with iritis when his second child, a daughter, was born on 26 July. The birth took place in a public ward and when Nora took the baby home she was given a pauper's gift of twenty crowns.

Nora became pregnant again in 1908 but she was not greatly upset when she miscarried on 4 August. Her husband, the doctor *manqué*, examined the foetus minutely and remarked that he was probably the only one to regret its truncated existence.

Giorgio was taken to Ireland by his father in the summer of 1909 and when the latter went back to Dublin in the autumn he lovingly instructed Nora to

> Tell my handsome little son that I will come to kiss him some night when he is fast asleep and not to fret for me and that I hope he is better and tell that comical daughter of mine that I would send her a doll but that 'l'uomo non ha messo la testa ancora'.

To a man of Joyce's sensibility parentage brought immeasurable joy alloyed with an apprehension of mutability which found outlet in some of the verses in *Pomes Penyeach* one of which recalls a winter walk with his son on the beach at Fontana:

> From whining wind and colder
> Grey sea I wrap him warm
> And touch his trembling fineboned shoulder
> And boyish arm.
>
> Around us fear, descending
> Darkness of fear above
> And in my heart how deep unending
> Ache of love!

As the years passed the boy grew to be a sixfooter ('the "child" Giorgio is taller than his father') a handsome young man, a champion long-distance swimmer, and a gifted bass vocalist. His parent gave news of him to all and sundry in his letters. 'Then my son was busy looking for a position here with the help of some friends. He found one in the *Banque Nationale de Credit*. The motto of the company seems to be: All work and no play makes Jack a bright boy. The hours are from 9 to 8 with an interval for lunch but he tells me many of the staff stay on till midnight.'

The office job proved tedious and Giorgio went instead to have his voice trained at the *Schola Cantorum*. 26 April 1929: 'Giorgio made his debut last night. He had no stage fright and even scowled round on the pianist when the latter (wilfully, he says) made a mistake. He sang quite well.'

Giorgio married Helen Kastor Fleischmann (who was ten years older) on 10 December 1930. The Joyces became devoted to their American daughter-in-law although at first Nora had disapproved of the marriage. When Stephen Joyce was born on 15 February 1932 (some weeks after the lonely death of his great-grandfather

in Dublin) his grandfather wrote a poem which he sent with the
following note to Louis Gillet: 'Here is the tiny poem. For eight
years I had not written a single verse . . . You will tell me if you like
it a little. I am *papa mais pas poète*.' It was the exquisitely poignant
Ecce Puer.

Of the dark past
A child is born;
With joy and grief
My heart is torn.

Calm in his cradle
The living lies.
May love and mercy
Unclose his eyes!

Young life is breathed
On the glass;
The world that was not
Comes to pass.

A child is sleeping
An old man gone.
O, father forsaken,
Forgive your son!

There is not a redundant syllable but the superb economy serves to
underline rather than to conceal the host of memories which enveloped
Joyce as he gazed into that cradle. And the cry, 'O, father forsaken,'
with its echo of Golgotha, hints of a plenary act of contrition for
filial shortcomings.

For Giorgio it was a period of affluence. He drove about in a Rolls
Royce (which Joyce personalised to a 'Jolls Joyce') but sold it in 1934
before going to America with Helen and little Stephen. Their departure caused heartache. From then until their return Joyce was an
authority on the sailing times of the liners which bore the mail to
and fro between Europe and New York. 'Babbo' refused to allow
worry to obtrude itself in his correspondence with his children and
kept up, as he explained to Harriet Shaw Weaver, 'a tone of almost
gay irresponsibility.'

Our best wishes to you both and regards to your host and tri-
lingual greetings to your lively charge. I shake all your amal-
gamated hands several times over in rapid succession with that

charming grace for which I have always been noted and blow to you in valediction my parentolegal blessings from this little old log cabin down the Seine.

His amusing, unstudied letters reveal Joyce without a mask, affectionate, fatherly, and playful. 'Good children, who read this in peace and joy, Breathe a prayer, drop a tear for The Crockery Joyce,' But he had to explain why he sometimes wrote to his son in Italian.

Dear complimentary but most suspicious daughter-in-law.
The reason I write to Giorgio in Italian is not to conceal anything from your keen swift flashing infalible eye but because when he was introduced to me 30 years ago by Dr Gilberto Sinigaglia I said: Toh! Giorgio! To which he replied: Baaaa Boooo. Our conversation has continued in that tongue.

And on another occasion he asked Helen

Why you give me grammatick lessons. He was me friend Le Hon [pidgin English for Paul Léon] send you that wire. Le Hon very nice chap but he not know the Englisch grammatick like me and you, missus. Also why for you make me big speech stuff about Frankee Doodles? *Pipe pas*! But, say, you's grown to be a swell orator, missus. I'll tell the woyld you is.

Giorgio received advice and encouragement from his father when he resumed his career as a singer in New York. 'Dear Giorgio : Good luck! Cheer up! Courage! Forward Savoy! Remember me to the little one.' John MacCormack promised to help but was powerless to do so. 'Dear Giorgio: Be patient! These things happen. Let Stephens and MacCormack go towards their sunset. For you it is still dawn. I think the contretemps is due first of all to that imbecilic N.B.C. official. By the way, you have merely changed the order of the letters. *Banque Nationale de Credit* and now National Broadcasting Corporation.

Joyce expressed himself more bitterly to Miss Weaver:

And speaking about the bass voice in general and my son in particular he went over to America, we were told, for four months. He has been there now a year. He is at present on crutches. He sang twice over the radio to the natives who love poor old Ireland and insist that, if he is to please them, he must forget all about the unmusical [sic] countries of Europe and croon to them about *Mother Machree* and *A Little Bit of Heaven*.

He has earned in all 35s. This amount he could have got in any southern French town for one performance before an audience which, however redolent of garlic, unlike the halfcastes in Covent Garden and the Metropolitan really does know the difference between a B and a bull's foot. They insist that he is from Erin's green isle and must sing that classical aria *Blatherskite*.

Giorgio was in poor health suffering from rheumatism[3] and an overactive thyroid gland but young Stephen was thriving.

We read with pleasure that your son is becoming more and more handsome and more and more attractive and I see a lot of paternal pride in your letter. I too have known that joy in the years that were. And before me your grandfather. And before him your ancestors who are shut up in a cellar of the Rue Claire wondering what on earth this move means and hoping and praying not to end up in the Middle East.

I see also that your health is better but I am really glad the surgeons did not cut off your four limbs. . . .

The young people returned to Paris in September 1935 and in the following year Giorgio submitted to an operation which Joyce mentioned when writing to Mary Colum: 'Giorgio was operated on a week ago for his thyroid gland. The vocal chords seem to have been quite unaffected at any rate. He is making good progress and it is believed that this will radically change his whole health.'

Giorgio and Helen went to the United States again in January 1938 when Mr Kastor fell suddenly ill. They returned in April but by this time they were growing estranged. Towards the end of 1939 Helen became mentally deranged and was committed to a *maison de santé* at Suresnes near Paris.

To Joyce with his lifelong persecution complex and his ability to sense insult where none was intended his daughter-in-law's breakdown might well have appeared a final monstrous affront at the hands of fate but he had grown accustomed to tribulation. For years, with infinite patience, he had watched his own daughter's erratic behaviour deteriorate into something far more serious. When Lucia was a child he had written:

Be mine, I pray, a waxen ear
To shield me from her childish croon
And mine a shielded heart for her
Who gathers simples of the moon.

But in the tragic event of her disturbed sanity his affection remained unprotected and vulnerable. Patiently, hopefully, he had taken Lucia from clinic to clinic. And to one of her doctors in a moment of self-searching he confided that he was 'a man of small virtue inclined to alcoholism.'

CHAPTER 10

INCLINED TO ALCOHOLISM

Louis Gillet, a close friend of the middle-aged Joyce, has said that Joyce did not drink. 'I never saw him take anything other than lime-blossom tea, or at table, some very light wine.' Ernest Hemingway, on the other hand, told Scott Fitzgerald, 'You're no more of a rummy than Joyce is and most good writers are,' which may have consoled Fitzgerald, but, if correct, would have placed Joyce in a very advanced category of alcoholism indeed, for Fitzgerald's career was eclipsed by drink. The truth about Joyce's drinking seems to lie somewhere between those opposed viewpoints. If an alcoholic is defined as a person whose drinking habits have proved harmful physically, economically, or socially then Joyce was an alcoholic but with good insight into his situation, managing to control the tendency in his later years.

Just as his first verses echo the Elizabethan age, his early drinking emulated the poets of the Mermaid Tavern, sack his favourite tipple. After his mother's death he began to drink heavily changing to the more commonplace but less expensive Guinness's porter. He had been abstemious as a student but in the latter part of 1903 he frequently reeled home 'glassy-eyed and slobbery-mouthed.' The description is Stannie's who rebuked him for his behaviour. 'It makes me sick,' Stannie said, 'just to look at you.' 'Try Bile Beans,' Joyce replied sarcastically. 'I'm sure they'd be the proper diet for you.' 'For the life of me I can't imagine what you have to say to these drunken Yahoos of medical students,' Stannie said. 'At least they don't bore me as you do,' said Joyce.

Dressed in Bohemian attire, a flowing bow, a round wide-brimmed felt hat rather like those worn by Protestant ministers, and carrying an ash-plant he was the hero of many drunken exploits. Once he was mistaken by street-urchins for a parson. The incident is mentioned in *Ulysses*—'Jay, look at the drunken minister coming out of the maternity hospital!'—which also records an incident when he passed into an alcoholic coma: '—O, the night in the Camden hall when the Daughters of Erin had to lift their skirts to step over you.'

His escapades were legendary. His feckless companions laughed at his waywardness but Stannie was distressed by his folly.

I hate to see Jim limp and pale, with shadows under his watery eyes, loose wet lips, and dank hair. I hate to see him sitting on the edge of a table grinning at his own state. It gets on my nerves to be near him then. Or to see him sucking in his cheeks and his lips, and swallowing spittle in his mouth, and talking in an exhausted husky voice, as if to show how well he can act when drunk, talking about philosophy or poetry not because he likes them at the time but because he remembers that he has a certain character to maintain, that he has to show that he is clever even when drunk, and because he likes to hear himself talking. He likes the novelty of his role of dissipated genius. I hate to hear him making speeches, or to be subjected to his obviously and distressingly assumed courteous manner. He is more intolerable in the street, running after every chit with a petticoat on it and making foolish jokes to them in a high weak voice. . . .

When Stannie joined him in Trieste he found him with the same intemperate habits and was determined to cure them. He would seek his brother out in the dockland bars and find him arguing with dockers about socialism and buying them drinks. Stannie would sit with them until he could find an excuse to make Joyce leave the bar. Then, using force if necessary, he dragged him home. Under Stannie's influence Joyce reformed temporarily.

Joyce lived in Zurich during the first World War and in 'Athens on the Limmat' as Frank Budgen called it he wrote much of *Ulysses*. There, too, he found companions less ascetic than Stannie with whom he made carousel.

The white wine at the Pfauen was excellent [Budgen wrote]. I never saw Joyce drink red wine unless white was unobtainable, and then he did it with a bad grace. It is one of the few things on which he is rigidly doctrinaire. When I asked him the reason for his preference he said: 'White wine is like electricity. Red wine looks and tastes like liquified beefsteak.

When Joyce returned to Trieste after the war he described himself to his brother as 'the foolish author of a wise book.' Saddened to find him more intemperate than ever Stannie was no longer prepared to act as his custodian. Their ways parted when Joyce, at the instigation of Ezra Pound, went to live in Paris where among his many acquaintances were two other Americans; Hemingway, who on the grounds of a single visit with him to the Deux Magots where Joyce ordered a dry sherry, has taken exception to the generalization that he drank only Swiss dry wine; and Robert McAlmon[1] whose *Being Geniuses Together* gives an uninhibited account of their evenings.

For a time this splendidly-built young writer had subsisted in New York by posing in the nude for art classes at Cooper Union at a dollar an hour. He was planning to sign on as a deck-hand aboard a freighter bound for China when Dr William Carlos Williams introduced him to Bryher, an English authoress who was visiting America with the poetess Hilda Doolittle. He became engaged to Bryher who turned out to be the daughter of Sir John Ellerman one of England's wealthiest men. The marriage was unhappy. Bryher resumed her tour with H. D. and McAlmon found himself alone in Paris but with ample funds at his disposal and in a position to help other impecunious writers including Joyce.

Almost every night Joyce and I met for aperitifs, and although he was working steadily on *Ulysses* at least one night a week he was ready to stay out all night and those nights he was never ready to go home at any hour . . . Sir Thomas Browne, not to speak of Ezra Pound and Eliot and Moore and Shaw, we discussed, but sooner or later Mr Joyce began reciting Dante in sonorous Italian. When that misty and intent look came upon his face and into his eyes I knew that friend Joyce wasn't going home till early morning.

He was fascinated by McAlmon's slang and by the twist the American gave to the English language. One night when in his cups he wept while explaining his love or infatuation for words. On another occasion Joyce collapsed with fright after seeing a rat. McAlmon hailed a taxi and took him home. 'There was a huge iron gate to the courtyard, and a key which was about a foot long. I wobbled it back and forth in the lock for ten minutes and finally got the gate open.' The taxi-driver carried Joyce across the courtyard and up two flights of stairs. Nora began to scold him but became tender when she realised that he was more upset by fright than drink.

When McAlmon saw that excessive drinking was harming Joyce's eyes he decided to stay away from the Gipsy Bar off the Boul' Mich', their favourite meeting place. He did so for a while but when Joyce had finished *Ulysses* McAlmon found him anxious but lively ('Like myself when Joyce wants to drink he will drink . . .') and by this time McAlmon had forgotten his good resolutions.

His *The Revolving Mirror* (1926) contains some fragments labelled 'Romances'. Joyce is the subject of 'Romance V.'

> That he had been and continued to be praised
> pleased his vanity at moments
> but when drunk,
>   a drunk distinguished foreigner
>   distinguishably drunken
>   drinking
> he wept.
>   That his father,
>   and his father's father
>   and fathers before them
>   were parents of families
>   twelve to seventeen in number,
>   But his economic circumstances—
>
> Nevertheless:
>   'I'm a young man yet,
>   and my wife is strong.
>   I'll make me a few more
>   before it's ended by the grace of God.'

One night they were still in the Gipsy Bar at five a.m. and the *patron* asked them to leave.

Out we got, and ensconced ourselves in a small bistro on the Boulevard St Germain. We bought cigars and we drank. Joyce began dropping his cigars. At first I leaned to pick them up and returned them to him. When I could no longer lean without falling on my face, I took to lighting the cigars and handing them to him. He almost immediately dropped them and I lighted cigar after cigar until they were all gone, and we took to cigarettes. At ten in the morning we sat alone in the small bistro, the floor covered with some twenty cigars, innumerable cigarettes, and the table with the forty glasses which had held our various drinks. The *patron*, whom I saw later, could not believe that such animals as we were had ever lived. He thinks he dreamed that early morning, but he helped Joyce into a taxi, and Joyce and I drove to his hotel.

The taxi-driver was less sympathetic and McAlmon had to carry Joyce up to his room unaided. Nora was angry. 'Jim, you've been doin' this for twenty years, and I'm telling you it's the end,' she said. 'Do you understand? You've been bringing your drunken companions to me too long, and now you've started with McAlmon in the same way.'

The American managed to placate her. He undressed the recumbent Joyce and put him to bed. Then he went back to his hotel 'to sleep, to die, to know agony, to curse Joyce, life, drink and myself. My head was vertiginously in torment; my eyes revolved in red-hot sockets; my stomach quivered with nausea.'

A telegram boy woke him in the early afternoon. With bleary eyes he read a command from Joyce to present himself without fail for tea at four-thirty.

Although it took me three months to get mildly into order with health after that night I did struggle into my clothes and went to Joyce's hotel. As I entered the room Joyce sat looking owl-like and earnest. 'And McAlmon, what have you been hearing to-day about the apartment the man said we were to have?'

In a second which was a million years my mind received the idea that Joyce had been telling Nora a cover-up story. 'Oh, he's seeing about it now. I'm to meet him at six o'clock,' I answered.[2]

Les Trianons near the Gare de Montparnasse was another of Joyce's favourite places. Once settled there he was loth to leave which annoyed Nora. And when his friends intervened she said, 'It's you who see him in a jolly state, but it's me who has to bear the brunt of it if his eyes are ailing, and what a martyr that man can be you've no idea.' He had a favourite table at *Les Trianons* and a favourite waiter who saw him safely home if Nora was not there.

Sometimes Nora was put out of patience. She visited a bistro one evening with her husband and William Bird. Eventually she remonstrated: 'Jim, do you hear me, you've had enough. Jim I'm telling you this has been going on for twenty years and I'll have no more of it. It's me that has to look after you when your eyes are giving trouble and raising a nuisance for us all. I'll take the children, Jim, an' go back to Ireland, I'm telling you. Mr Bird, you see how it is. His eyes'll be bothering him. Come on, Jim, be sensible for once in your life.'

Joyce insisted on going on to Fouquet's without Nora. At five in the morning Bird got him into a taxi which drove to his apartment. The elevator was out of order but Bird managed to haul him up to the fifth floor. Once there Joyce went into the bathroom, locked the door and sulkily refused to come out.

Nora pleaded with him. Bird cajoled him but it was fifteen minutes before he emerged.

'What are you to do with such a man?' Nora asked Bird. 'And to think I've put up with him like this for all these years. What a damn fool his admirers would think me if they knew the half of it. He may be a genius to them, but look at him—what is he to me?'

But mindful of his alcoholic heritage Joyce took steps to control it. He made a strict rule never to drink before evening. At a luncheon party Sylvia Beach noticed that Joyce was not drinking despite many attempts on the part of other guests to fill his glass. Finally he turned his glass upside down but reddened with embarrassment when Ezra Pound began to line up all the bottles on the table in front of him.

Sorrow had matured and sobered Joyce by the time that Louis Gillet came to know him. They used to meet at a café in the late afternoons. Joyce always arrived punctually; he would sit down, sigh, and order lime-blossom or vervain tea, never coffee or liquor. Then the celebrated French Academician and the world-famous author talked about their children.

'Joyce emphasized family affection to an extreme degree,' Gillet wrote. 'This terrible nay-sayer was a family man; in the chaos of the universe, as in the Deluge, his family was for him a sheet-anchor, the sacred Ark.' He talked to Gillet endlessly about Lucia and he accused himself of transmitting the evil strain that caused her madness.[3]

CHAPTER 11

SCHIZOPHRENIA

Only in occasional moments of candour did Joyce accept that his daughter was schizophrenic. Understandably he preferred to cast doubt on the diagnosis, to seek some physical explanation, or to use a euphemism. 'Her case is cyclothymia dating from the age of seven and a half,' he informed Jacques Mercanton in August 1940. 'Her character is gay, sweet and ironic, but she has sudden bursts of anger over nothing when she has to be confined in a straitjacket.'

Any oddities of behaviour in childhood had been dismissed as vagaries of temperament consistent with Lucia's upbringing. She was pretty in an unusual way, a slight squint hardly taking from her attractiveness. Later she appeared to be a pleasant if unpredictable young woman, but Stuart Gilbert thought the intellectual *milieu* centred on Joyce may have been uncongenial to her, despite her devotion to her father. 'Several times, when I persuaded her to come with me to the nearby bar *Chez Francis* (in the Place de l'Alma) for a cocktail, I was struck by the change in her manner when I switched the conversation over to ordinary topics and encouraged her to talk about herself. Her ambition was to strike out on her own . . . "I want to *do* something," she would say, and though I could understand her feelings and sympathise with them, there were no openings I could think of for a young girl who at the age of twenty-five had still the inexperience of half that age.'

She did some dress designing and with a little help from Valéry Larbaud she published an article on Charlie Chaplin in 1924 in *Le Disque Vert*. Later she showed talent as a ballet dancer and took instruction from Lois Hutton. On 19 February 1928 she appeared in 'Ballet Faunesque' at the Comédie des Champs-Elysées, in the part of a wild vine. In July she joined Raymond Duncan's school of the dance in Schloss Klessheim near Salzburg.

Her next interest was *lettrines*. Louis Gillet wrote: 'She used to dance. Those who saw her declared that she was enchanting. I can well believe it; I have seen her walk. Then her fancy changed. She wanted to prove that she had as much wit in the tips of her fingers as in the tips of her toes. She bestirred herself and began to draw. She ornamented her father's collection of songs entitled *Pomes Penyeach* with charmingly fantastic initials. These initials seemed alive.

They were like insects, weird butterflies of unknown species thrown on to the page and about to fly away. They were oriental, faery-like and withal extremely Irish.'

Lucia fell in love with Samuel Beckett and when this came to nothing Paul Léon encouraged his brother-in-law Alexander Ponisovsky, a Russian bank clerk, who had just had a broken love affair, to take an interest in her. Eventually, apparently at Léon's instigation, Ponisovsky proposed marriage and was accepted. Mary Colum remembered Lucia's earnest rather formal way of speaking, 'as if she had considered matters and had come to conclusions,' but because of her background her speech was deracinated. In the course of a few sentences she might slip from English into French, from French into Italian and her idioms were faulty. 'She and I are in the same boots,' she said of an Irish friend who was also engaged to a man with a Russian name. Mrs Colum thought her solitary and hesitant with a reflective air about her. 'Lucia,' she said explaining her name, 'it means Light —like Paris, the City of Light, you know.'

Despite Giorgio Joyce's protests to his parents that Lucia was not in a fit mental state, an engagement party was held at the Restaurant Drouand but when the girl returned to the Léon apartment after the party she lay on a sofa and passed into a state of catatonia. After her recovery the engagement was tacitly allowed to lapse. She agreed to go to London with her parents but on 17 April she had a *'crise de nerfs'* at the Gare du Nord. She screamed that she hated England and refused to board the train. When persuasion failed Joyce had the trunks taken off the train and abandoned the journey. He wrote to Miss Weaver a few days later: 'I have arranged for Lucia to see Dr Fontaine and a nerve specialist. I shall try to set up a home for her here though she is terribly difficult but she is really a child . . .'

Soon after this she went to stay with the Colums who had taken the Jolas's apartment in the rue de Sevigné. It was night when she arrived and she stood by the window. 'That star means something,' she said, standing there quiet and pathetic. The Colums obtained a job for her as translator for an American entomologist but after a single morning's work she rebelled. 'Is that the sort of work for me?' she asked in an aggrieved tone. 'Why should I, an artist, waste myself on that kind of work?'

When Sunday came Lucia went to Mass with Padraic Colum. Joyce telephoned when they were out and he remarked, when told where they had gone—'Now I know she is mad'—which is quite out of character with his usual denial of her illness.

Fearful that the girl might be suicidal Mrs Colum slept with her, pinning her nightdress to her own with a safetypin. Lucia refused to see a psychiatrist but it was arranged that he should call to the apartment each morning ostensibly to advise Mrs Colum who was not well. The latter sat beside Lucia on the sofa and the doctor addressed his questions to them both. When Lucia volunteered an explanation for her hostess's illhealth, *'Madame est très nerveuse,'* the psychiatrist said, *'Madame est artiste'* and evoked from Lucia, *'Mais m'sieu, c'est moi qui est artiste.'* Sometimes Mrs Colum managed to slip out of the room leaving Lucia alone with the doctor. She thought he did not understand the girl and, indeed, she was prepared to back her own assessment of how matters stood and contradicted the psychiatrist flatly when he told her that whatever it was it was not serious and that Lucia would soon recover.

Joyce came round every day and although he would sit at the piano and play and sing to himself he was obviously desperately unhappy. To bring him peace of mind and for the girl's own sake the Colums were anxious to keep her with them but when Mrs Colum had to go to hospital it was necessary to make other arrangements for Lucia.

Without informing her of their destination Giorgio Joyce and Mrs Colum took her to l'Hay-les-Roses, a sanitarium. Mrs Colum hated the deception: 'We entered the office of the director of the Sanitarium, and as he began to talk to me Lucia threw me a look of bewildered appeal which I can never forget. Later the director sent both of us upstairs to a room where Lucia was received by a pleasant nurse of her own age, for whom she took an immediate liking. The young nurse made her feel at ease, told Lucia she would be with her all the time, and her presence in the room made the good-bye I had dreaded pass off more easily.

This was the first of many admissions for mental treatment but her stay on this occasion was short. Joyce expressed his dissatisfaction to Edouard Dujardin:

Les choses ne vont pas bien. On a même proposé l'isolement total pour ma fille, proposition contre laquelle tout mon instinct se révolte. Il y aura justement demain une consultation entre les médecins et je propose d'emmener ma fille de cette maison et de l'envoyer à l'étranger accompagnée par son infirmière et une famille de notre conaissance [Eugene and Maria Jolas] afin qu'elle puisse se distraire.

Joyce wrote to Miss Weaver from Zurich on 10 July 1932: 'I

smuggled Lucia and her nurse out of the clinic, through Paris and
to Austria. Here is the first result. Everyone in Paris is huffy because
I would not allow her to be seen while she was there . . . We have to
prepare a retreat for her in case she has a fresh collapse. So we want
to go to Neuchâtel to see a place there. We ourselves want to stay
near Lucerne. The moving out of Paris with fees and fares and
pensions in advance cost me 10,000 frs.' But when Lucia expressed
the intention of joining her parents Joyce was alarmed. 'I wish she
would stay where she is. I have written to Dr Codet about her as, of
course, I am nervy all the time at having taken her out of his hands
on my own responsibility.' He sent Miss Weaver further details on
July 22:

> Jolas sends good news from Feldkirch but I never know whether
> these letters are rigged or not. Lucia writes announcing her
> arrival with the nurse on Friday next. I hope she does not decide
> to stay. I wish she would not come. She runs the risk of two
> more station scenes.
>
> I thought if she sent three letters GBS to Shaw on the 26th
> (they have the same birthday) he might like her talent. But I am
> afraid Shaw has lived too long on the boreal side of La Manche
> to appreciate silly things like that. Perhaps he is right too.

He visited Feldkirch and in a letter to John Sullivan he wrote on
August 25th: 'Lucia, I think, is out of the danger zone but will need
many months of surveillance. She and her friend are going in a week
or so to Venice on condition that we go to Nice for a few months so
as to be near them. So we said yes.'

Joyce continued to foster her flair for *lettrines* and to seek a market
for her work. Much to his disgust the British Customs seized ten
copies of the *de luxe* edition of *Pomes Penyeach* as 'silk luxury goods'
imposing a tax of £4 per copy. Back in Paris Miss Moschos was in
charge of her in the morning and another girl took over in the afternoons. Her father tried to take her lightly and gave her the price of
a fur coat which he thought would relieve her inferiority complex
more than any psycho-analyst could. He persuaded her to take an
interest in book-binding and during 1933 she studied painting with
Marie Laurencin.

Paul Léon kept Miss Weaver informed of Joyce's problems:

> . . . he still has to fight against pressure brought to bear on him
> from all sides with regard to placing his daughter under a certain

restraint in a sanatorium which he absolutely refuses to do and he has placed her in the care of a doctor here and has engaged a girl-companion for her. The opinion of this doctor is that she ruined her nervous system by five years dancing strain something which he always combated and tried to discourage as far as he could while recognising her great talent. He tells me that she is encouraged by certain people to go and pass the winter alone in Zurich—this he regards as lunacy but every time I meet him some new origin of her condition has been discovered the only thing which does not vary is the fact that he is the culprit.

She was admitted under the care of Dr Oscar Forel to Les Rives de Prangins at Nyon on 30 July but Joyce took her away again on 4 August against Forel's wishes. Later he wrote optimistically to Stanislaus: 'Lucia is much better (touching wood) in excellent health but as *stramba* as a March hare and as proud as ever she can be. But devil a hapworth else that I can see after her ten doctors.' At the end of 1933, however, he remarked, 'What a year! Fog, illness, disaster, madness.'

During the following April he sought a further knowledge of his daughter's character from Max Pulver, a graphologist, but soon after this she was re-admitted to the mental home at Nyon and his letter to Giorgio held an air of mystification about her treatment: 'They called in a German specialist at Nyon and he advised them to treat Lucia as if she had something or other, though there is no trace of it. And this is apparently doing her good.' She remained there for some months improving slowly but in a letter to his daughter-in-law Joyce reported: 'Lucia seems to have fallen for some undesirable gent in the Nyon shop who either lives in Dublin or London. They are being kept apart and he is going away. This has for the moment upset her. But they say it will soon pass. I see nothing crazy in that, as women go.'

He visited Nyon in August and was flabbergasted by a mix-up which he described to his son:

I asked Forel to prepare Lucia for our visit. He said no, he would have an interview with us first. He told me therefore to come on Sunday at 2.30 to his villa Hautes Rives, while Lucia was at Les Eglantines, and he would keep her away so he could speak with us before allowing us to see her. We arrived at 2.30 at Forel's home. Mama saw Lucia at once, standing on the grass near the door. Mama said to me: Quick, let's go in before she sees us. And she slipped in. I followed as best I could, the entrance being full of people. I thought I had made it when I heard Lucia cry, 'Babbo! Babbo!' And in a moment she was upon me, hugging me and sobbing. I calmed her and then she went on to Mama. I stayed to swear violently at a doctor who happened to be near. It seems they had told Lucia I was coming at 2.30. What do you think of this little tale?

He told Giorgio that his sister was well, 'her face fuller, no more grey hairs etc.' but to Mrs Giedion he wrote: 'We found Lucia after 7 months of the clinic almost on the verge of collapse. Utter despair. The doctor says after all the time he can make no diagnostic. They are helpless in the case. The only hold she seems to have on life is her affection for us. She is under restraint, that is her windows are barred, and she is always *surveillée*. But I feel if she stays there she will simply fade out.' He looked to Budgen for advice: 'Some time ago you wrote me of some case you heard of. It was a friend? and your letter spoke of a treatment for reduction of white corpuscles. Lucia has 4 times the normal number of these. They say there must be a source of infection. They have put her to tests for syphilis, tuberculosis, glands, etc., but the result is always the same, negative. If this seat of infection could be found and treated they think the battle might turn.'

She was admitted to Burghölzli the Zurich mental asylum on 20 September 1934 and Professor Theodor Naegeli, a haematologist was called in consultation. A week later she was transferred to a private mental home at Küsnacht where Carl Jung was on the staff. Joyce was impressed by Jung but the latter was uncertain as to what line to take with Lucia. After a month his assistant explained that Jung would start psycho-analysis if he insisted but that it might cause a deterioration. This was Joyce's own feeling in the matter. He confided to his son and daughter-in-law that the expenses were high. 'Küsnacht is like Prangins 7000 a month and Jung's bill for October was 3600. So hurry up as I want the loan of a million.' He added that Lucia sometimes had 'the wisdom of the serpent and the innocence of the dove.' He was convinced that she was clairvoyant.

She was allowed to spend Christmas with her parents at the Carlton Elite Hotel, Zurich and in January 1935 she was well enough to move into Villa Elite (an annex of the hotel) with a nurse. 'The great danger is past but the doctors had nothing to do with that,' Joyce wrote in a letter. He explained to Helen that he would soon send

away the nurse, 'as my sister Eileen is coming from Dublin to try out
a stay of a month or so at Lucia's constantly repeated request. Have
just wired her her fare. Please ask all the jews in America to get up
a subscription for me as I am planning to enter the poorhouse on S.
Patrick's Day next.'

In February an endocrinologist in Paris diagnosed a deficiency of
the adrenal glands and his régime (which included two tepid baths
daily) was adhered to even when she visited London with her aunt
as guests of Miss Weaver. Details of her behaviour and emotional
state at this period are given in Jane Lidderdale and Mary Nicholson's
Dear Miss Weaver; depressed, she threatened to buy a pistol but
laughed when her aunt, who handled her well, said she should buy
two in case one did not work. During this visit Miss Weaver took
her to see Mr. John Swift Joly, F.R.C.S., a Dublin graduate who
practised in Harley street and specialized in urology.[1] She found the
consultation a disturbing experience; afterwards she insisted to going
to Piccadilly alone and to the distress of her hostess remained away
until the following morning.

Later she accompanied her aunt to her home in Bray, Co. Wicklow.
Joyce gave permission for the visit to Ireland but told Eileen that
Nora had misgivings. 'She is not very keen on Lucia's going to Galway as she anticipates trouble when her people find out that she
doesn't go to holy mass, holy confession, holy communion and holus
bolus. However she thinks the air will do her good. Also Irish eggs
are famous all over the world.' He was distressed to think that Lucia
had been rude to Miss Weaver and tried to make excuses for her
behaviour. 'Possibly Lucia, not having been brought up as a slave
and having neither Bolshevik nor Hitlerite tendencies, made a bad
impression on you and she certainly does not flatter.' He insisted that
Eileen must always be straight-forward and honest with her, 'as she
is herself in spite of her loony ways,'

She was forever in his thoughts and was the main topic of a letter
written to Miss Weaver on 1st May.

> I am only too painfully aware that Lucia has no future but that
> does not prevent me from seeing the difference between what is
> beautiful and shapely and what is ugly and shapeless. As usual
> I am in a minority of one . . .
>
> While I am glad in a way that Lucia is out of the dangers of
> Paris and especially of London, every ring of the doorbell gives
> me an electric shock as I never know what the postman or tele-

graph boy is going to bring in. And if it is bad news all the blame will fall on me. . . . She behaves like a fool very often but her mind is as clear and as unsparing as the lightning. She is a fantastic being speaking a curious abbreviated language of her own. I understand it or most of it. Before she went to London she spoke to me about you and what you had done for me. She wanted through herself to establish a final link between the dissolute being who is writing these lines and your honourable self. Then she went on to Ireland with the same idea. Whatever she may have succeeded in doing with you she will do nothing over there. How well I know the eyes with which she will be regarded! Léon is concerned with what she may do to prejudice my name there. And my wife who personally is probably worth both of her children rolled together and multiplied by three thinks that this is the chief reason for my constant state of alarm. So far as I know myself it is not so.

So long as she was within reach I always felt I could control her—and myself. And in fact I could. But now though I have the faithful support of my wife and Léon's loyal friendship and that of some others here to say nothing of your own patience and sympathy there are moments and hours when I have nothing in my heart but rage and despair, a blindman's rage and despair.

I cannot be such an utter fool as to be inventing all this. But I can no longer control matters. On many sides I hear that I am and have been an evil influence on my children. But what are they doing away from that evil influence? On the other hand what can I honestly ask them to come back to? Paris is like myself a haughty ruin or if you like a decayed reveller. And any time I turn on the radio I hear some British politician mumbling inanities or his German cousin shouting and yelling like a madman. Perhaps Ireland and the U.S. are the safe places. And perhaps this is where the gas is really going to be turned on. Well, so be it.

He wrote to Lucia frequently. He made her a generous allowance but was left unaware that her behaviour was disturbed and unpredictable. She was missing for days and Constantine Curran, sensitive to her father's feelings, used his influence as an officer of the Law Courts to warn the police not to inform the press if she was found wandering. Then a letter from her cousin alarmed Joyce; he implored Michael Healy, Nora's uncle, to send him reliable news.

Healy's letter was vague but disquieting and Mrs Jolas went to Dublin to see the girl. She returned with bad news and Lucia herself wrote asking to go to a nursing-home which Joyce arranged by telephone.

He was enraged by Eileen's well-intentioned 'deception' and uncertain about letting Lucia stay with Miss Weaver to break the return journey to Paris, 'as the latter has been for months past in collusion with Eileen "not to write this to Paris etc.," keeping me in ignorance of all the sordid squalor of the case and of the warning of the authorities that their next step would be to commit her or intern her. I was told always "she is getting on fine" and Miss Weaver, as with her other female charms, walked blue-eyed and prim-mouthed into my sister's booby-trap.' He would not hear of Giorgio's suggestion that she be sent to a mental hospital.

> If you had seen Lucia's condition after seven months of confinement at Nyon you would not advise me to put her back in such an institution. I shall do it if and when there is no other recourse. Nothing serious happened in Ireland. Everyone who saw Lucia there agreed that she was stronger and less unhappy. But she lived like a gipsy in squalor. All this was known to Eileen and the other two and to Miss Weaver and they all were in league to conceal it from me. It was a good thing that Mr Healy saw her. But he changed his mind very quickly for during the last two years he as well as your grandmother have been writing continually: No doctors, no sanatorium, no blood examinations etc.

Finally she did go to stay with Miss Weaver and had a course of injections from her latest doctor. Her father expressed the conviction 'that he will be for you what Vogt has been for me. That is to say the man who does his business and comes at the end of a series of "botchers".' In a letter to Constantine Curran he dwelled on the same theme: 'For more than a year I have been harping on the subject of a glandular disturbance. Nobody seemed to listen, I mean of the so-called mind doctors—about two score of them in all. The instant I touched her hand at Nyon after a forced separation I knew some change had set in.' And to Curran again ten days later: 'It is terrible to think of a vessel of election as the prey of impulses beyond its control and of natures beneath its comprehension and, fervently as I desire her cure, I ask myself what then will happen when and if she finally withdraws her regard from the lightning-lit revery of her clairvoyance and turns it upon that battered cabman's face, the world. Our hope is that the gaiety and gentleness that we always remember will once again be her companions, as they were through her happy childhood but then grown into another and warmer youth.' He added that 'the medical faculty of half Europe has very considerately and very considerably lightened my bag of marbles to the extent of about £5000 in the last 4½ years and see the result. *Un bel niente*!'

He should have blamed his own credulity, to some degree, for the mounting medical expenses. It is unlikely, for instance, that had he sought their opinions his own medical advisers would have approved of the latest course of treatment with Professor N. E. Ischlondosky's bovine serum which, with Miss Weaver's help, he had arranged for Lucia; nor would they have agreed that she should be placed under the care of a doctor who appears to have had scant understanding of her case.

Wm. George Macdonald, M.B., Ch.B., Aberdeen (1908) a general practitioner of Boxmoor, Herefordshire, was honorary surgeon to the West Herts. Hospital, Hemel Hempstead. He took rooms in London, in the Harley Street area, in 1931 and was recommended to Joyce by Ischlondosky, a Russian scientist who had settled in Paris, in whose work he had an active interest. When Miss Weaver called on Dr Macdonald in Queen Anne Street he agreed, without having actually seen the patient, to administer the course of twenty-five injections personally. In due course, after a violent struggle, the first injection was given; to aggravate matters the doctor insisted that the restless girl should stay in bed throughout the period of treatment, and that in hot weather and without sedatives.

Miss Weaver looked after Lucia as best she could, with the assistance of her friend Edith Walker, a trained nurse. They nailed the windows so that they could not be opened fully; they moved her into a back-room, for she tended to throw books down into the street. They pacified the neighbours, annoyed by constant singing in any one of four different languages, as best they could. And when necessary additional nurses were employed.

Joyce never ceased to encourage his daughter with wonderfully gentle letters, occasionally hinting that she should mend her ways.

My dear little daughter: 'Hariosement,' as Mama says, your blessed treatment has come to an end. Now it is simply a question of changing surroundings and air (everything has been settled) and then of allowing time to take its course. You know,

139

all things come to him who waits. A short stay in the country will be the right thing for you.

I think you have stood very bravely all the inconveniences of this endless spell of heat and the continuous imprisonment. But now you must forget all about it. Miss Weaver has been very conscientious and considerate towards you and I am sure you appreciate her sincere and simple kindness. If I have anything to say to you it is not concerning her but concerning your nurses.

Each time I get a letter from you you have another one. Gracious! How greedy you are. Prince Norindett Norodum Doum Doum is entitled to hoist seven umbrellas over his bald head because he is of kingly race. Perhaps you have the ambition of making a collection of seven nurses' caps because you are the daughter of Apelles, son of Apollo. All right. But I beseech you not to exceed the holy number of seven because all these good females—English, Scotch, Welsh, Irish, Mulatto, Indo-Chinese, Ethiopian, Red Indian (and whoever knows of more should put more on this list) depend on me personally, except, of course, Miss Weaver's friend.

He wrote to her in Reigate where she was convalescing, on 17 October:

Dear Lucia: We received your postcards and the two photographs also, of you and of Miss Weaver. Thank you. Miss Weaver is always the same and as for you, you look as if you did not care in the least about the *terrestial globe*, absorbed as you are in your reading and swimming. If only all the inhabitants of the above mentioned rolling ball were so peaceful!

I think the next number in your programme of convalescence should be a nice fur coat. How does that strike you? I have written to Mrs Budgen who spent several years as secretary of a London firm that dealt with these articles and is therefore an expert. You must have good advice, otherwise you run the risk of buying, one might appropriately say, a *cat* in a poke . . .

If your picture is indicative of your state of health you must be much, much better. And now, dear Lucia, every day in every way you must get—well, it doesn't sound right in Italian but it is what the most reverend and most wise Dr Coué preaches.

Macdonald who had visited Joyce in Paris came down to Reigate to see Lucia. Although he declared her improved he was at last sufficiently realistic to arrange for her admission to St Andrew's, Northampton, a celebrated mental hospital. While she was there an unfortunate incident occurred.

Edith Walker had seen patients like Lucia with hidden cancers and when she and Miss Weaver visited her in Northampton she glanced at the case-notes and saw that a doctor had written, '?carcinoma'. Pressed by the two ladies the young doctor said that the possibility, however remote, had to be considered. Accordingly, intending to spare him pain, Miss Weaver arranged that a mutual friend should break the news gently to Joyce. When Macdonald came to hear what she had done he wrote a furious letter rebuking her for her interference and forbidding her to see the girl again.

Lucia returned to Paris towards the end of February, 1936, but her condition deteriorated and in March she was taken in a straitjacket to Le Vésinet from where she was transferred to Maison de Santé at Ivry. Joyce did not despair of her recovery. When the Obelisk Press published *A Chaucer ABC* with Lucia's *lettrines* he suggested to Mrs Giedion that she might 'send her a few lines, perhaps about her book *et la pluie et le beau temps* and seeing her again in Zurich *when* she is better as you hear she is making progress.' He avoided giving Herbert Gorman, his biographer, any details of her visit to Ireland.

On Bastille Day 1937, he sent Constantine Curran a case of wine and mentioned that 'some doctors and people who saw Lucia lately agree that she is much better than $2\frac{1}{2}$ years ago. What a dreadful trial to be laid on any girl's shoulders! I had arranged for her to go out on a motor ride today but there's the rain in bucketfulls! *Pas de chance!*' In the following month he commiserated with Adolf Kastor, father of his daughter-in-law, whose son had developed schizophrenia, pointing out that Nijinsky, an apparently hopeless case, had recently benefited from insulin treatment. He wrote elsewhere to find if the cure was authentic. 'If it is I believe it will or ought to revolutionise the treatment of mental-moral maladies which are also clearly physical.'

Lucia had a further set-back in November and remained in the Maison de Santé. When writing to Louis Gillet in September 1938 Joyce hinted of new troubles.

Mon long silence n'est pas dû seulement au travail fou qui m'a accablé depuis bien des mois mais aussi au fait que depuis quelque temps nous nous voyons—ma femme et moi—confronté par la possibilité d'un autre grave événement dans notre famille comme si la presque tragédie de ma fille ne suffisait pas. De cela je préfère vous parler de vive voix et quand nous serons tous les deux de rétour à Paris. Pour le moment je vous prierai de n'en parler à personne. Je ne partage pas le pessimisme qui m'entoure mais peut-être je me trompe.

Quant à ma fille je suis la seule personne qu'elle voit ou qu'elle veut voir. J'y vais tous les dimanches après déjeuner et je reste là jusqu'a la nuit.

The authorities planned that in the event of war the patients at Ivry should be transferred to La Baule and during the 1938 crisis Joyce waited there for Lucia's arrival. The war-clouds passed temporarily but in September 1939 the distracted Joyce sent a wire to his son.

ABSOLUMENT ACUNE PROVISION FAITE ICI POUR RECEVOIR MAISON SANTE STOP DELMAS PENSE POUVOIR ARRANGER EVENTUELLEMENT D'ICI HUIT A QUINZE JOURS STOP EN ATTENDANT LUCIA ABANDONNEE SEULE IVRY MALGRE TOUS MES PREPARATIFS STOP ESSAYE TE METTRE EN RAPPORT AVEC PERSONNEL MAISON NOUS SOMMES HOTEL CHRISTOPHE ICI TELEPHONE 21 — 30 COURAGE BONNE CHANCE   BABBO

Eventually the patients were transferred to the Hôtel des Charmettes[2] at Pornichet near La Baule where Joyce and Nora remained until November when, as he explained in a letter to Mr and Mrs V. A. Sax, his daughter-in-law's acute derangement obliged him to return to Paris.

Chers amis: Merci de votre gentille pensée. Vous semblez être presque les seules personnes en ce moment qui pensent à nous. Nous avons dû quitter La Baule en hate à cause de la grave maladie de ma bru et n'y rentreons que d'ici quelques semaines. Elle est maintenant dans une maison de santé à Suresnes, près de Paris, et son frère arrive ici demain de New York et il tâchera de l'emmener avec lui en Amérique. L'enfant a été placé dans une école près de Vichy. Une histoire lamentable et qui a semé le désastre à droite et à gauche. Mon fils et moi avons passé trois semaines angoissées pour ne parler pas de ma femme. Ma fille me croît souffrant et toujours à La Baule. Il ne nous manquait que cela vraiment. Nous sommes à l'hotel parce que l'appartement n'est pas chauffé.

En somme, du courage!

Helen Joyce was taken back to the United States on 2 May 1940. Meanwhile Joyce and Nora had settled in Saint-Gérand-du-Puy. Lucia did not see her father again but she was never far from his mind and he was indefatigable in his efforts to have her transferred to a *maison départmentale* at Moulins, or later, when he had decided to leave France, to a clinic in Switzerland.

Eventually he obtained an exit permit for her but it had expired by the time the Swiss authorities granted her a visa. He was obliged to leave her behind him in Pornichet, not far from Saint Nazaire, an important bombing target. After the war she was admitted to St Andrew's Hospital, Northampton, where she still is today. She has benefited greatly from treatment with modern drugs and her good wishes were read out at the International James Joyce Symposia held in Dublin in 1967 and 1969.

CHAPTER 12

DOCTORS AND HOSPITALS

When there was a fire in the Irish Sweepstake Office in 1935 Joyce wrote sardonically to Lucia: '. . . it seems to me that the lady Anna Livia did not do her duty even if the firemen did theirs. Much smoke and little water. But they will find another edifice in which to continue their noble work for the benefit of the Dublin hospitals and the poor doctors, the poor sisters, the poor sick people and the poor priests, consolers of these latter. Let me weep. And cheers for the race-horse.'

Many medical institutions are mentioned in *Ulysses* those alluded to most frequently being the Mater, Holles Street, and Mercer's Hospitals.

Leopold Bloom, whose meanderings are followed throughout 16 June 1904, lives in Eccles Street. Passing along Berkeley Street in the morning he muses: 'The *Mater Misericordiae*. Eccles Street. My house down there. Big place. Ward for incurables there. Very encouraging.' Later he hears a medical student discoursing on the affectations of the profession. 'The bedside manner it is they use in the Mater hospice. Demme does not Dr O'Gargle chuck the nuns there under the chin?'

Bloom has had firsthand knowledge of 'the house of misericord.' He has been to the Casualty Department with a bee sting. The student —'Dixon yclept junior of saint Mary Merciable's'—who treated him, has moved to Holles Street Hospital, then under the Mastership of Dr Andrew Horne.

> Seventy beds keeps he there teeming mothers are wont that they lie for to thole and bring forth bairns hale so God's angel to Mary quoth. Watchers they there walk, white sisters in ward sleepless. Smarts they still sickness soothing: in twelve moons thrice an hundred. Truest bedthanes they twain are, for Horne holding wariest ward.

Walking through Molesworth Street Bloom notices a placard advertising the Mirus Bazaar. 'In aid of funds for Mercer's hospital. *The Messiah* was first given for that. Yes Handel. What about going out there. Ballsbridge.' In the afternoon he encounters the Viceroy who 'on his way to inaugurate the Mirus bazaar in aid of funds for Mercer's hospital, drove with his following towards Lower Mount street.' Many others view the Viceroy and his Countess: from the Ormond Hotel 'gold by bronze' the barmaids watched and admired; Simon Dedalus 'stood still in mid-street and brought his hat low;' Blazes Boylan 'offered to the three ladies the bold admiration of his eyes and the red flower between his lips.'

Late in the evening Bloom is again reminded of Mercer's when '*Mirus Bazaar fireworks go up from all sides with symbolic phallopyrotechnic designs.*' Meanwhile two minor characters, M'Coy and Lenehan, have passed along Sycamore Street beside the Empire Music Hall: 'At the Dolphin they halted to allow the ambulance car to gallop past them for Jervis Street.' Phillip Gilligan, one of Bloom's friends, died in Jervis Street Hospital.

M'Coy worked on the *Freeman's Journal* before he got the job in the morgue under Louis Byrne. 'Good idea a postmortem for doctors. Find out what they imagine they know. He died of a Tuesday.'

There is an inexplicit reference to Sir Patrick Dun's Hospital; Dr Steevens' Hospital is not included but the founder's sister, Madame Grissel Steevens (according to an ill-informed legend she had a face like a pig's snout) is recalled in a discourse on monstrous births. Our Lady's Hospice for the Dying, the Royal Hospital, Kilmainham, and 'Simpson's Hospital for reduced but respectable men permanently disabled by gout or want of sight' are briefly mentioned. And is not Joyce's description of neglected senility a more oppressive reality today than in 1904? 'Nadir of misery: the aged impotent disfranchised ratesupported moribund lunatic pauper.'

There is a reference to Hampstead, Glasnevin—'Dr. Eustace's private asylum for demented gentlemen'—at present supervised by Dr. H. Jocelyn Eustace whose uncle, Henry Marcus Eustace, was Superintendent in 1904; 'the nun's madhouse' where in *A Portrait* Stephen Dedalus heard 'a mad nun screeching' is, probably, St. Vincent's Asylum, Fairview. The Richmond District Asylum, Grangegorman (today called St. Brendan's Hospital) and its R.M.S. are spoken of by Buck Mulligan: 'He's up in Dottyville with Conolly Norman. General paralysis of the insane.' Dr. Conolly Norman, F.R.C.P.I. (b. 12 March 1853 son of the Rev. Hugh Norman of Newtown Cunningham, Co. Donegal), a distinguished psychiatrist, was also a collector of books, engravings and pewter. He was subject to angina pectoris which he mistakenly attributed to beri beri. He died suddenly on 23 February 1908.

The Westmoreland Lock Hospital, Townsend Street, which has

closed its doors, had a hundred beds for females with venereal diseases; in the Circe episode a whore speaks of 'Mary Shorthall that was in the lock with the pox she got from Jimmy Pidgeon in the blue caps had a child off him that couldn't swallow and was smothered with the convulsions in the mattress and we all subscribed for the funeral.'

Stanislaus Joyce was a clerk at the Apothecaries' Hall, an item duly fitted into the mosaic of *Ulysses* a book in which, as in life, irrelevance is relevant: 'Where is your brother? Apothecaries' hall. My whetstone.'

Stephen Dedalus who plays Telemachus to Bloom's Odysseus lives in the Martello Tower, Sandycove, with Buck Mulligan. 'And what is death?' Mulligan asks rhetorically. 'You saw only your mother die. I see them pop off every day in the Mater and Richmond and cut up into tripes in the dissecting room. It's a beastly thing and nothing else.'

During the course of the day Bloom meets an old flame. He asks about a mutual acquaintance, Mrs Purefoy, to be told, 'She's in the lying-in hospital in Holles street. Dr Horne got her in. She's three days bad now.'

After their marriage the Blooms had lived in Holles Street. Unknown to Leopold his wife ogled the students from her window but found them slow on the uptake: '. . . not a notion what I meant arent they thick never understand what you say even youd want to print it up on a big poster for them . . . where does their great intelligence come in Id like to know grey matter they have it all up in their tail if you ask me. . . .'

The College of Surgeons is referred to in *Dubliners*. Lenehan a character in 'Two Gallants' is waiting for a friend. 'He went as far as the clock of the College of Surgeons. It was on the stroke of ten.' Another story features Baggot Street Hospital where the inquest on the body of the alcoholic Mrs Sinico was held. 'Dr Halpin, assistant house-surgeon of the City of Dublin Hospital, stated that the deceased had two lower ribs fractured and had sustained severe contusions of the right shoulder. The right side of the head had been injured in the fall. The injuries were not sufficient to have caused death in a normal person. Death, in his opinion, had been probably due to shock and sudden failure of the heart's action.'

In the first draft of 'A Painful Case' the scene of the inquest on Mrs Sinico was St Vincent's Hospital but with his customary attention to detail Joyce wrote to Stannie for information: 'Would the city ambulance be called out to Sydney Parade for an accident? Would an accident at Sydney Parade be treated at Vincent's Hospital?' Stannie's suggestion that 'in all probability the body would have been sent in on the tram' may not reflect the inadequacy of the ambulance service but indicate a measure of expediency in the days of horse-drawn ambulances. Meanwhile it probably occurred to Joyce that accident cases are taken to the *nearest* hospital and the Royal City of Dublin Hospital, Baggot Street, is a good deal nearer to Sydney Parade than is St Vincent's Hospital.

The background to 'Araby' is a bazaar held in aid of Jervis Street Hospital. This was the first of an annual series of bazaars and we have already seen that from noon to night in *Ulysses* Bloom is reminded of another of these great bazaars. 'A long lost candle wandered up the sky from Mirus bazaar in search of funds for Mercer's hospital and broke, drooping, and shed a cluster of violet but one white stars. They floated, fell: they faded.'

The *Report of Mercer's Hospital* for 1903 contains an anticipatory reference to the event: 'Many of the friends of the Hospital are making strenuous efforts to raise a sum of money for the benefit of the Hospital by the "Mirus" Bazaar to be held at Ball's Bridge. . . .' Unfortunately the *Report* for 1904 is not available but from that of the following year we learn that the success of the Fête enabled the Governors to provide a new operating-theatre, an anaesthetic room, an X-ray department, and four bedrooms for the Sisters—'all of which will be electrically lighted.' The bazaar was held in splendid weather (the total attendance was 54,565 and Mercer's received £4,399. 3. 4.) but it commenced on 31st May and if on 16th June 'bronze by gold' heard 'the viceregal hoofs go by, ringing steel,' the Earl of Dudley's purpose was not to open the Mirus Bazaar. Furthermore, had Blazes Boylan been about on the actual opening-day his leer would have disconcerted two ladies rather than three. Countless Dudley, who was pregnant, did not attend.

For the general reader *Finnegans Wake* is still as impenetrable as a mediaeval palimpsest. Who knows what topographical riches lie hidden in its pages? There is a fairly obvious reference to the late Dr Bethel Solomons[1] and the Rotunda Hospital: 'in my bethel of Solyman's I accouched their rotundaties.'

Madame Steevens and a number of hospitals are referred to in the following passage:

> . . . he after having being trying all he knew with the lady's help of Madam Gristle for upwards of eighteen calendars to get

out of Sir Patrick Dun's, through Sir Humphrey Jervis's and into the St Kevin's bed in the Adelaide's hosspittles (from these incurable welleslays among those incarable wellasdays through Saint Iago by his cocklehat, good Lazar, deliver us!) without after having been able to jerrywangle it anysides.

As we have already seen there is an allusion in *Finnegans Wake* to the Medical School in Cecilia Street where Joyce was enrolled so briefly as a student. He never 'walked the wards' of the Dublin hospitals but he would have known several of the faculty by name and reputation. Many medical practitioners and scientists are mentioned in *Ulysses* the latter group including Pasteur and Röntgen who made discoveries of epic importance. Some are historical, some fictional; a number were Dublin celebrities of Joyce's youth; and there is one quack, Henry Franks, a purveyor of pills for V.D.

All kinds of places are good for ads. That quack doctor for the clap used to be stuck up in all the greenhouses.[2] Never see it now. Strictly confidential. Dr Hy Franks. Didn't cost him a red . . . Got fellows to stick them up or stuck them up himself for that matter on the q.t. running in to loosen a button. Fly by night. Just the place too. POST NO BILLS. POST 110 PILLS. Some chap with a dose burning him.

The earliest historical medical figures included are Empedocles (504-443 B.C.) and Maimonides (1135-1204) the latter a famous Jewish physician, philosopher, and Rabbi whom Bloom mimics. And Joyce utilises the well-known saying, 'from Moses to Moses there was none like Moses,' which refers to the Biblical Moses, Moses Mendelssohn, and Moses Maimonides respectively.

Next we find mention of some of the Irish families in which the role of physician was hereditary:

It is not why therefore we shall wonder if as the best historians relate, among the Celts, who nothing that was not in its nature admirable admired, the art of medicine shall have been highly honoured. Not to speak of hostels, leper yards, sweating chambers, plague graves, their greatest doctors, the O'Sheils, the O'Hickeys, the O'Lees, have sedulously set down the divers methods by which the sick and the relapsed found again health whether the malady had been the trembling withering or the loose boyconnell flux.

The O'Sheils who lived at Ballysheil (in the present Co. Offaly) were physicians to the McMahons of Oriel and are credited with the *Book of the O'Sheils* c. 1657. The O'Hickeys were physicians to clans living in what is now Co. Clare. Nicholas O'Hickey translated *Lilium Medicinae* during the last quarter of the fifteenth century. The O'Lees lived in Connacht. They, too, had a book, a translation of a Latin text.

Paracelsus—the most original medical thinker of the sixteenth century, according to Garrison—is included among a list of notabilities in the Cyclops episode. J. S. Atherton (*The Books at the Wake*) thinks it improbable that Joyce ever read Paracelsus but if Gogarty is to be credited Lyster urged the medicals who used the National Library to read him. 'Before perusing Osler, who is quite a modern author and divorced from European tradition[3] might I not suggest that you dip for a little into Paracelsus, that Doctor of both Faculties neither of which he deigns to define? Surely your mind is not impervious to the charm of those inadequately appreciated Middle Ages?' Is it likely that Joyce could have resisted the Librarian's challenge?

R. M. Adams has pointed out in *Surface and Symbol* that it was Rualdus Columbus who first recognised the clitoris as an anatomical entity, an item which Joyce uses with comic effect. 'All possess bachelor's button discovered by Rualdus Columbus. Tumble her. Columble her.' Columbus (1516-59) whose anatomical work was published posthumously in 1559 was assistant to Andreas Vesalius the founder of modern anatomy and succeeded him in the chair of anatomy in Padua. He showed that the lens of the eye is not situated in the centre of the globe and proved experimentally that blood flows from the lungs into the pulmonary vein.

Nicholas Culpepper (1616-54), Lazaro Spallanzani (1729-99), Johann Friedrich Blumenbach (1752-1840), Graham Lusk (1866-1932), C. G. Leopold (1846-1911), Oscar Hertwig (1849-1922), and G. Vallenti (1860-19—) are referred to as embryologists although only the last three merit the title. Hertwig proved that the spermatozoon enters the ovum accomplishing fertilization by union of male and female pronuclei.

Must we accept the view of Empedocles of Trinacria that the right ovary (the postmenstrual period, assert others) is responsible for the birth of males or are the too long neglected spermatozoa or nemasperms the differentiating factors or is it, as most embryologists incline to opine, such as Culpeper, Spallanzani,

149

Blumenbach, Lusk, Hertwig, Leopold and Valenti, a mixture of both?

Charles Lucas (1713-71) who has been called 'the Wilkes of Ireland' is better remembered as a politician than as a doctor. In 1747 he started a weekly paper the *Citizen's Journal* but had to flee the country because of his opinions. He took a medical degree in Leyden and practised in London before returning to Ireland. For a time he was Member of Parliament for Dublin and as Joyce recalls he founded *The Freeman's Journal*: 'Grattan and Flood wrote for this very paper, the editor cried in his face. Irish Volunteers. Where are you now? Established 1763. Dr Lucas.'

In the funeral cab Bloom listens to his companions but he is watchful by habit. Passing through College Street he notes: 'Plasto's. Sir Philip Crampton's memorial fountain bust.[4] Who was he?' The question, like so many questions in life, is left unanswered. Joyce tells us nothing about the distinguished surgeon to the Meath Hospital who had been Surgeon General, President of the Royal College of Surgeons in Ireland, and a chief founder of the Dublin Zoo, but later in the afternoon Bloom, pondering on communal kitchens, recalls Crampton: 'After you with our incorporated drinking-cup. Like Sir Philip Crampton's fountain. Rub off the microbes with your handkerchief. Next chap rubs on a new batch with his.'

Crampton was born at 16, William Street, Dublin on 7 June 1778. At the age of twenty one he qualified at the Royal College of Surgeons in Ireland. Three days later he was appointed Surgeon to the Meath Hospital. He did postgraduate work at Glasgow (where he took an M.D. degree), Edinburgh, and London. For a brief period he saw army service under the command of Sir John Moore. Attending a soirée at Dublin Castle after being appointed Surgeon General in 1819 his uniform was so impressive that someone asked, 'Who is the man in that splendid uniform?' 'He's the Surgeon-General.' 'I suppose that's a General in the Lancers,' a wit interjected.

He had country house at Bray, Co. Wicklow, and as a very old man, drawing on his memories, he boasted that many times he had swum Lough Bray, ridden into the city and amputated a limb before breakfast. He died from uraemia on 10 June 1858.

Two landmarks used to guide us in Cashel Boyle O'Connor Fitzmaurice Tisdall Farrell's walk through the city are 'Mr Lewis Werner's cheerful window'[5] (Louis J. Werner, F.R.C.S.I., Ophthalmic Surgeon to the Mater Hospital, lived at 31 Merrion Square) and 1

Merrion Square, the corner house formerly occupied by Sir William Wilde whose distinction as a surgeon and antiquarian has been overshadowed by the notoriety and literary achievements of his famous son.

Sir Andrew Horne's prominence in the Oxen of the Sun episode has already been noted. He was Master of the maternity hospital where on 16 June Mrs Purefoy was in labour. In selecting that surname for his fictional patient Joyce had his tongue in his cheek: Richard Dancer Purefoy (1847-1919) of 62 Merrion Square was an ex-Master of the Rotunda Hospital, a rival maternity institution. Incidentally he established the hospital's first pathology laboratory by organizing the 'Lucina' Bazaar.

Other medical notabilities of the time who figure in *Ulysses* are Louis A. Byrne[6] the Dublin coroner, Sir Charles Cameron,[7] Surgeon McArdle,[8] Sir Thornley Stoker[9] (whose brother wrote *Dracula*), George Sigerson,[10] and Austin Meldon. The last-named who was surgeon to Jervis Street Hospital and President of the Royal College of Surgeons in Ireland in 1889-90 was famous for his dinner-parties at which exotic items such as kangaroo tail and shark's fin were served. His corpulence explains Joyce's reference of 'a wolf in the stomach' and also a riddle current in the Dublin of the 1890s: 'What is more wonderful than the passing of a camel through the eye of a needle?' 'Dr Austin Meldon getting into a fly.'

Stephen Dedalus's reference to his mother's last illness—'Dr Bob Kenny is attending her'—derives, of course, from Mrs Joyce's terminal illness. She died from cancer and her doctor was Robert J. D. Kenny, F.R.C.S.I. of 30 Rutland Square, West, Visiting Surgeon to the North Dublin Union Hospital and to Cabra Auxiliary Hospital.

Metchnikoff ('And to such delights has Metchnikoff innoculated anthropoid apes') and A. Conan Doyle ('The Stark-Munro letters by A. Conan Doyle, property of the City of Dublin Library 13 days overdue' was on Bloom's bookshelf) are well-known celebrities but a number of the doctors in *Ulysses* are fictional. The latter may include Dr Finucane[11] who certified Paddy Dignam's death, 'snuffy Dr Murren,' Dr Francis Brady, Dr Rinderpest (*rinderpest*=cattle plague) 'the best quoted cowcatcher in all Muscovy,' and the Rt. Hon. Sir Hercules Hannibal Habeas Corpus Anderson, F.R.C.P.I.

We cannot, however, designate as fictional any character in *Ulysses* without hazard. Leopold Bloom's reflections on the vogue of Dr Tibble's Vi-coca suggests a fiction or a quack and *Ulysses* had already been published before Joyce consulted Sydney Granville Tibbles

(1884-1960) a London ophthalmologist. A more questionable fiction is young O'Hare for whom, as Bloom recalls, Nurse Callan had a soft spot.

> Her he asked if O'Hare Doctor tidings sent from far coast and she with grameful sigh him answered that O'Hare Doctor in heaven was . . . he was died in Mona island through bellycrab three years agone come Childermas.

The young doctor had died from cancer but in the Spring of 1902 John J. O'Hare of Mayo Bridge, Newry, Co. Down took a degree at the Royal University and was appointed to the Mater Hospital. In the following February *St. Stephen's* included a news item: 'Dr Jack O'Hare the popular Bohemian[12] footballer is at present in Holles Street Hospital.' And at the Mater 'smoking concert' at the Rotunda on Shrove Tuesday 1904 O'Hare sang a ditty with an obstetrical theme: 'The kiddie's still there but the waters are gone. . . .'

Dr O'Hare was Assistant Master in Holles Street Hospital from 1903-06 before setting up in practice at 36 Hill Street, Newry. But with unexpected suddenness his name disappears from the medical directory, presumably due to the premature death from cancer which Joyce set at an earlier date.

Dr Collins whom Molly Bloom recalls with vivid detail poses a particularly interesting conundrum:

> When I had that white thing coming from me and Floey made me go to that dry old stick Dr Collins for womens diseases on Pembroke Road your vagina he called it I suppose thats how he got all the gilt mirrors and carpets getting round those rich ones off Stephens Green running up to him for every little fiddle faddle her vagina and her cochin china. . . .

It has been said that Joyce's model for Dr Collins was Dr Joseph Collins of New York whom he met in Paris in 1921 but R. M. Adams points out that there was an actual Dr J. R. Collins, M.B., B.S., Dub. at 65 Pembroke Rd. On looking further into the matter we find that in 1904 the Rev. T. R. S. Collins lived at that address. His son, Jonathan Rupert Collins, who did not graduate from Dublin University until 1901 and cannot have been a dry old stick, had left Ireland and was practising in Cheltenham.[13]

It is pointless to analyse Joyce's motives too closely. The search for correspondences should not be pursued too rigorously. However ardent Joyce's desire for verisimilitude it must be remembered that he had a novelist's licence to trim his facts to suit his purpose. *Ulysses* is a superb prose cathedral richly adorned with a multitude of decorations; presumably its author was moved by the impulse that led mediaeval masons to chisel the faces of their patrons and enemies on the soaring walls, depicting them at a whim as saints or devils, the reality sometimes altered by mere caprice.

Crampton ('so inseuladed as Crampton's peartree') Tibble, Lucas, Sigerson ('Sigurd Sigerson Sphygmomanometer Society for bledprusshers') Horne ('Ho, he hath hornhide!') and possibly Gogarty ('Gougerotty') re-appear in *Finnegans Wake* and the names of several doctors and scientists are woven into the text of this book where one word may have many meanings, for instance 'through all Lavinia's volted ampire' commemorating Volta and Ampere.

One of the most unequivocal allusions is to Sir Dominic Corrigan[14] a leading nineteenth century Dublin physician—'Corrigan's pulse and varicoarse veins;' perhaps the best-known—'when they were yung and easily freudened'—concerns Jung and Freud who also perform a tandem act in 'Jungfraud's Messongebook.' Carl Jung whom Joyce consulted about Lucia and who wrote a critique of *Ulysses* which displeased its author is also referred to in 'the law of the jungrel,' 'the jest of junk the jungular,' 'no junglegrown pineapple,' and 'Junglemen in agleement.' Vogt who operated on Joyce is worked into Ann van Vogt an amusing modification of Ireland's legendary Shan Van Vocht, and Virchow, pathologist, anthropologist, and politician, author of the celebrated *Cellular Pathology* is referred to in 'by virchow of those filthered Ovocnas.'

A British affectation in the pronunciation of certain surnames (e.g. Home pronounced H*u*me) amused Joyce and Gustavus Hume who gave his name to Dublin's Hume Street affords scope for punning: 'hume sweet hume,' 'and send him to Home Surgeon Hume.'

Because he extolled the virtues of oatmeal porridge Gustavus Hume (1730-1812) was called 'Stirabout Gusty'. He remained in practice when he had attained a great age:—

> *Hume, twice as ancient as the College Charter*
> *Scours Death with Stir-a-bout from every quarter.*

He was on the Staff of Mercer's Hospital for more than fifty years and for some months in 1785 was President of the R.C.S.I.

Another Dublin worthy included is Rutty, an austere man who extolled the virtues of mineral waters. 'The use of cold water, testificates Dr. Rutty, may be warmly recommended for the subjugation of cungunitals loosed. Tolloll, schools!' John Rutty (1697–1775) born in Wiltshire to Quaker parents, graduated M.D. at Leyden and settled in Dublin in 1724. His *Essay towards a Natural History of the County of Dublin* was published in 1772. An austere scientist of religious temperament his practice included 'a pretty handsome supply of paupers, but few of the rich.' He instructed that his *Spiritual Diary* should be published after his death. It shows that his patients often omitted to pay him. 'Eleven patients, and not one fee, and patience abused considerably. I muttered a little, I hope not unrighteously.' The winter of 1774 found him in poor health and he made his last entry in the Diary: 'The voice of God now sounds louder in my great infirmity of being scarcely able to bear the cold.'

The threat that 'this ogry Osler will oxmaul us all' echoes the indignation aroused by Dr (later Sir William) Osler's valedictory address in Baltimore in 1905. The newly-elected Regius Professor of Medicine at Oxford University, who was then fifty-five years of age, referred facetiously to an ancient law in certain Greek states which decreed that sexagenarii should be thrown from a bridge, and added: 'In that charming novel, *The Fixed Period*, Anthony Trollope discusses the practical advantages in modern life of a return to this ancient usage, and the plot hinges upon the admirable scheme of a college into which at sixty men retired for a year of contemplation before a peaceful departure by chloroform.' Next day, to his discomfiture, the newspaper headlines—OSLER RECOMMENDS CHLOROFORM AT SIXTY—misinterpreted his humorous intention.

The reference to 'the skall of a gall' becomes clearer when it is recalled that Gall was a prominent phrenologist, and that to Hairductor Achmed Borumborad is a tribute to the audacity of a Kilkenny man.

In 1771 an impressive, bearded Turkish physician, Dr. Achmet Borumbodad, arrived in Ireland and proposed to set up baths in Dublin. Obtaining support among the local medical fraternity and receiving grants from the House of Commons and the College of Physicians he established 'Dr. Achmet's Royal Baths' on the quays at Bachelor's Walk. They were well patronised and Borumbodad claimed that from 1775 to 1781 '10,000 destitute and miserable objects have been restored to the blessings of health.' His charges were modest and the expense of enlarging the baths led him into insolvency. Meanwhile the Turk had fallen in love with a Miss Hartigan. He offered to shave off his great black beard and to become a Christian. This was not enough to win the lady and eventually he disclosed that he was no foreigner but Patrick Joyce of Kilkenny.

Details of many other scientists who have been identified by Adaline Glasheen in Joyce's pages—'thought he weighed a new ton when there felled his first lapapple' (Sir Isaac Newton) 'Charley, you're my darwing!' (Darwin) 'ignerants show beneath suspicion like the bitter halves of esculapuloids' (Aesculapius)—can be found in her *A Census of Finnegans Wake*.

CHAPTER 13

THE PURPLE ISLAND

Every novelist makes some use of simple surface anatomy for descriptive purposes but anatomical allusions are frequent and sometimes remarkably detailed in *Ulysses*.

> He unbuttoned successively in reversed direction waistcoat, trousers, shirt and vest along the medial line of irregular incrispated black hair extending in triangular convergence from the pelvic basin over the circumference of the abdomen and umbilicular fossicle along the medial line of nodes to the intersection of the sixth pectoral vertebrae, thence produced both ways at right angles and terminating in circles described about two equidistant points, right and left, on the summits of the mammary prominences.

The pituitary body, solar plexus, sacral region, buccinator muscles, colon, blind intestine and appendix are mentioned and a remarkable adjective is coined, the 'scrotumtightening' sea. Naturally the brain is alluded to, 'the incommensurable categorical intelligence situated in the cerebral convolutions.'

Joyce claimed, in conversation with Budgen, that 'Among other things my book is the epic of the human body. The only man I know who has attempted the same thing is Phineas Fletcher. But then his *Purple Island* is purely descriptive, a kind of coloured anatomical chart of the human body. In my book the body lives in and moves through space and is the home of a full human personality.'

J. S. Atherton has identified a number of references to Fletcher and his *Purple Island* in *Finnegans Wake*. R. M. Adams has shown that a phrase in the Sirens episode, 'Well it's a sea. Corpuscle islands,' was 'Blood is a sea, sea with purple islands,' in the (University of Buffalo) manuscript. Stuart Gilbert has listed the organs symbolised in the various episodes and Ellmann has recently made available Carlo Linati's list which differs in minor respects. But the success, or otherwise, of Joyce's aspirations in anatomy and his disparagement of Fletcher's achievement do not appear to have received critical appraisal.[1]

*   *   *   *

Phineas Fletcher whom Izaak Walton referred to as 'an excellent divine and an excellent angler' was born on 18 April 1582 in Cranbrook, Kent, where his grandfather was vicar. He was the eldest child of Giles Fletcher, sometime Member of Parliament for Winchelsea, a wandering diplomat and remembrancer for the city of London. His uncle, the Reverend Richard Fletcher, D.D., father of John Fletcher the dramatist, stood at the scaffold of Mary, Queen of Scots, and vainly urged her to abjure Catholicism. Subsequently this worldly man became Bishop of London but when, after the death of his first wife, he married a wealthy widow of ill-repute, Queen Elizabeth banished him from Court and temporarily suspended him from his episcopal functions.

Phineas was educated at Eton and King's College, Cambridge, where in 1611 he took Holy Orders and was elected Fellow. Failing to secure preferment he left Cambridge and became chaplain to Sir Henry Willoughby at Wood-Hall, Hillgay, Norfolk, and later at Risley Hall, Risley, Derbyshire, where in 1615 he married Elizabeth Vincent. He obtained the living of Hillgay, the gift of Sir Henry Willoughby, in 1621 and resided at Hillgay Rectory until his death in 1650.

The Purple Island or the Isle of Man: together with Piscatorie Eclogs and other Poetical Miscellanies was published in 1633 but had been written much earlier. In the dedication Fletcher refers to 'these raw *Essayes* of my very unripe yeares, and almost childehood.'

The Romans not uncommonly wrote philosophical and scientific treatises in verse but *The Purple Island* a poem in twelve cantos is primarily poetical and theological rather than didactic. So that his meaning shall be clearer Fletcher added copious marginal notes.

An edition of the collected poems of Giles and Phineas Fletcher was prepared by Professor Frederick S. Boas. The second volume containing the *Purple Island* was published in 1909 the year in which Joyce made two visits to Ireland. Whether he became acquainted with it then or earlier is of little consequence. Evidently it intrigued him and he borrowed from it without acknowledgement when in reply to a conventional remark from Budgen concerning the heart he said, 'The seat of the affections lies lower down, I think.' Fletcher disposing the abode of love in the liver where ' 'tween the *Splenions* frost and th' angry Gall/The joviall *Hepar* sits,' adds that 'lust (which some perversly call love) be otherwise seated. . . .'

It is, perhaps, presumptuous to suggest that Joyce's unwillingness to credit Fletcher with more than 'a kind of coloured anatomical chart' was due to his inability to see the *Island* as a significant salient revealed against the horizon of the dawn of scientific anatomy. Others, however, have made this error. An anonymous writer in the *British Medical Journal* regarded it with amused contempt and A. T. Pohlman lightly decided that it derived from Galen whose great intellect dominated medicine to its detriment. Fortunately A. B. Langdale's penetrating study achieved redress.

Langdale adduces reasons for thinking that Fletcher may have been influenced by Francis Bacon and that he was at least on speaking terms with William Harvey. Admittedly the *Purple Island* gives no definite indication that Fletcher had read *De Motu Cordis* but certain lines—

> Circling about and wat'ring all the plain,
> Emptie themselves into th' alldrinking main;
> and creeping forward slide, but never turn again—

appear to indicate at least an intimation of circulation.

He shows that although classical anatomy contributes largely there are details of more recent discoveries: 'the Vas breve, or the short vessels,' the short branches of the splenic artery and vein; the cerebral aqueduct; the vermiform appendix discovered by Jacobus Berengarius—'The first of the baser is called blinde: at whose end is an appendant;' the description of the inner ear including the stapes or stirrup discovered by Ingrassias in 1548:

> The first an Hammer call'd, whose out-grown sides
> Lie on the drumme; but with his swelling end
> Fixt in the hollow Stithe, there fast abides:
> The Stithes short foot doth on the drumme depend,
> His longer in the Stirrup surely plac't;
> The Stirrups sharp side by the Stithe embrac't
> But his broad base ti'd to a little window fast.

When reading the *Purple Island* it is essential to recall that for centuries anatomy had been hindered by prejudice and obscurantism. Dissection of the human cadaver was forbidden and when the law was changed dissection remained controlled by licence. After 1540 the Barber Surgeons Company was permitted to dissect the corpses of four criminals in public, annually, and the Royal College of Physicians of London was granted a like privilege. Medical students were outnumbered at the dissections by the *beau monde* attracted by the novelty.

Surprisingly, the licence to hold public dissections secured by the great medical corporations was given also to Gonville and Caius College, Cambridge, and Langdale underlines the fact that twice a year a body was anatomized within a hundred yards of Fletcher's lodgings. Once this is realized we can discern in the poet's pages the actual pattern of a dissection which invariably began with the abdominal viscera, the first to decay, proceeding next to the thorax and finally to the brain, the last to mortify.

> The whole Isle, parted in three regiments,
> By three Metropolies is joyntly sway'd;
> Ord'ring in peace and warre their governments
> With loving concord, and with mutuall aid:
> The lowest hath the worst, but largest See;
> The middle lesse, of greater dignitie:
> The highest least, but holds the greatest soveraigntie.

Langdale points out that, 'In general he works from the outside of the body inward, as if he were actually handling the scissors, sponges, and scalpels. After brief remarks about the skin, flesh and muscles, he discusses the parts of the ventral cavity in the following order: skin, fat, 'panniculus carnosus' muscles, vessels of the tunicle, bladder, stomach, intestines, pancreas, liver, blood vessels of the liver, gall bladder, spleen, kidneys. They have been treated in the sequence of their appearance under the instruments of the dissector.'

Certain of Fletcher's images, for instance, his description of the flesh of the liver, 'Built all alike, seeming like rubies sheen,' and his account of the cave of Auditus, 'The last passage is called the Cochlea, snail, or Periwincle; where the nerves of hearing plainly appeare,' are unlikely to derive from books. It seems clear that he was an absorbed spectator at the Cambridge dissections. Langdale has excellent grounds for declaring that 'Nothing intervened between the cadaver and the poet, and his writing was a reporting of what he had seen with his own eyes.'

Joyce's cursory dismissal of Fletcher was ill-judged. Rather does the scientific-minded divine deserve Langdale's encomium: 'These cantos are the climax of the poetry and the life of Phineas Fletcher. They rescue him from the slough of the commonplace and set him upon the high plain where he walks, humbly as was his wont, with Sir Francis Bacon, Galileo Galilei, William Harvey, and the other soldiers of science who warred against holy edicts, superstitions, lethargies, and all that vagrant rout. *The Purple Island* is a vindication of England's share in the progress of anatomical study, of certain mute, inglorious anatomists of Caius College, and of Phineas Fletcher's original genius.'

*   *   *   *

'Most of all he liked grilled mutton kidneys which gave to his palate a fine tang of faintly scented urine.' 'A kidney oozed bloodgouts on the willowpatterned dish . . .' 'His hand accepted the moist tender gland . . .' There is no organ for the first three episodes of *Ulysses* but the kidney is mentioned twenty times in the Calypso episode which features excretion. We read of the 'flop and fall of dung' in the cattle market and of its virtues in cleaning kid gloves; we see a book fall against a chamberpot, and are made aware of Bloom's 'flowing qualm' and follow him to the jakes.

The correspondences for the genitals, the organ of 'Lotus-Eaters' are vague ('venereal disease' 'Women all for caste till you touch the spot' 'Gelded too: a stump of black guttapercha wagging limp between their haunches' 'Angry tulips . . .' 'Eunuch') until we see Bloom in his bath 'the dark tangled curls of his bush floating, floating hair of the stream around the limp father of thousands, a languid floating flower.'

By contrast the heart, organ of 'Hades' is mentioned at least forty-one times ('He took it to heart' 'Wear the heart out of a stone' 'good-heartedness' 'the Sacred Heart' 'Heart on his sleeve' etc.) and Bloom's attitude is just as detached as a modern cardiologist's: 'Seat of the affections. Broken heart. A pump after all, pumping thousands of gallons of blood every day. One fine day it gets bunged up and there you are. Lots of them lying around here: lungs, hearts, livers. Old rusty pumps: damn the thing else.'

The lung is the organ of 'Aeolus' but structure is less evident than the subsidiary functions: 'flatulence' 'wind off my chest' 'inflated windbag' 'blowing out' 'loud cough' 'puffing' 'panting' 'grunting'. We encounter 'breathless' 'breath of life' and 'you take my breath away' but there is no indication of the interchange of gases which is the essence of pulmonary function. Ellmann has indicated additional devices—paired phrases and words, e.g. 'Scissors and paste', 'Way in. Way out'; opposed actions, doors opening and closing, trains stopping and starting, people coming and going; inflated newspaper headlines —which represent respiratory inspirations and expirations.

According to Stuart Gilbert we are to expect to find the oesophagus high-lighted in 'Lestrygonians' but Joyce told Budgen that 'the

160

stomach dominates and the rhythm of the episode is that of the peristaltic movement.' Food and drink, feeding and nutrition are prominent. We find 'tummies' 'rumbling stomach' 'gullet' and 'entrails' but as in the previous episode crude physiology is more apparent than anatomy: 'cram' 'gulp' 'swilling, wolfing' 'bolting' 'scoffing up' 'digestion' 'dyspepsia' and 'chewing the cud' are illustrative terms.

The brain, the organ of 'Scylla and Charybdis', is mentioned only three times in the episode where we also find 'mystic mind' 'myriadminded' 'dullbrained' 'soul' 'skull' and 'pineal glands.' Neither is the symbolism of blood in 'the Wandering Rocks' well developed.

The ear is an appropriate organ for 'Sirens,' richer in word music than anything in literature, occurring twentythree times in its own right and present, too, in other words (an*ear*, h*ear*d, end*ear*ing, an*ear*by) synonyms ('red lugs' 'Lugugugubrious' 'purple lobes' 'peeping lobe') and by implication in the imperative 'Listen!' as well as negatively in 'deaf Pat' 'Pat doesn't hear.'

'Cyclops' is understood to represent muscle—'broadshouldered deepchested stronglimbed' 'brawny forearm' 'meat' 'muscular bosom' 'corpora cavernosa'—but either in deference to the one-eyed monster for whom Joyce may have had a soft spot, or by way of preamble to 'Nausicaa' the references to the eye are more numerous and ingenious: 'Balor of the evil eye' 'cod's eye' 'eye of heaven' 'gave him an eye' 'eyes glowered' 'eyes of the law' 'eyetallyano' 'walleye' 'oxeyed' 'whiteeyed kaffir.' And pertaining to the eyes: 'glowered' 'glaring' 'tears' 'lachrymal ducts' 'peep' 'starting out.'

'Nausicaa' has at least thirtynine further ocular references and according to Stuart Gilbert represents the eye and nose. The tokens of the latter include 'exquisite nose' 'end of her nose' 'piquant tilt of her nose' 'carbunckly nose' 'under her nose' 'an acquiline nose or a slightly retrousse,' and Bloom also deliberates on smells.

The Oxen of the Sun which represents the womb has been considered in an earlier chapter. In 'Circe,' the episode of the locomotor apparatus, we find abnormal and normal gaits: 'jerks past' 'hobbles off' 'take your crutch and walk' 'scuttle off' 'blunders stifflegged' 'sprint' 'saunters' 'strides out' 'leap out' 'toe heel, heel toe;' and there are ample allusions to structure: 'feet' 'ankles' 'foreleg' 'cloven hoof' 'spine' 'shoulders' 'bones' 'gluteal muscle' 'thighs fluescent, knees modestly kissing.'

The intimations of the nervous system in 'Eumeus,' which embodies the nerves, are 'brains' 'mind' 'nervousness' and 'sensation.' The skeleton is symbolised in 'Ithaca' rather by recapitulation providing an outline of the day's happenings than by more unequivocal images although these do occur: 'nasal and frontal formation' 'cranium' 'pelvic basin.' The flesh of fish ('plaice' 'eelscod') and of animals ('butchers meat from Buckleys loin chops and leg beef and rib steak and scrag of mutton and calfs pluck' 'veal and ham') as well as human flesh are celebrated in 'Penelope'. The symbols for human flesh are venal and include 'bottom' 'barebum' 'breasts all perfume' and 'round and white.'

* * * *

Joyce certainly managed to interweave a remarkable number of anatomical symbols into his novel, albeit so unobtrusively that even perceptive readers may miss them. Given a hint that they are there, however, they will be found in abundance by anyone with the endurance for the search. But the concentrated pursuit, although rewarded by increased appreciation of detail, detracts from the reader's general pleasure in *Ulysses* and is not for beginners.

As a technical achievement it is remarkable, but comparisons that come to mind are the patient Chinese craftsman carving an unending series of concentric ivory spheres, or a painstaking tailor lavishing infinite care handstitching seams that will lie hidden, unseen by any eyes except his own.

Unfortunately Joyce's symbolism will not convince those with professional knowledge of anatomy who are more likely to prefer Phineas Fletcher's exposition of body structure. Such critics will hardly agree that repetitive mention of 'kidney' recreates the *viscus elegantissimus* or be satisfied by a heaping of synonyms for gluttonous swallowing as an adequate representation of well-adjusted peristalsis.

However intrigued they may be with Joyce's melodic employment of 'ear' or sympathetic towards his preoccupation with 'eye' they will be unimpressed by the portrayal of brain and nerves. They may grant the palm to Joyce for Bloom's objective treatment of the heart in 'Hades' but will be less than satisfied with the anatomical depiction of flesh in the Penelope episode.

CHAPTER 14

PENELOPE

Proust's society hostesses knew how to behave, Madame Leroi being no exception. ' "Love?" she had once replied to a pushing lady who had asked her: "What are your views on love?"—"Love? I make it constantly but I never talk about it." ' Certain subjects were taboo, and in mixed company many topics and some words were prohibited by general consent. The same sanctions affected nineteenth century literature. A result has been to denude the language of simple acceptable terms to describe reproductive and excretory functions.

Good-taste, admittedly, calls for sparing usage, or, indeed, avoidance of such words in general conversation but their total exclusion from polite speech and literature is indefensible. There are occasions when bodily functions must be discussed, an object ill-served by an emasculated vernacular. In a recent study of urinary incontinence, a frequent cause of great human distress, *The Lancet* pointed out that 'Lack of socially acceptable words for the excretory functions made communication between doctor and patient difficult.' Among the many causes of the prudery and awkwardness which the medical journal deplored, literary censorship must take a high place.

It may be countered that medical needs should not dictate the rule but this is only one instance of the harmfulness of restriction and if literature is to mirror life its reflections should not be marred by puritanical, not to say hypocritical, exclusions. William Cartwright, a seventeenth century English poet, was in no doubt about this:

As some strict down-look'd Men pretend to fast;
Who yet in Closets Eat;
So lovers who profess they Spirits taste,
Feed yet on grosser meat;
I know they boast they Soules to Soules convey,
Howe'er they meet, the Body is the Way.

The indecency of *Ulysses*, according to the *Pink 'Un*, was 'enough to make a Hottentot sick'[1] and Dr Joseph Collins[2] declared that 'Odo of Cluny never said anything of a woman's body in life that is so repulsive as that which Mr Joyce has said of Marion's mind: a cesspool of forty years accumulation.' The comment in the English sporting paper, the majority of whose readers, we may suppose, were not lily-tongued, is an excellent example of a curious paradox—foul words may be uttered but not written—but Collins, an American neurologist, might have been expected to ponder more deeply why an author should choose to defy the conventions of his time, and as a man of science to ask if those conventions and the related censorship were well founded.

It is pointless to enumerate again the vicissitudes which *Ulysses* encountered before the Honourable John M. Woolsey cleared it of the charge of pornography but it may be noted that the Judge said, 'In many places it seems to me to be disgusting . . .' He agreed that that it was not aphrodisiac; sometimes its effect on the reader 'undoubtedly is somewhat emetic.' Woolsey's legal definition of obscenity was: 'tending to stir the sex impulses or to lead to sexually impure or lustful thoughts'; but this is too narrow an interpretation of a word which also means 'offensive to the senses or the mind' (*The Shorter Oxford English Dictionary*). The latter interpretation is intended in the present chapter in which the significance of Joyce's unquestionable preoccupation with the obscene is considered and the suitability of Molly Bloom as a model for feminine psychology challenged.

*   *   *   *

Dr. Marshall B. Katzman of St. Louis has attempted to quantify obscenity but a scientific phenomenological study has not yet been accomplished. It is to be hoped that sooner or later this will be remedied. Meanwhile, however salutory the convention of discouraging it in books, the universality of obscenity[3] as a natural occurrence in life must be accepted. The range of human behaviour is wide—at one extreme we find a saint who fainted if he heard a dirty word; at the other the peculiar *maladie de Gilles de la Tourette* the symptoms of which are sudden involuntary movements accompanied by obscene verbal utterances—and the average man (and woman) is quite easily and naturally visited by thoughts which could be called lascivious or obscene.

How could it be otherwise? Each of us has a brain area which keeps us conscious of the 'body image', the genitals, perinaeum and anus being adequately represented; we are all subject to the physiological necessity of excretion; from an early age we are aware of and have experienced in varying measure the sexual function. A commendable and legitimate object of civilized communities, hygienic and aesthetic, has caused excretion to become a regulated function and

164

favours privacy for courtship and coitus. Unfortunately, in the process, these manifestations of life have become heavily tinged with shame. Meanwhile powerful forces have conspired to exalt the spiritual, drawing a veil over carnality, but through our nervous systems we are constantly reminded of our nagging or exulting flesh. And, as Simone de Beauvoir has said, 'The erotic experience is one that most poignantly discloses to human beings the ambiguity of their condition . . .'

It is many years since Swinburne said that, 'if literature is not to deal with the full life of man and the whole nature of things let it be cast aside with the rods and rattles of childhood.' Meanwhile his plea for freedom of expression has been amplified by other authors and the distinction between pornography and obscenity clearly defined. Norman St. John Stevas pointed out that: 'A pornographic book can be easily distinguished from an obscene book. A pornographic book, although obscene, is one deliberately designed to stimulate sex feelings and to act as an aphrodisiac. An obscene book has no such immediate and dominant purpose, although incidentally this may be its effect. A work like *Ulysses* certainly contains obscene passages, but their insertion in the book is not to stimulate sex impulses in the reader but to form part of a work of art.'

But if the case has been made for literary freedom[4] and the artists distinguished from the pornographers one may still ponder the motivation of the former in the deployment of obscenity. Were these avantgarde writers rebels defying convention, crusaders for freedom of expression, or realists who despite their powers of literary inventiveness found it more honest to call a spade a spade? Or were they influenced, consciously or subconsciously, by personal angularities? D. H. Lawrence has been viewed as a pioneer insisting on his right to describe sexual intercourse, but Lytton Strachey 'saw him as a kind of Puritan standing on his head, an evangelist of sexual obsession.' And does not the biographical material now available suggest that *Ulysses* was influenced by Joyce's self-admitted partiality for the obscene?

His confidences in 1904 to Stannie concerning his bride might conceivably be excused as the indiscretions of immaturity—'her boot was pinching her' i.e. she was menstruating. 'I really can't write. Nora is trying on a pair of drawers at the wardrobe. Excuse me.' 'She has told me something of her youth and admits the gentle art of self-satisfaction.'—but apparently the trait persisted. Years later Frank Budgen found him 'a man of quite rare candour in talking to his more intimate friends. His frankness was sometimes embarrassing when he talked about himself and those nearest to him.'

In 1922 the by then mature and disenchanted Stannie asked his brother, 'Isn't your art in danger of becoming a sanitary science . . . Everything dirty seems to have the same irresistible attraction for you that cow-dung has for flies.'

Joyce once said to Budgen, 'My cloacal obsession . . . How right Wells was!' Ezra Pound thought that Joyce wrote 'with a certain odeur-de-musk-rat' and that he could have drawn Bloom quite effectively 'without such detailed treatment of the dropping feces.' In a letter to Joyce he said: 'I have had as much Trouble as you do in getting printed—tho' I am much milder & far less indecent—au moins je suis peutêtre un peu plus phallique, mais mi interessent moins les excremens et les feces humains et des bestiaux.' His advice to Joyce was: 'Abnormal keenness of insight O.K. but *obsessions* arseoral-ial, cloacal, deist, aesthetic as opposed to arsethetic, any obsession or tic shd. be very carefully considered before being turned loose.'

Despite the statistical information gleaned from Kinsey and the anatomical and physiological details more recently supplied by Masters and Johnson, sexual behaviour remains shrouded by reticence. As Katherine Whitehorn puts it '. . . no one really knows what other people do—they know what they say they do, or what Nell Dunn says they do, or what everyone *thinks* the others do.' And apart from what they do it is equally difficult to know what they think about it, how much and how often, but we may take it that some degree of sexual fantasy is a normal occurrence especially in adolescence.

Sexual curiosity, perhaps, is more particularly a male preoccupation; the earthy male is interested to know how closely his own development and base desires have been paralleled in what he regards as the more aethereal female. This question certainly tormented Joyce. In *Giacomo Joyce* we read, 'Those quiet cold fingers have touched the pages, foul and fair, on which my shame shall glow forever. Quiet and cold and pure fingers. Have they never erred?'

In Joyce's youth (indeed until much later in the century) the fantasies of puberty were considered regrettable, potentially harmful to body and soul, and to take pleasure in them was sinful. To the modern mind their inevitability and universality exonerate them from blame. When exaggerated they may indicate psychological imbalance, but recalling sexual inventiveness and variety of taste one hesitates to draw a line between normal and abnormal.

Fugitive and impermanent, the average man's fantasy troubles or titillates nobody but himself. Joyce's fantasy overflowed into letters written to Nora in 1909 unintended for the public eye. A number of

166

these have been published but it is in the suppressed letters—'unprintable and all but unreadable' in the opinion of Mary T. Reynolds —that his cloacal obsession is most clearly seen.

They were, as Richard Ellmann points out, 'intended to accomplish sexual gratification in him and inspire the same in her, and at moments they fasten intently on peculiarities of sexual behaviour, some of which might be technically called perverse.' The masturbatory intent of the letters is unmistakable. They are turgid with squalid images and reek of sordid desires. When relief has been obtained (and duly noted) the change in tone is immediate. The girl who has been addressed in terms that would offend the coarsest strumpet becomes, 'my love, my life, my star, my little strange-eyed Ireland!'

Under the stress of passion a degree of masochism and a coprophilic tendency are disclosed. There is a compulsion to degrade and soil the beloved and a demand that her out-spokenness shall rival his. He pleads that her letters shall be as dirty as his own.

There is a passage in *Finnegans Wake*, '[he] knew her fleshly when with all my bawdy did I whorship' which aptly sums up the many paradoxes contained in the normal human sexual relationship where male tenderness and adoration culminates in vigorous subjugation of a compliant female; where adventurousness is rewarded by extraordinary delights and the ultimate pinnacle of orgiastic feeling may dissolve in a gale of mutual laughter. The letters posted from Dublin to Trieste contain no such general insights. They are personal, erotic, and ugly. And they are also guilty letters, for Joyce was aware that they were coarse, obscene, filthy, and bestial—the adjectives are his own—at variance with his usual manner of expression.

As you know, dearest [he wrote,] I never use obscene phrases in speaking. You have never heard me, have you, utter an unfit word before others. When men tell, in my presence here filthy or lecherous stories I hardly smile. Yet you seem to turn me into a beast . . .

It is unnecessary to ask if Joyce's sexual fantasy was abnormal (could *l'homme moyen sensuel* demanded by Judge Woolsey answer other than in the affirmative if he had read the suppressed letters?) for the relevant question is does this strongly developed fantasy erupt in *Ulysses*? We can hardly doubt that it does. Molly Bloom's recollections of Lieutenant Mulvey, for instance—'I made him blush a little when I got over him that way when I unbuttoned him . . .'— are exactly paralleled by Joyce's own experiences in a field in Ringsend in 1904, of which he reminds his 'darling little convent-girl' when writing to her on 3 December 1909. The relevant passage has not been published. An ellipsis in another letter refers to a toilet detail which Molly also favours: 'I think I'll cut all this hair off me there scalding me I might look like a young girl.'

And in Circe, too, we encounter a crude passage—'He implored me to soil his letter in an unspeakable manner, to chastise him as he richly deserves . . . to give him a most vicious horsewhipping'—which faithfully echoes the unprintable letters.

*　　　*　　　*　　　*

Writing to Joyce in 1932 Carl Jung said, 'The 40 pages of nonstop run in the end is a string of veritable psychological peaches. I suppose the devil's grandmother knows so much about the real psychology of a woman. I didn't.' A remarkable tribute from one who had access to the hidden secrets of the mind! Nora Joyce, on the other hand, said her husband knew nothing about women.[5] As a generality her remark is insupportable but in the particular of feminine sexual psychology Nora may have been correct. The female, whether she be Judy or the Colonel's lady, seldom reveals her true sex thoughts, even to her doctor, and it is doubtful if the most perceptive male novelist can discern them.

From Kinsey we learn that females are less susceptible than males to erotic art and less industrious scribblers of graffiti, but for deeper insights into feminine thought we must turn to female authors. At once we find a disparity of attitudes relating to age, environment, and upbringing rather than to basic physiology. We are told by Lenore Kandel: 'All parts of you are beautiful. All the parts of your body are beautiful. All of you is divine.' But a character in Edna O'Brien's *Girls in their Married Bliss* feels helpless and obscene in a gynaecologist's consulting-room:

> 'Relax,' he said, sort of bullying then. Relax! I was thinking of women and all they have to put up with, not just washing napkins or not being able to be high-court judges, but all this. All this poking and probing and hurt. And not only when they go to doctors but when they go to bed as brides with the men that love them. Oh, God, who does not exist, you hate women, otherwise you'd have made them different.

Clara, in Margaret Drabble's *Jerusalem the Golden*, is younger than these. After a swim she sees her naked image in the wet tiled floor of a dressing-cubicle:

> But Clara had not cried out, originally, through vanity . . . she had been truly moved by herself, by her own watery image, by her grotesquely elongated legs, her tapering waist, and above all by the undersides of her breasts, never before seen. She stood there and stared at herself, seeing herself from that unexpected angle, as though she were another person, as though she were a dim white and blue statue on a tall pillar, a wet statue, a statue in water, a Venus rising from the sea, with veined white marble globes for breasts. She had never expected to be beautiful, and she was startled to see how nearly she approached a kind of beauty.

At puberty, according to Simone de Beauvoir, the girl child 'undergoes her metamorphosis into a woman not only in shame but in remorse.' Temporarily she feels embarrassed and defiled:

> Usually, though with some resistance, the young girl accepts her femininity . . . vanity is soon mingled with the shame her flesh inspires. That hand, that look which stirred her feelings, was an appeal, a prayer; her body seems endowed with magic virtues; it is a treasure, a weapon; she is proud of it.

Hélène Deutsch maintains that female psychology depends on a harmonious co-operation of masochism and narcissism and regards woman's sexuality as more spiritualized than man's.

And the psychology of Molly Bloom?

A fictional character would hardly merit such serious attention had not Stuart Gilbert, referring to Molly's soliloquy, written: 'the force of this long, unpunctuated meditation, in which a drowsy woman's vagrant thoughts are transferred in all their naked candour of self-revelation on to the written record, lies precisely in its universality.' Most Joycean scholars appear to have accepted Gilbert's equation of Molly Bloom and Gaea-Tellus without demur but to J. Mitchell Morse this is the apotheosis of a slut.[6] He sees Molly as 'a woman who lacks sufficient energy to be effective in the ordinary tasks of daily life, whose health is declining, whose fertility is below par, whose capacity for sexual enjoyment is questionable, who considers the sexual act dirty and in fact makes it dirty, whose heart is cold and whose atttude is generally negative and censorious.'

If Morse is right—and his assessment certainly appears more level-headed than that of Gilbert, who had Joyce looking over his shoulder when he wrote his book—we must ask, at the risk of offending several splendid women, how representative are the disgusting thoughts of such a woman? It seems inconceivable that they are typical of normal, mature, healthy sexuality. Rather do they represent the thoughts of a woman whose sex fantasy is arrested at an infantile level.

And if it be impossible for a male to enter the secret places of the female mind what models did Joyce use for Molly? He must have known a great many women, respectable and otherwise, but recalling his reserved and formal manner in adult life it is difficult to imagine him swapping confidences about physical matters with the former. Even towards the outspoken whores of Nighttown his attitude seems to have been declamatory and incongruous. He may have picked up a good deal in Paris in the Gipsy Bar which he frequented with Robert MacAlmon who recalled those bibulous nights in *Being Geniuses Together*:

> The *patron* and the 'girls' knew us well and knew that we would drink freely and surely stay till four or five in the morning. The girls of the place collected at our table, and indulged in their Burgundian and Rabelasian humours. Jeanette, a big draught horse of a girl from Dijon, pranced about like a mare in heat and restrained no remark or impulse which came to her. Alys, sweet and pretty blonde, looked fragile and delicate, but lead Jeanette to bawdier and altogether earthy vulgarities of speech and action. Joyce, watching, would be amused, but inevitably there came a time when drink so moved his spirit that he began quoting from his own work or reciting long passages of Dante in rolling sonorous Italian.

Joyce's first sentimental attachment was to Eileen Vance, the little girl from Bray mentioned in *A Portrait* ('When they were grown up he was going to marry Eileen.') In his 'teens he silently admired Mary Sheehy. Then he met Nora Barnacle.

He may have been more than a little in love with a young pupil in Trieste. ('Who? A pale face surrounded by heavy odorous furs. Her movements are shy and nervous. She uses quizzing-glasses.') He had a tepid affair in Zurich with Martha Fleischmann, the model for Gerty McDowell. Ungallantly, he described to Budgen the circumstances in which he first saw Martha. 'First I saw of her,' said Joyce, 'was at the back of the house. She was in a small but well lit room in the act of pulling a chain.' Later, having spent an evening with her, Joyce told Budgen 'that he had explored that evening the coldest and hottest parts of a woman's body.'

According to Herbert Gorman there were two models for Molly Bloom: a Dubliner and an Italian whose passionate wartime love-letters passed through Joyce's hands in Zurich.[7] Be that as it may one cannot help wondering if Nora unwittingly contributed something to the creation. Her care of her middle-aged ailing husband was admirable, but in Trieste as a young woman she displayed something of Molly's indolence and incapacity and had a similar tendency to grammatical errors.

Bloom's acceptance of his cuckolding is paralleled by Joyce's subconscious wish to be made a cuckold by Nora, manifested by his instant acceptance of Cosgrave's claim that he had courted her ('You stood with him: he put his arms round you and you lifted your face and kissed him. What else did you do together?'), his suspicion that she may have succumbed to the persuasion of Mr. Holohan, a guest in Finn's Hotel, and his outpourings in the elided passage of a letter dated 3 December 1909. Frank Budgen's recollection of an evening in Zurich seems to indicate that this bizzare expression of his sexual curiosity rose above the subconscious level. 'Going home from the Pfauen one night. A straggling party, Joyce bringing up the rear. At my side a woman's voice, bewildered, tearful. Wants me to know other men. Help his writing . . .'

Like many men Joyce required of his wife that she should not be only a lover but a mother:

> Guide me, my saint, my angel. Lead me forward. *Everything* that is noble and exalted and deep and true and moving in what I write comes, I believe, from you. O take me into your soul of souls and then I will become indeed the poet of my race. I feel this, Nora, as I write it. My body soon will penetrate into yours, O that my soul could too! O that I could nestle in your womb like a child born of your flesh and blood, be fed by your blood, sleep in the warm secret gloom of your body!

He asks her to defend him and make him strong ('I gave others my pride and joy. To you I give my sin, my folly, my weakness and sadness.') He says, 'I am your child as I told you and you must be severe with me, my little mother.' A whipping is not only richly deserved but vehemently desired. Bloom, too, aspired to flagellation.

His love for Nora exalted him and in this mood he is aware of the sublime qualities which man has always found in the loved one:

> Every coarse word in speech offends me now for I feel that it
> would offend you. When I was courting you (and you were only
> nineteen, darling, how I love to think of that!) it was the same.
> You have been to my young manhood what the idea of the
> Blessed Virgin was to my boyhood.

When the mood changed he wrote, 'Love is a cursed nuisance
especially when coupled with lust also;' and during his absence from
Trieste in 1909 lust was dominant.

22 August 1909: 'There is a letter which I dare not be the first
to write. . . .' The compulsion was irresistible and on 1 September
he wrote her a letter (it has not survived) which, remembering it next
day, caused him to feel disgusted. Once started, however, the practice of onanism by writing ('Secret satieties and onanymous letters'
Finnegans Wake) was not to be set aside. He persuaded Nora to
adopt a similar style, her participation a further stimulus. Her letters
were not kept but it is clear that she replied with equal candour.

> My darling [he wrote on 2 December 1909] I ought to begin by
> begging your pardon, perhaps, for the extraordinary letter I wrote
> you last night. While I was writing it your letter was lying in
> front of me and my eyes were fixed, as they are even now, on a
> certain word in it. There is something obscene and lecherous in
> the very look of the letters. The sound of it too is like the act
> itself, brief, brutal, irresistible and devilish.

Apart from the enumeration of his desires in coarsest detail the
most striking feature in this series of letters is his insistent enquiry into
her subjective response and previous experiences. What he learned
from their correspondence (and their conversations) cannot be said but
Molly Bloom's 'by the hour question and answer would you do this
that and the other with the coalman yes with a bishop yes I would',
and 'then he wrote me that letter with all those words in it', and again
'his mad crazy letters my Precious one everything connected with your
glorious Body everything underlined that comes from it is a thing of
beauty and a joy forever', are derivative.

Detumescent, Joyce waxed lyrical, and Nora was 'my beautiful
wild flower of the hedge, my dark-blue rain drenched flower.' Molly,
too, remembered Bloom's compliments: 'he said I was a flower of
the mountain yes so we are flowers all a womans body yes that was one
true thing he said in his life and the sun shines for you today. . . .'

Ulysses is a lyrical and comic masterpiece; it is, to borrow Niall Montgomery's brilliant phrase, 'more a public labyrinth than a celtic toilet.' But Joyce's overall representation of woman is distorted and ugly. 'Always open sesame. The cloven sex.'

Arnold Bennett ('talk about understanding "feminine psychology" . . . I have never read anything to surpass it, and I doubt if I have ever read anything to equal it.') like Jung and Stuart Gilbert was impressed by Joyce's understanding of women. But the limitations of the male mind in certain respects have already been stressed and if we are to be guided by the generalities of Hélène Deutsch or Simone de Beauvoir regarding female development, Molly Bloom cannot be seen as representative of mature well-adjusted sexuality.

Joyce's models for Molly remain conjectural and it is also arguable what degree of his own unbridled fantasy has entered her soliloquy. It is regrettable that within that marvellous passage, like a canker in the rose, there lies the soiled sexuality of an immature and inadequate woman. And because, to cite Hélène Deutsch, 'the inability to say no may express nothing more than an infantile ability to give up an immediate pleasure for the sake of a greater but delayed one,' it is sad to reflect that the final famous 'Yes' was the assent of a weakling.

CHAPTER 15

FINNEGANS WAKE

Even those who saw more than a *succès scandale* in *Ulysses* threw up their hands when the chapters of *Work in Progress* appeared and today, despite the endeavours of numerous interpreters, the general reader still looks askance at *Finnegans Wake*.

Can he be blamed for his perplexity when the literary *élite* did not conceal theirs? 'Nothing so far as I can make out,' wrote Ezra Pound, 'nothing short of divine vision or a new cure for the clapp can possibly be worth all the circumambient peripherization.'[1] Stanislaus Joyce, to his later regret, refused to accept a presentation copy and George Bernard Shaw, viewing the book, muttered 'Sheer madness!' into his beard.[2] But other critics acclaimed it as a masterpiece, among them Joyce's friend Louis Gillet who wrote:

> Beyond life, occupied solely by his vision and his 'Ireland, we two will have it out!' he drew out from his magic ink-pot (the haunted Inkbottle) an arch of a thousand colours and built a bridge out of dreams, clouds and night, an iridescent boreal dawn where in brilliant atoms are depicted the eternal nothingness and vain phantasmagoria of the universe.

Adaline Glasheen, a perceptive, open-minded, and fruitful student of Joyce's last book admits that 'for the first year or two' it is very difficult. After that, apparently, the magic casements open a little. For she is honest enough to admit that her understanding of the narrative is still 'weak, uneven, full of holes, crawling with mistakes and ignorance . . .'

The general reader lacking the stamina of the true Joycean can nevertheless extract a great deal of amusement and interest from a quite superficial reading of *Finnegans Wake*. The Irish reader will readily detect topographical details—'So pool the begg and pass the kish for crawsake' (7.7) 'the Dullkey Downlairy and Bleakrooky tramaline' (40.29) 'Issy-la-Chapelle! Any lucans, please?' (80.36)—and even a smattering of Gaelic will enable him to translate 'Guinness thaw tool in jew me dinner ouzel fin?' (35.15) He will recognise, too, economic and social references: 'to help the Irish muck to look his brother dane in the face' (86·21) 'Bejacob's, just a gent who prayed his lent' (89.15).

The Catholic reader hears the echo of familiar prayers: 'haloed be her eve, her singtime sung, her rill be run, unhemmed as it is uneven!' (104.2) 'So in the name of the balder and of the sol and of the hollichrost' (331.14) 'Mirror do justice, taper of ivory, heart of the conavent, hoops of gold!' (527.22) 'Mildew, murk, leak and yarn now want the bad that they lied on' (598.22). Any reader will find a measure of satisfaction in recognising some of the innumerable references to old songs and nursery rhymes and the copious literary allusions: 'Psing a psalm of psexpeans, apocryphul of rhyme!' (242.30) 'Chinchin Childaman Chapchopchap!' (304.33) 'For a burning would is come to dance inane' (250.16) 'do you kend yon peak with its coast so green?' (317.35) 'To slope through heather till the foot. Join Andersoon and Co.' (318.27).

The temptation to multiply these examples for the joy of it must be resisted. Their identification is usually easy although their significance in their context may remain obscure. But occasionally, even at the level of simple understanding, adequate appreciation is not possible without biographical information not generally available when *Finnegans Wake* was first published. The identity of a number of famous Irishmen is lightly concealed in the passage: 'This is Steal, this is Barke, this is Starn, this is Swhipt, this is Wiles, this is Pshaw, this is Doubblinnbbayyates' (303.5). Further illumination is added, however, when we learn that Joyce was endlessly amused by the way in which W. B. Yeats's name was pronounced 'Doublevé Vé Yats' by little Hélène Moschos.

The wilful obscurity of *Finnegans Wake* irritates readers trained in the sciences whose constant object is clarification and precise expression. The apparently chaotic pages will, at first sight, remind any medical practitioner who looks at them of brain-damaged patients with speech disorders. Jargon aphasia, a senseless hotch-potch of words, hardly seems less meaningless than some of Joyce's sentences. But aphasia is a breakdown of language whereas in *Finnegans Wake* a synthesis of languages is being attempted.

Discussing psychotic speech Dr Macdonald Critchley remarks: 'Before leaving the subject of schizophrenic writing we can scarcely refrain from referring to something which is on the face of it at least, analogous. I refer to the unorthodoxies of obscure and reiterative writing as a deliberate art form. Taking first the latter aspects we readily find in avant-garde literature a studied paligraphia which defies traditional syntax.' After citing an example from a modern novel he adds: 'Similar instances are common enough in Joyce and more especially so in Gertrude Stein.'

Jung, too, appreciated that 'Even the layman would have no difficulty in tracing the analogies between *Ulysses* and the schizophrenic mentality.' But he drew attention to a 'singleness of aim and rigorous selectivity' which are the antithesis of psychotic thought. Joyce himself had sufficient insight to be aware that *Finnegans Wake* would strain his supporters' credulity. 'These twentyfive pages,' he told Louis Gillet, 'have cost me sixteen hundred hours of my life. Perhaps it is folly. One will be able to judge in a century.' It distressed him immeasurably to think that his book might be regarded as a leg-pull and Jung appears to have hit the nail on the head when he wrote, 'what seems to be mental abnormality may be a kind of mental health which is inconceivable to the average understanding; it may even be a disguise for superlative powers of mind.'

Joyce's vocabulary was phenomenal.[3] George Steiner points out that 'his work, more than any since Milton, recalls to the English ear the wide magnificence of its legacy. It marshalls great battalions of words, calling back to the ranks words long asleep or rusted, and recruiting new ones by stress of imaginative need.'

He was interested, to some degree, in the physiological basis of speech ('lesbiels, dentelles, gutterhowls and furtz' (16.28) and in Paris attended the lectures of the Abbé Jousse, a proponent of a theory that speech had its origin in gesture.[4] 'In the beginning was the rhythmic gesture,' Joyce used to say. Add to this his knowledge of languages—according to Sylvia Beach he had at least nine: English, Italian, French, German, Greek, Spanish, Dutch, and the three Scandinavian tongues apart from some knowledge of Yiddish and Hebrew—and *Finnegans Wake* may seem a logical development.[5] He took every opportunity to augment his knowledge of foreign tongues; when the International Theatre played in Paris he attended nearly every night and he sometimes went to the Danish Church near the Tour Eiffel to listen to the Sunday evening service.

There seems no reason why the phonemes of a consummate polyglot should not coalesce to produce something idiosyncratic and incomprehensible to the general. It is tempting, therefore, to view *Finnegans Wake* as an organic speech development, but when we learn that Joyce visiting Stuart Gilbert borrowed a Burmese grammar it looks like addition rather than accretion. This, to be sure, is not a denigration of the polyglot who presumably will lose no opportunity to add to his word store.

In every branch of knowledge there have been men with quite exceptional powers—the Indian mathematician Srinivasa Ramanujan treated the positive integers as his special friends, Lord Rutherford could 'see' the structured atom in his mind's eye—and Joyce was a prodigy where words were concerned.

It is not yet possible to define the histological basis of genius but it is unlikely that particular aptitudes are fortuitous; presumably they result from unusual dispositions of brain cells and rich endowments of association fibres in the cerebral cortex. 'I have something inside of me talking to myself' (522.26). *Finnegans Wake* should be approached with the realization that it is the unique product of a unique mind which saw language with an added dimension and interwove into his pages the obsession and delights of a tortured personality mercifully sustained by an enormous sense of fun. 'Can you not distinguish the sense, prain, from the sound, bray?' (522.29).

*   *   *   *

Its elucidation requires corporate efforts and according to J. Mitchell Morse, 'In the reading of *Finnegans Wake* everybody teaches everybody else.' It has been ransacked for books by J. S. Atherton, for people by Adaline Glasheen; others have catalogued the food and the advertisements and a similar exercise regarding its medical content is overdue: certainly a medical reader finds a good deal of intriguing material and notices again Joyce's ability to present in 'idioglossary' (423.9) recognisable clinical pictures. What could be more descriptive of chronic ill-health than 'his spittyful eyes and his whoozebecome woice'? (240.5) 'Calorrubordolor' (445.18) contains the elements of inflammation. 'His braynes coolt parritch, his pelt nassy, his heart's adrone, his bluidstreams acrawl, his puff but a piff, his extremeties extremely so' (74.13) is a compendium of degenerative diseases. Tuberculosis, not by any means a 'Ballade Imaginaire' (177.26) causes 'a cough and a rattle and wildrose cheeks for Piccolina Petite MacFarlane' (210.9); 'all the colories fled from my folced cheeks!' (365.36).

'His watch was bradys' (35.19) 'involucrum' (50.13) 'strabismal' (189.8) 'salmofarious germs' (79.32) 'rheumaniscences in his netherlumps' (319.17) 'pudendascope' (115.29) 'mortisection or vivisuture' (253.34) 'somatophage merman' (171.3) and 'traumaturgid' (496.24) derive from medical terminology. Biology and anatomy lend something to the amusing rhyme (418.10):

He larved ond he larved on he merd such a nauses
The Gracehoper feared he would mixplace his fauces

And 'duodisimally' (6.16) 'duedesmally' (566.12) and 'Juan Dyspeptist' (453.15) are appropriate neologisms to have been minted by an author suffering from duodenal ulceration; 'billiousness has been billiousness during milliums of millenions' (117.21).

We find reflected in Joyce's pages well-being and desolation ('sick or whole, stiff or sober' (289.14) the contemplation of death ('I was thinking fairly killing times of putting an end to myself and my malody' 279.12) and its reality—'quite beetly dead' (100.1) 'when the angel of death kicks the bucket of life' (170.12)—a solemn moment when the soul is at the brink of eternity ('ere the death he has lived through becomes the life he is to die into' 293.3) and the body faces interment 'In the orchard of the bones' (453·29). The cause of death is given in at least one case: 'after a lenty illness the roeverand Mr Easterling of pentecostitis' (130.8).

What Hélène Deutsch called 'the destiny of woman as the servant of reproduction' a destiny which may be softened by romance but places her physical well-being in jeopardy is referred to by Joyce: 'she who has given his eye for her bed and a tooth for a child' (101.34). In Dublin, as likely as not, the infant will be delivered by one of an 'internatural convention of catholic midwives' (128.26) in a 'Sweeps hospital' (618.11) 'that grandnational goldcapped dupsydurby houspill . . . with its vomitives for our mothers-in-load and stretchers for their devitalised males' (448.14).

Among the sub-standard males 'noon inebriates' (542.10) an all too common 'dieoguinnsis' (421.26) is alcoholism:

> how he has the solitary from seeing Scotch snakes and has a lowsense for the production of consumption and dalickey cyphalos on his brach premises where he can purge his contempt and dejeunerate into a skillyton be thinking himself to death (422.5).

Others as a result of deprivation—'from the slime of their slums and artesaned wellings, rickets and riots' (209.33)—fall prey to 'flu, pock, pox and mizzles, grip, gripe, gleet and sprue, caries, rabies, numps and dumps' (523.28) and are puny specimens:

> No, before your corselage rib is decartilaged, that is to mean if you have visceral ptossis, my point is, making allowances for the fads of your weak abdominal wall and your liver asprewl, vinvin, vinvin, or should you feel, in shorts, as though you needed

178

healthy physicking exorcise to flush your kidneys, you understand, and move that twelvefinger bowel and threadworm in-
hibitating it, lassy, and perspire freely, lict your lector in the lobby
and why out you go by the ostiary on to the dirt track and skip!
(437.8)

The ideal state of 'all-too-lyrical health' (452.3) 'Health, chalce,
endnessnessessity' (613.27) is vulnerable. 'He wandered out of his
farmer's health' (589.21) 'blueygreen eyes a bit scummy developing
a series of angry boils with certain references to the Deity, seeking
relief in alcohol and so on, general omnibus character with a dash of
railwaybrain, stale cough and an occasional twinge of claudication'
(443.36).
    'And the greater the patrarc the griefer the pinch. And that is
what your doctor knows' (269.28) whether he is one of the 'low-
quacks' (99.2) 'mudical dauctors' (413.7) 'working medicals' (333.24)
'post-wartem plastic surgeons' (263.13) or any of that 'noblesse of
leechers' (495.26) whose concern is 'bausna beatha in Miracle Squeer'
(384.9) Joyce's playful name for Merrion Square where in his day
the medical consultants lived.
    'How a Guy Finks and Fawkes When He Is Going Batty' (177.28)
is a question to be put to the 'psychoanolised' (522.32) or to the
'special mentalists' (96.32) 'we grisly old Sykos who have done our
unsmiling bit on 'alices' (115.21) who 'psoakoonaloose' (522.34) in a
'single minded men's asylum' (124.7). A common disorder needing a
'nursetendered hand' (392.9) and 'massoeurses' (432.23) for 'the
travaillings of his tommuck' (344.34) is one of 'tummy moors maladies'
(492.34).
    Whooping cough is featured in 'cacchinic wheeping caugh' (511.14)
'He was down with the whooping laugh at the age of the loss of
reason the whopping first time he prediseased me' (423.25) 'since
the phlegmish hoopicough, for all a possabled, after ete a bad cramp
and johnny magories, and backscrat the poor bedsores and the far-
thing dip' (397.24). The mysterious sweating sickness of the Middle
Ages is recalled by 'famine with Englisch sweat and oppedemics'
(539.36) Wearing apparel rather than pathology is intended in 'with
their trench ulcers open' (529.27). 'Gout' (229.3) is God, taste, and
go-out (530.11) but we also encounter 'gouty hands' (143.5) 'gouty
old galahat' (389.23) and 'her togglejoints shuck with goyt' (199.21).
    Allergists will appreciate, 'And Sunfella's nose has got rhinoceritis
from haunting the roes in the parik' (96.2); 'eelsblood in his cold toes,

179

a bladder tristended' (169.19) may appeal to urologists; 'your soreful miseries' (527.10) applies to what women all the world over tersely call *the curse*.

The medical content of *Finnegans Wake* is too extensive for serial comment. Instead, what might be termed an anthology of the abnormal is presented. 'It is infinitesimally fevers, resty fever, risy fever' (597.25) 'scalds and burns and blisters impetiginous sore and pustules' (189.31). 'O, my back, my back, my bach! I'd want to go to Aches-les- Pains' (213.17); 'all's dall and youllow' (427.17) 'he was shocking poor in his health, he said, with the shingles falling off him' (39.26) 'like the narcolepts on the lakes of Coma' (395.8) *'Or Culex feel etchy if Pulex don't wake him?'* (418.23)

'Heel trouble and heal travel' (620.13) 'call a blood-lekar!' (301.1) 'Where's Dr Brassenaarse?' (301.2) 'M.D· made his antemortem for him' (423.20) 'X-ray picture' (530.8) 'Only a bone moving into place' (522.22) 'medical assassiations' (146.14) 'Dr Chart of Greet Chorles street he changed his backbone at a citting' (603.22) 'suffering genteel tortures from the best medical attestation' (557.31).

'Just press this cold brand against your brow for a mow. Cainfully! The sinus the curse' (374.32). 'The pantaglionic affection through his blood like a bad influenza in a leap at bounding point?' (513.17) 'And I see by his diarrhio he's dropping the stammer out of his silenced bladder' (467.19) 'hiccupping, apparently impromptued by the hibat he had with his glottal stop' (171.9) 'tone-deaf in our noses' (522.28) 'sorestate hearing, diseased, formarly with Adenoiks' (242.1) 'a neurasthene nympholept, endocrine-pineal typus' (115.29).

Venereal diseases are well represented:

An infamous private ailment			
(vulgovarioveneral)	98.18	a vile disease	33.17
casehardened testis	87.34		
gonorrhal	349.2	clap	117.5
primary taincture	286.5	grenadier's drip	192.15
undeleted glete	183.36	Ructions gunorrhal	192.3

Many other symptoms and diseases are mentioned:

Acoustic						
Disturbance	71.18	Ague	150.8	Alcoholic		
amnesia	122.6	arch trouble	459.16	amblyopia	545.10
bennyache	302.28	berri-berries	542.2	aphasia	122.4

<table>
botulism 170.29   boils 137.28   Bheri-Bheri 200.14
</table>

botulism	170.29	boils	137.28	Bheri-Bheri	200.14
buboes	198.29	carbunckley	224.36	bronxitic	536.13
carmp	392.5	cholera	463.30	cataleptic	
circumcivicise	446.35	cock eye	363.3	mithy-	
crusted hoed	385.33	deaf	200.14, 331.5	phallic	481.4
delysiums	379.17	dizzy spells	373.27	circumcised	483.33
esophagous		Gall stone		collera	
regurgitation	558.3	belly	393.18	morbous	211.1
gliddinyss	318.35	gobbos	319.20	deff . . .	
howdrocephal-		hypnotised	320.2	dumm	517.2
ous	310.6	infirmierity		eczema	260.f.n,
Insomnia	193.29,	complexe	291.37		380.25
	120.14	Lazar's Walk	429.6	gibbous	531.1
king's evils	616.29	lupus	480.35	headnoise	535.23
luppas	403.16	measles	459.5	hysteria	528.14
mackerglosia		neuralgia	286.1	itch	231.3
and		palsied		lepers 350.4,	355.33
mickroo-		priamite	513.20	manias	289.18
cyphyllicks	525.8	pediculously		melancholia	40.24,
nettlerash	306.34,	so	88.13		449.1
	439.7			pains	65.3
palsied	440.24			phthisis	305.22
thishis	356.11			pneumonia	434.20
morbus					
pedeiculo-		Potts Fracture	73.8	Prost bitten!	424.9
sus	466.31	pulmonary		quartan agues	555.8
prickly heat	570.27	T.B.	172.13	suicide	462.36
rheumatic	544.10	rickets	293.5	ulcers, ill-con-	
tse tse	423.4	tuberclerosies	541.36	ditioned	521.28
vomit	89.17	boosy cough	555.12		

*　　*　　*　　*

In the sphere of anatomy there are numerous references the most amusing of which is a description of swallowing:

the faery pangeant fluwed down the hisophenguts, a slake for the quicklining, to the tickle of his tube and the twobble of his fable (319.12)

and the most ingenious a detailed account of the ear:

to pinnatrate inthro an auricular forfickle (known as the Vakingfar
sleeper, monofractured by Piaras Ua Rhuamhaighaudhlug, tym-
pan founder, Eustache Straight, Bauliaughacleeagh) a meatus
conch culpable of cunduncing Naul and Santry ... up his corpular
fruent and down his reuctionary buckling, hummer, enville and
cstorrap (the man of Iren, thore's Curlymane for you!), lill the
lubberendth of his otological life (310.9).

Eyes: 'We are all eyes. I have his quoram of images all on my retinue'
(443.1) 'by the humdred and sixty odds rods and cones of this even's
vision' (405.12).

Locomotor system: 'assuary as there's a bonum in your osstheology!'
(341.28) 'when you've bled till you're bone it crops out in your flesh'
(373.36) 'that's pectoral, his mammamuscles most mousterious' (15.32)
'I messaged his dilltoyds sausepander mussels on the kisschen table'
(531.5) 'not one of the two hundred and six bones and five hundred
and one muscles in his corso was a whit the whorse for her whacking'
(84.26).

Miscellaneous: 'diagonally redcrossed nonfatal mammalian blood'
(84.20) 'a blind stomach, a deaf heart, a loose liver, two fifths of two
buttocks' (169.17).

A number of brief anatomical references are listed below:—

acoustrolobe	419.22	aural eyness	623.18	auricles	412.15
arraky bone	368.14	blood	424.8	blood donor	425.10
bowels	563.14	C_3 peduncle	211.28	cerebrum	172.18
chessgang-		cokeblack bile	447.5	constant	
lions	571.36	estomach	192.22	lymph	577.11
entrails	231.35	feast of Saint		eustacetube	36.36
eyeballs	523.12	Pancreas	550.13		535.26
Gubbernathor	525.15	halluxes	429.17	groin	319.18
Larynx	419.23	lymphing	367.13	juggaleer's	
oncemaid		pectorals	137.25	veins	300.31
sacral	433.28	Vulva!	482.7	occiput	107.12
portal vein	614.33			*pelves*	551.13

*   *   *   *

'Derg rudd face should take patrick's purge' (582.28) refers to St.
Patrick's purgatory on Lough Derg in Co. Donegal rather than the

treatment of costiveness which is dealt with later: 'wreathe the bowl to rid the bowel' (613.24). There is sage advice, too, about nutrition—'If we could fatten on the elizabeetons we wouldn't have teeth like the hippopotamians' 437.23 'Deal with Nature the great greengrocer and pay regularly the monthlies, 437.16—and comments on the dietary habits and housing of the lower-income group:

> calories exclusively from Rowntrees and dumplings, one bar of sunlight does them all january and half february, the V. de V's (animal diet) live in five-storied semidetached but rarely pay tradesmen, went security for friend who absconded, shares same closet with fourteen similar cottages and an illfamed lodginghouse (544.34).

'Eulogia, a perfect apposition . . . from Boileau's I always use in the wards after I am burned' (527.12) recalls the Dublin firm of Boileau and Boyd 'cash chemist and family drugger' (492.21) 'chemicalled' (621.27). Here the numerous medicines referred to in the *Wake* could have been supplied. Here, as in other 'drogueries' (358.35) Joyce's characters could have collected their 'pansements' (443.14) and been 'dosed, doctored and otherwise' (438.36) with 'jesuit bark and bitter bite, calicohydrants of zolfor and scoppialamina by full and forty Queasisanos' (182.36) or with any of the following:

a little judas tonic	193.9	bluebutterbust	165.28
Castor's oil on the		codliverside	563.1
Parrish's syrup	432.1	Huster's micture and	
drugs	355.36	Yellownan's embroca-	
halibut oil or jesuit's tea	382.6	tion	184.22
poultice	302.4	The Pills, the Nasal	
		Wash (Yardley's)	156.27

When necessary 'some lotion or fomentation of poppyheads would be jennerously exhibited to the parts' (84.17) and he 'drinks tharr and wodhar for his asma and eats the unparishable sow to styve off reglar rack' (130.4). There are 'spas and speranza and symposium's syrup for decayed and blind and gouty Gough' (211.23). And Joyce adds: 'be advised by mux and take your medicine. The Good Doctor mulled it. Mix it twice before repastures and powder three times a day. It does marvels for your gripins and it's fine for the solitary worm' (193.5).

Toxic effects may occur: 'deadleaf brown with quicksilver appliques'

(271.36) 'salivarium' (286.21); but 'she shuk the bottle and tuk the medascene all times a day' (413.11).

The chemicals mentioned include:—

acid and alkolic	393.2		
antimonian manganese	184.36	alum	423·23
chrystalisations of alum	86.4	carbolic	67.34
corrosive sublimation	185.36	cohlorine	359.10
H$_2$O	495.26	globules of mercury	183.35
hevantonoze	392.6	heliose	67.10
iodines	253.18	iodine	200.36
magnegnousioum	397.26	lithium	131.36
prussic blue	305.14	nitrience of oxagiants	67.7
Sulphate de Soude	184.29	sulfeit of copperas	86.2
white arsenic with		sugars of lead for the	
bissemate alloyed	577.4	chloras ashpots	616.12

* * * *

Joyce also had something to say about physics. It is, of course, a far cry from the 'moisturologist of the Brehon's Assorceration for the advauncement of scayence' (608.2) to nuclear physics, 'split an atam' (333.24). The folk at the *Wake* include Max Planck—'Let's hear what science has to say, pundit-the-next-best-king. Splanck!' 505.27—and Lord Rutherford. '*The abnihilisation of the etym by the grisning of the grosning of the grinder of the grunder of the first lord of Hurterford explodotonates through Parsuralia with an ivanmorinthorrorumble fragoromboassity . . .*' (353.22).

When we finally consider what a great deal about medicine and the sciences has been packed into the book it seems appropriate that through Professor Murray Gell-Mann's borrowing from '*Three quarks for Muster Mark!*' (383.1) to name 'the quark', his postulated sub-unit of the neutron and proton, *Finnegans Wake* has effectively bridged the gap between 'the two cultures'.

CHAPTER 16

THE MILTONIC AFFLICTION

His intimates have said that Joyce credited his writing with a prophetic quality. On the second page of *A Portrait* his surrogate Stephen Dedalus is threatened with the blindness which later affected Joyce.

> . . . He hid under the table. His mother said:
> —O, Stephen will apologise.
> Dante said:
> —O, if not the eagles will come and pull out his eyes—
>> Pull out his eyes,
>> Apologise,
>> Apologise,
>> Pull out his eyes.

Joyce was myopic and wore glasses as a child. At Clongowes he was knocked down by accident on the cinderpath: the spectacles were 'broken in three pieces' and a few days later the prefect of studies punished him unjustly, an incident recounted in *A Portrait*.

> —Lazy idle little loafer! cried the prefect of studies. Broke my glasses! An old schoolboy trick! Out with your hand this moment!

Eye complaints were a family defect. John Stanislaus Joyce, the author's father, was treated for conjunctivitis and iritis in Jervis Street Hospital. Writing to her son in March 1903 Mrs Joyce informed him:

> I have just come from the Eye Hospital Mays eyes were giving trouble the Dr says she has small ulcers but did not alarm us. (Dr Benson[1] same as prescribed yr glasses) My own sight has become so bad I can hardly see what I am writing, glasses and all . . .

The exact date of onset of Joyce's iritis does not seem to have been established. It probably occurred first as a complication of an illness described as 'rheumatic fever' in Trieste in 1907. Dental sepsis—'My mouth is full of decayed teeth, my soul of decayed ambitions'— troubled him for years. He may have had a venereal infection in 1904 and again in 1909. And the myopia necessitated a change of glasses now and then.

I was examined by the doctor of the Naval Hospital here last week [he wrote from Trieste in 1905] and I now wear pince-nez glasses on a string for reading. My number is very strong—could you find out what is Pappie's. As soon as I get money I shall get my teeth set right by a very good dentist here. I shall then feel better able for my adventures.

On another occasion he expressed irritation:

My glasses annoy me. They are crooked and there is a flaw in both of the glasses. It is a bloody nuisance to have to carry bits of glass in your eye.

Joyce hymns 'the ineluctable modality of the visual' in *Ulysses* but he had already considered in *A Portrait* how myopia may have influenced his art.

Did he then love the rhythmic rise and fall of words better than their associations of legend and colour? Or was it that, being as weak of sight as he was shy of mind he drew less pleasure from the reflection of the glowing sensible world through the prism of of a language manycoloured and richly storied than from the contemplation of an inner world of individual emotions mirrored perfectly in a lucid supple periodic prose?

His resistance may have been undermined by privations to which he alluded repeatedly in his letters. From Paris in 1903 he wrote to his mother: 'I try to eat as much as I can, for Synge [who developed Hodgkin's disease] told me fasting cost him £30 for an operation.' From Rome in 1906 to his brother: 'I don't know what the hell I'm going to do this time. I can't go beyond Tuesday evg. I have eaten nothing to-day except a soup in order to economise.' And again to the long-suffering Stanislaus: 'It is Xmas Eve. 7 o'clock. I have eleven lire in my pocket.'

After returning to Trieste in 1907 Joyce fell ill and was in the Ospitalo Civicio from mid-July until September. He received a letter of commiseration and advice in November 1907 from Oliver St John Gogarty who was doing post-graduate work in Vienna.

Dear Joyce, I am very sorry to hear you had such a little time in bed to fight rheumatic fever. At least 6 months are necessary to ensure safety of the cardiac valves. If you could come to this place they would give you the best medical advice. London has done most in the attempt to cure the disease and there Paignton

[F. J. Poynton] isolated the bacillus: but Vienna is first rate . . .
Avoid strains and physical work as much as may be, in order that
your heart may 'compensate' for the longest possible period.

In the following year there was a relapse of the iritis which had
complicated the acute illness and there were other symptoms to which
he referred in a letter to his sister Margaret: 'I feel a little better of
the rheumatism and am now more like a capital S than a capital Z'

When Joyce visited Dublin in the summer of 1909 his friends'
comments about his appearance differed: 'in splendid health,' said
one; 'looking very ecclesiastical,' said another, and Gogarty ran a
clinical eye over him and remarked, 'Jaysus, man, you're in phthisis.'
But he remained free of rheumatism even in wet weather and attributed the improvement to drinking lithia. He rejoined his family
in Trieste in September but returned to Dublin six weeks later, agent
for a syndicate which set up the Volta Cinema in Mary Street.

Writing to Stanislaus on 28 September he reported, 'I am rather bad
with sciatica along the leg.' And the iritis relapsed again during this
visit.

Professor Richard Ellmann, Joyce's biographer, refers to 'a minor
complaint probably contracted from a prostitute,' in explanation of
the following passage from Joyce to his wife on 1 November 1909:

It is very good of you to enquire about that damned dirty affair
of mine. It is no worse anyhow. I was alarmed at your silence
first. I feared you had something wrong. But you are all right,
are you not, dearest? Thank God! Poor little Nora, how bad I
am to you!

The cinema was a flop. The Joyce ménage continued a penurious
existence in Trieste and later in the lovely city on the Zurichsee
where

The moon's greygolden meshes make
All night a veil,
The shorelamps in the sleeping lake
Laburnum tendrils trail.

Ezra Pound wrote to W. B. Yeats in July 1915:

Re/James Joyce. Joyce writes in regard to his eyes that he is
subject to 'irido-something or other' as a consequence of malarial
fever contracted in Rome, and that these attacks may incapaci-
tate him for work for three or four weeks at a time.

187

Early in 1916 he was again laid up with rheumatism; in October he wrote to his benefactress, Miss Harriet Shaw Weaver:

> Kindly excuse me for my delay in answering your letter. I have been ill lately. I had had three or four collapses which I feared were due to syncope but the doctor says I am not a cardiac subject and that the collapse is due to nervous breakdown.

And in November he reported: 'I have had no more attacks and feel better and am making a kind of cure.'

February 1917 brought a further relapse of iritis; the doctor seemed optimistic in March but in April Joyce's news for Miss Weaver was not good.

> I am still under doctor's care and rather depressed that the attack —possibly on account of the infamous weather—is lasting so long. I never had an attack that lasted so long as this one. I have no pain but the consequences this time seem to be rather serious —but I hope always that an operation may be avoided. I can read and write however and am continuing my book at the usual snail's pace.

Writing to Forrest Reid in May he stated: 'I am recovering from a very long and tiresome illness of the eyes (rheumatic iritis complicated with synechia and glaucoma) . . .'

The chronic sufferer seldom lacks advisers. Well-meaning friends tell him what to eat, what not to eat and what is said by so-and-so to be the very latest cure. Their gratuitous and often conflicting advice is sometimes almost mischievously interfering.

Ezra Pound exerted a most helpful influence on James Joyce's literary career. Never a man to do things by half he also concerned himself with Joyce's eye disorder and urged him to write to Dr George Milbry Gould, an American ophthalmologist, biographer, poet and essayist. Gould, who had written a medico-biographical study of Lafcadio Hearn, saw a connection between eye-strain and genius and this caused Pound to see him as Joyce's chief hope.

Pound wrote: 'I never know where I am with English doctors and I have never been to an oculist on this side of the atlantic. I don't know whether they are still in the XVIIIth century or not.'

He also suggested that Joyce should visit an osteopath:

> One other thing you can try before being operated on, IS there a trained osteopath in Zurich? Atrophy of the deltoid and biceps

shows that the trouble is not necessarily local and confined to the eye. I know an increasing number of people whom 'regular' physicians have bungled, who have been cured and renovated by having a vertebra set right side up and thus relieving blood or nerve pressures.

Joyce let Pound have a written account of his symptoms which the latter, unable to remember Gould's address and not quite sure if he was living, sent to America to John Quinn to forward to him, but with a lawyer's instinct for the practical, Quinn consulted his own doctors instead. In due course he wrote to Nora Joyce declaring the unwisdom of consulting anyone three thousand miles away about an acute condition.

Most of the people spend more time getting the right tailor or the right barber or getting the right restaurant than they do in getting the right doctor. Zurich is a good sized city and there ought to be a good specialist in Switzerland somewhere. . . .

By this time Pound, too, pointed out that urgency precluded waiting for Gould's advice but Joyce persisted. He sent 'the facts' of his case to Quinn who consulted Dr John R. Shannon, a New York ophthalmologist, passing on Joyce's 'facts.' In his reply Shannon pointed out that his information must be incorrect: 'Atropine is not used in Glaucoma—indeed it is absolutely contraindicated.' He recommended two Zurich specialists.

In a letter written in May 1917 Pound informed Joyce: 'I have written to Dr Gould direct. But heaven knows what he will be able to do at such a distance. He may perhaps know who is who among continental oculists, anyhow.'

Eventually after all the fuss and pother Pound had a note from Gould and on 27 June 1917 he passed on to his friend the American ophthalmologist's down-to-earth opinion that Joyce 'should have gone to some trustworthy ophthalmic surgeon and been treated perhaps operated upon.' Gould suggested that he might consult Sir Anderson Critchett in London but in war-time that would have been difficult.

On 24 August Professor Ernst Sidler Huguenin of Zurich performed an iridectomy (paid for by Edward Marsh) which was followed by haemorrhage and 'a nervous collapse which lasted three days,' but Joyce then recovered and wrote limericks in the dark.

He reported to James B. Pinker, his literary agent, from the kinder climate of Locarno in November: 'My health is much better and my sight improving here. . . .' The improvement did not last and in June 1918 he told Pinker, 'My health is very poor lately. I have been laid up again with my eyes and so am obliged to dictate this to you.'

He informed another correspondent in August:

Vous devez avoir une très mauvaise opinion de ma politesse! Mais la vérité est que j'ai été presque deux mois et demi à lit avec une très grave maladie des yeux—une double iritis avec glaucome. Maintenant elle est passée, dieu merci, et je puis de nouveau lire et écrire.

By now he was thirty-six, approaching middle age, and 'Bahnhofstrasse', a poem written in 1918, takes something of its mood and imagery from his ocular disorder.

The eyes that mock me sign the way
Whereto I pass at eve of day,

Grey way whose violet signals are
The trysting and the twining star.

Ah star of evil! star of pain!
Highhearted youth comes not again

Nor old heart's wisdom yet to know
The signs that mock me as I go.

Writing to Mlle Guillermet in February 1919 he said, 'You will think me very remiss for not having written ere now. I have been ill again with my eyes for the sixth time! If I am a sun, as you say, it is a sun which is often under an eclipse.'

The operation was an unpleasant memory which he recalled in a letter to Miss Weaver in 1920.

I was sorry to hear that any relative of yours should have to undergo the operation of iridectomy. It is a dreadful ordeal— or was so for me but there were complications in my case that made it almost impossible. I hope it has been successful. That is the only thing to be said for it.

Having moved to Paris in 1920, Joyce wrote to his friend Budgen in December from an apartment in the Boulevard Raspail: 'An eye attack was hanging on and off for a fortnight owing to cold and damp of the hotel so we took this flat for six months. It has about 100 electric lamps and gas stoves but how I am going to pay for it damn me if I know.'

'I am nearly dead with work and eyes,' he told Valery Larbaud in September 1921. Early in the following year he was attending Dr Victor Morax. On an occasion when the latter was not available, his assistant Dr Pierre Mérigot de Treigny called on Joyce to find him squatting on the floor of his room at 9 rue de l'Université wrapped in a blanket and beside him a stewpan with a chicken carcass and a half empty bottle of wine. All the chairs being taken up with odds and ends Mérigot de Treigny was obliged to squat while examining his patient. On his next visit the doctor told Joyce that another operation was necessary.

The story is taken up by Sylvia Beach who in *Shakespeare & Co.* related how the young Joyces came running to fetch her.

> Hurrying to the little hotel in the rue de l'Université, where they were living at the time, I found Joyce very ill. He was suffering terribly. Mrs Joyce was tending him. With a bucket of ice water beside her, she was constantly renewing the compresses on his eyes. She had kept this up for hours and looked worn out. 'When the pain is unbearable he gets up and walks the floor,' she said.

Miss Beach saw that fear as much as pain was responsible for Joyce's agitation. The prospect of another operation during an acute attack terrified him. He implored her to intervene.

> I scooted over to the rue de la Paix, where, among all those dressmaking establishments, my oculist had his office. Dr Louis Borsch, a compatriot of mine, had been very kind when I once consulted him at the little clinic he ran on the Left Bank for students and working people. He listened very kindly now to the account I gave him of Joyce's woeful situation, but though I beseeched him to go to him at once, he said he was sorry, he couldn't go to the bedside of a patient another physician was looking after. Seeing my despair, he said he would see Joyce, but Joyce must come to him. I told him that Joyce was too ill to leave his bed, but Dr Borsch was firm. 'Get him over here as soon as you can,' he said.

When informed of Borsch's decree Joyce said 'Let's be off,' and with the help of Nora and Miss Beach he made his way across Paris by taxi and slumped into an armchair in the doctor's waiting-room. 'Oh the wait in that waiting-room [Miss Beach recalled] under the gaze of those silver-framed crowned heads with grateful inscriptions that adorned the grand piano.' But to Joyce's relief Borsch agreed to postpone the operation.

The acute iritis subsided and in August 1922 Joyce informed another correspondent, 'Am writing this beside the window with half an eye. Have got leave to start for London on Thursday but am not cured. The nebula in the pupil will take some time yet to disappear . . . 1,000 drops of stuff in my eye, profuse nightly perspirations and pain have made me for the moment very fatigued and irritable. . . .' Some weeks before this Ezra Pound had arranged for Dr Louis Berman, an American endocrinologist who was visiting Paris, to examine Joyce. Endocrine therapy and dental attention were advised for spinal arthritis.

While in London he consulted a Dr Henry and Mr Robert Rutson James of 46, Wimpole Street, Ophthalmologist to St George's Hospital. They recalled to his mind Henry and James's drapery shop in Dublin and gained a place for themselves in *Ulysses* ('. . . Henry and James's wax smartsuited freshcheeked models, the gentleman Henry, *dernier cri* James.')

More to the point they advised an immediate operation but on his return to Paris Dr Borsch temporised. Dental extractions and a rest in Nice were prescribed. During this holiday he had a further setback and consulted Dr Louis Colin whose treatment he described to Miss Weaver.

> I took a flat on Wednesday . . . An hour afterwards I felt the first sign of trouble in my eye and on the following day I was again in the doctor's hands, one recommended to me by Dr Borsch in case of need. He attributes the relapse chiefly to the rain and wind-storms of the past week. It had not rained for nine months before my arrival. I am to have the visit of five leeches in an hour from now and he hopes that by relieving the congestion the attack will not develop. There is no tension. He thinks that as soon as practicable I ought to be operated as the risk is too great. My sight has improved very much even during the inflammation. By raising my head to a certain angle I can see as well through the bad eye as through the good. This means that there is a clear space in the lower part of the nebula on the lens. It seems the operation is not likely to have as damaging an effect as if it had been made when the sight was almost totally effaced.

He wrote to her optimistically in February 1923:

> At last I have some kind of good news though not much. The dionine treatment prescribed by Dr Colin of Nice has dissipated a fair part of the film. Dr Borsch, however, will not apply it in the strong solution which the Nice doctor prescribed partly I suppose because he is older and more prudent but also because he knows better the pusillanimous nature of his patient. He prefers to continue the treatment gradually and to wait and see if the film will thin more. He does not believe the dionine will dissipate the film wholly nor was Dr Colin positive of that either. He was, however, as you see a very clever man and all the London doctors who said the film was 'organised' (that is not fluid but irremovable) were wrong. Unfortunately this does not mean any improvement in my power to read or write and for this reason. I had before 1/10 of normal vision in that eye. Now I have 1/7 or 1/6 but this is only good enough for longrange vision. It enabled me a few nights ago to see the lights of the Place de la Concorde which before had been only a blur. Dr Borsch believes that after the operation I will have 1/2 normal vision. Personally I am sceptical about the result of the dental one but since Dr Borsch will not do his operation till the dentist has done his let it be so. The latter will get to work as soon as Dr Borsch is convinced that the dionine can do no more. The threatened attack in the right eye has been kept under partly by Dr Borsch's treatment, partly by Dr Colin's cure.

Borsch performed a sphincterectomy on 28 April 1923. Joyce was disappointed by the slowness of the improvement but by June he was writing and reading again. He submitted to another iridectomy on the left eye on 10 June 1924, which he mentioned when writing to Miss Weaver from St Malo.

> I left Paris after a final interview with Dr Borsch. I am to go back there in a couple of months to see the result of the operation and to get other glasses. Meanwhile I am to continue the treatment here or wherever we stop. No further operation, he says, is necessary or would do any good. The sight will come back, he says. I will say nothing more on this subject till then.

By October he was left in no doubt that the operation had been unsuccessful.

During these last two days the sight of my eye has been wretched. I see less than before. It is very irritating. I cannot understand why part of this deposit cannot be removed when they can remove everything else in the eye. I shall try to see the doctor to-morrow or Tuesday.

He wrote to Robert McAlmon on 21 November.

There is unpleasant news for me. I have a cataract and am to be operated next Saturday. This came on me as a surprise. Borsch did not tell me and I could not understand how my sight went on failing. He says I will get my sight back. These continuous operations are dreadful.

Borsch operated on 29 November. Later Joyce wrote

I saw splendid sights for a minute or so. Dr Borsch says the sight cannot come back quickly but it will come . . . There is to be an electric cure when the broken window of my soul can stand more shocks. He is positive as to the result.

When he closed his eyes he had visual hallucinations. On New Year's Day he wrote to Miss Weaver.

Here is another Borsch dialogue of yesterday.

Dr B.: How is your eye?
J.J.: *Semper idem.*
Dr B.: (business): Not to me. I have still a fortnight.
J.J.: Ten days, doctor. You still think you'll win.
Dr B.: Sure I'll win.
J.J.: (baffled, beaten, vanquished, overcome, pulverised) smiles broadly.
Dr B.: You'll see all right.
J.J.: It's an obstinate eye, doctor, no?
Dr B.: No fellow's any good if he's not obstinate.
J.J.: (checkmated, silenced, overpowered) smiles broadly:
and when do you think you can prescribe for the lenses?
Dr B.: Three weeks or a month after.

I don't know what he means. But he ought to be Ambassador for the two Americas. I asked him then if the woman from Bordeaux who was operated about the same time would get her sight. She is a bad case, he said, but there is a little hope for her.

Later in January he sent her a further instalment.

I report two dialogues:

Dr. Borsch. How are you?
J.J. Slightly inclined to pessimism.
Dr Borsch. You don't think etc.
J.J. Well. . . .
Dr B. What will you bet?
J.J. Fixing a date.
Dr B. A month. How much will you bet?
J.J. O well. . . .
                    (later)
    You removed the front wall of the capsule and the lens?
Dr B. Yes.
J.J. Can a cataract form on the back wall?
Dr B. Sure.
J.J. Is it likely in my case?
Dr B. No. If it did I'd win my bet quicker.
J.J. (prolonged smile).

He beats me every time. He ought to have written *Ulysses.*

He dictated a letter on 23 February 1925, from the *Clinique des yeux,* 39 *rue du Cherche Midi* (which he sometimes referred to as Mme de la Vallière's château) where he was laid up with conjunctivitis and episcleritis in the right eye.

Cher Mademoiselle Weaver je me trouve ici depuis 8 jours le trouble dans mon oeuil persiste mais l'on m'assure que ce n'est pas l'Iris et quil n'y aura pas de consequence je n'en sais rien la douleur est parfois intolerable et principalement Vendredi la nuit. Le docteur m'a assurer maintenant que le crise est passée. je l'espère bien.

Always intrigued by names, Joyce noted with approval that the clinic in the *rue du Cherche Midi*—Southern-seeking Street—stood on an intersection with the *rue du Regard.* He liked Borsch (according to Sylvia Beach he was 'as fat as Santa Claus') who bent over his patient mumbling in a Yankee drawl, 'Too bad ye got that kickup in your eye.' He liked Borsch's nurse, also corpulent, who assisted the doctor, cooked the meals, ran the establishment and the patients, bullying some of them but never Monsieur 'Joasse' who was one of her favourites. 'She grows garlic in a sponge on the window,' he told Sylvia Beach, 'to season our dishes with.'

Arthur Power (author of *From the Old Waterford House*) visited Joyce at about this time and recalls him lying in a low-ceilinged room with one single dim light burning over his bed. The air of dilapidation dismayed Power but prompted the irrepressible Joyce to write:

> The clinic was a patched one,
> Its outside old as rust
> And every place beneath its roof
> Lay four feet thick in dust.

Leeches were applied. They wriggled, but Mrs Joyce and the nurse prevented them from flopping to the floor, and kept them in place until they stuck on and relieved the congestion. At night time the pain was so bad that Joyce thought himself 'as near unreason as my worst critics think me,' but morphine gave relief.

In March a dental X-ray showed a sequestrum (piece of dead bone) which required removal and his patience was tried further by medical advice: 'I have now been put on a starvation diet by way of adding to my present pleasures. The weather here renders my cure almost impossible once an attack has set in. I am also advised to walk eight or ten kilometres a day. If I can do this with one eye sightless and the other inflamed in to-day's thick, damp fog through the traffic of Paris on an unfed stomach I shall apply for the legion of honour.' He managed to write in large black letters with a black pencil, and with a magnifying glass he could decipher pencilled words. Thus equipped he prepared a fragment of *Finnegans Wake* for the press.

Borsch did a capsulotomy on Joyce's left eye in April 1925 but the latter wrote plaintively to Miss Weaver in July: 'I saw Dr Borsch. He is surprised I cannot see better, is positive I will see. I asked if another operation might be necessary. He said, "I think not." ' Later in the same month Borsch advised another operation in September. 'He says it is boring but the only course and in the end I will see, he says.' At a stage when Joyce might have been forgiven for exasperation or worse he remarked wryly, 'I am going to ask the sea breezes at the coast what they think about it all.'

Rain spoiled his holiday in Normandy. At Fécamp in the ninth row of the stalls he could not see the actors' faces. On the beach his over-clouded vision tried his nerves. He encountered thunderstorms in Niort and Bordeaux *en route* to Arcachon.

But we shall have great times,
When we return to Clinic, that waste land
O Esculapios!
(Shan't we? Shan't we? Shan't we?)

Joyce did not 'jump through Hoop no. 7' until December and on New Year's Eve he wrote despondently to Miss Weaver:

I have been having a poor time, more or less constant pain in the wound, allayed by aspirin and pilocarpin (antidote of scopo), no sight whatsoever and 'blues.' Dr Collinson says he has no great hopes of it. Dr Borsch says I ought to see when the blood absorbs. It is doing so at about 1/20 of the normal rate.

In March 1926 Borsch was using 'some kind of new chemical stimulant (not chemical but acting by purely physical means, recently discovered here, I understand, synthol for massaging the temples and brow).' Joyce conceded that his eye was 1/1,000,000,000 better.

His general health, too, was unsatisfactory; he was prone to 'nervous collapses' and in 1927 spent a miserable Christmas because of 'inflammation of the intestines;' his weight was reduced to '8 st odd which is nothing for one who would be a sixfooter if mangled out, so I have to eat oysters, Turkish Delight, Butter Scotch, coal, strychnine, hypophosphates, etc., etc.' His eye gave trouble again in August and September to which he referred in a letter to Valery Larbaud.

I suppose Miss Beach told you about my collapse. I cannot see a single word of print and of course am dreadfully nervous on account of it. They are giving me injections of arsenic and phosphorus but even after three weeks of it I have about as much strength as a kitten and my vision remains stationary that is in the dusk with the light behind it. They examined 'all the internal organs of the beast' and his blood pressure and found everything normal except his nerves. Apparently I have completely overworked myself and if I don't get back sight to read it is all U-P up.

Towards the end of January 1929 he informed Stanislaus, 'My reading sight seems to have come to an end but I was informed that both eyes should be again operated. This will be operation nine and ten. Nevertheless with the help of about ten assistants I was able to check the next instalment for Transition which comes out this week.'

Joyce remained Borsch's patient until the ophthalmologist's death and attended his funeral. For a time he was under the care of Dr Arthur William Collinson, Borsch's former assistant, later he attended Dr Edward Hartmann. Then some friends advised him to consult Professor Alfred Vogt[2] and he did so early in April 1930. Vogt advised an operation and when Professor Pagenstecker of Wiesbaden confirmed the opinion Joyce submitted to the operation in Zurich.

Meanwhile George Moore had written to him:

My anxiety will be great till I hear from you that the Swiss oculist promises you the sight of one eye. One eye is quite sufficient: a man is as well off with one as with two.

Vogt wrote a detailed post-operative report.

Left eye. A ninth operation was performed on this eye for tertiary cataract by Professor Alfred Vogt at Zurich on the 15th of May 1930. The growth was cut through horizontally, but the proposed operation could not be completed as the vitreous body, most of which seems to have been lost during the last two operations, or during the attack of Scopolamine poisoning which immediately followed the eighth operation threatened to collapse completely by emergence. The dangers attendant on the ninth operation were successfully avoided as was an excessive haemorrhage. Ten days after the operation an attack of mechanical iritis due to the presence of blood occurred but lasted only ten hours and did not leave any exudate. A week later leeches were applied which successfully removed all the blood from the anterior chamber of the eye. On the 3rd of June it became possible to make a microscopic examination. This revealed that the incision made, contrary to what happened in other operations, had remained open and unclogged by exudate but that blood had entered into the vitreous body, which a much operated eye would take some months to eliminate. It also revealed however that at the last operation the back wall of the capsule of the lens had not been removed, possibly because its removal was too difficult and that in the time intervening between the eighth and the ninth operation, $1\frac{1}{2}$ years, it had been gradually over clouded so that it is now in a condition of almost *secondary cataract,* thereby occluding practical sight. At some future date which Professor Vogt cannot fix a tenth operation (capsulotomy) should be performed.

Right eye. This had not suffered appreciably in consequence of the operation on left eye, it still presents a complicated cataract on which an eleventh operation must ultimately be performed. *General observations.*

It has been decided to defer the 10th operation till middle of September 1930. The operation just performed will probably produce a slight amelioration of vision in the left eye, which before had a seeing power of 1/800 to 1/1000. On the other hand the seeing power of the right eye, estimated some months ago at 1/30, diminished constantly but slowly as the cataract developed. The most favourable factor in the case is, that, according to all medical opinions, in both eyes, optic nerve and periphery of the retina functioned perfectly normally. It is also, Professor Vogt believes, that the macula also is *normal* and that is, if the two operations still necessary are made with special instruments and when the eyes are in a non-glaucomatous condition, that there is every hope of obtaining ultimately a fair measure of clear and practical vision.

Vogt refused a fee remarking to Giorgio Joyce that he regarded himself well-repaid by being able to restore a great literary talent to the world. He asked only for a copy of *Ulysses* inscribed for his daughter. He examined his patient for nearly an hour on 15 June and was so pleased with the improvement that he sanctioned Joyce's return to Paris whereupon the latter concocted a publicity stunt to benefit an operatic tenor, John Sullivan, whose voice he greatly admired. Having kept his improvement secret he attended the Paris Opera where Sullivan was singing in *Guillaume Tell*: during the course of the evening Joyce stood up and leaned forward dramatically in his box; then, removing his dark glasses he exclaimed: *Merci, mon Dieu pour ce miracle! Après vingt ans je revois la lumière!*

He saw Vogt again in November 1930; the operation was postponed until the Spring and after his return to Paris he received an encouraging letter from the ophthalmologist.

Many thanks for your friendly letter. I am very happy to be able to state that the result of my operation is already favourable and that the new pupil which I put in will enlarge itself further. The main thing now is that you should not expose yourself to any colds, so that iritis will not recur.

Then later I will be able to begin first the removal of the cataract from the *right* eye, and finally, with all due precaution, the splitting of the post-cataract membrane of the left eye, in so far as this may still be necessary.

Joyce noticed a temporary visual deterioration in January 1931: in March 1932 he informed Frank Budgen, 'My eyes are not very well, a slight attack of episcleritis from a neglected blast but much better these last few days.' Despite Vogt's reminder Joyce did not go to Zurich again until July 1932; his daughter's mental illness and 'one damn worry after another' accounting for the delay.

When he arrived in Zurich Vogt was away.

Vogt was in Amsterdam for an operation but will see me tomorrow. It pours and pours and pours in floods here and I am nervous about my eye which everybody finds better. Why does the best ophthalmologist in Europe live in the worst eye-climate?

The professor's report was bad.

Professor Vogt saw my eyes on Monday 10 July. He says I should have come to him before and is afraid it is now too late. The right eye was still operable 20 months ago. Now the cataract is total and unfortunately complicated with glaucome (secondary) and a partial atrophy of the retina. I was wrongly advised, he says, to put an atropine in it which was pure poison. He says I must not even rub it. Retina and optic nerve were normal when he saw it in November 1930 but are not so now. He intends to observe it for some days and then decide whether he will allow it to go blind (erblinden) or attempt two very difficult operations in succession, the first early in September. In the latter course I may have to face a 5-6 months' residence in Switzerland. This means a total cessation of work, and a considerable expenditure of money. I am writing Vogt a letter explaining the events from April 1931 which prevented me from coming here to be visited and operated. He added that seeing the complicated condition of the neglected eye that he was reluctant to touch the other but that he would have done so had glaucoma and retinary atrophy not intervened in the other, resultant from interocular pressure unchecked by operation.

Joyce saw Vogt again in September.

He injected I don't know what and I had to go back in 3 hours. It was a test for tension. The result was favourable and then he said he could wait (bad eye). There was no room in the anterior chamber as it was, he would have to cut through the lens to work. This might produce a traumatic iritis which would probably pass over to the good eye and perhaps undo all. He says the capsule will shrink in about 1-1½ years and so leave him some space . . . He changed my glasses and insists I am to come back to see him every 3 months during that 1-1½ yr.

Nothing less would satisfy Vogt; he refused to accept interim reports from any other doctor. To which Joyce said, 'Damn well right, too. I wish I had met him 10 years ago.'

After a visit to Zurich in May 1933 Joyce wrote to Stanislaus:

> *1st consultation:* Left eye, the good one, slightly improved since Sept. 1932. No exudate or precipitation in gap. Artificial gradually opening upwards. Rate of progress slow. This is an advantage as rapid rate of progress might bring complications. It wd continue 3 or 4 yrs until pupil reached 4 mm. Could be hastened by operation but far too dangerous. After 3 yrs a tiny operation (removal of outer film) may be possible and advisable.
> Prognosis good.
> *2nd consultation:* Right eye disimproved. Cataract almost completely verkalkt (calcified), no vision. Little sensibility to light. Retina (invisible) certainly in part atrophied. Test of injection made at 1st consultation however gives not unfavourable result as regards probability of glaucoma. Therefore operation still possible—if not made, eye will be blind. If it is made—very difficult; also dangerous for operated eye which may go blind during op. because of loss of vitreous. If it succeeds still no means of knowing what vision eye may obtain, this depending on retinal condition. For such an operation greatest tranquillity needed.
> Asked advantage of such an operation, Vogt said 2 eyes better than 1. Asked about retour d'age and my physical state, Vogt said he found me looking younger and better (!!!) But that I shd have complete calm. Asked if op. might imperil left eye, V replied (reversing what he had said in Sept. consultation) that if there was a traumatic iritis in right eye after op. wd probably extend to left and undo all the good he believed.
> Refused to advise but sd if in my place and cd be sure of an operator like himself wd run risk.
> I am to reflect and let him know in a few days. He wd operate now or in Sept. when in any case I must return to Zurich to have my eye examined.

His devotion to St Lucy patroness of eyesight—surprising perhaps in a lapsed-Catholic—was unabated. He commemorated her feastday, 13 December, annually. 'Santa Lucia '33. Her candle is burning quietly in the drawing-room. She has rather a job looking after my occhi.'

After visiting Vogt in the Spring of 1934 Joyce expressed relief that 'operation No. 11 (world's amateur championship) has been staved off till the autumn'. He sent further details to Frank Budgen.

> I've just come here to Paris from the rainy southern shore. I to Monte Carlo went but I never played a cent. I saw Vogt in Z'ch. The right eye-lens almost calcified. He can't make up his mind. Two operations at least needed and he is not sure of the result. If good, I could see with a lens as well as most people. But any upset in the eye during the operation might pass to the other and close me up entirely. The other eye has slightly improved. He gave me a different glass to see better with. Have to go back in autumn.

'What a nuisance to have eyes like mine! Alarms all the time,' he wrote in February 1935 and in another letter: 'I can't write much as my eyes are troubling me—either the awful damp or the dust of the books I was unpacking.'

After a visit to Vogt in April 1937 he wrote to his son.

> I have seen Vogt at last. He found my sight much improved. The hole he made in my left eye is enlarged. He says it will become even larger and two years from now he proposes to make another cut. I should like to see better. He changed my lenses (3 dioptical points) and wants to keep me under observation to find out if I can get accustomed to new glasses. I put them on to-day. They feel a bit strange but I see better already. The right eye—non-sight—a little deteriorated because of hardening of the crystalline near the nose. Yes but he threatened me with one of those brief burning flashes once in a while. The climate here is really crazy. In fact a burning flash came an hour after I had seen Vogt. But I took aspirin and made hot compresses and today it's much better.

In the following February there was another alarm which he described to Ezra Pound.

> Retinal congestion suddenly developed in my left (the only one

really left) eye in consequence of months of day and (literally) allnight work in finishing *W i P* and I had to leave Paris and come here to see Prof. Vogt. All writing and reading were stopped but it was only strain and righted itself with a few weeks rest and I am now allowed 2 or 3 hours a day work.

The further operation which Joyce dreaded was not performed because more dire events interposed. It remains to consider the cause of the iritis and to recall some touching descriptions of his blindness.

A detailed analysis of the effect of ocular disease on Joyce's writing is beyond the scope of this book but a reference to Edmund Wilson's essay *The Dream of H. C. Earwicker* is pertinent. Wilson, mentioning with approval T. S. Eliot's judgement that James Joyce is the greatest master of the English language since Milton, who was mainly a writer for the *ear*, added that Joyce dealt 'principally in auditory sensations' in his later phase—'There is as little visualization in *Finnegans Wake* as in *Samson Agonistes*.'

Sylvia Beach, too, had something to say on this theme: 'as his sight diminished his hearing developed so that he lived more and more in a world of sounds, so, *Finnegans Wake*, to be comprehensible must be heard by the reader. Even in his earliest work, Joyce was always harping on sound. His sight as a child, as one remembers, was weak.'

*　　　*　　　*　　　*

When iritis (inflammation of the iris, the delicate contractile coloured diaphragm which surrounds the pupil) is combined with inflammation of the ciliary body it is termed 'irido-cyclitis' or 'anterior uveitis'; its causes are numerous and in a particular case it may be impossible to establish the precise cause with certainty. For doctors such a diagnostic challenge holds an endless fascination; for patients, on the other hand, the most acceptable explanations are the simplest. Thus in *Ulysses:*

> —Are you bad in the eyes? the sympathetic personage like the town clerk queried.
> —Why, answered the seafarer with the tartan beard who seemingly was a bit of a literary cove in his own small way, staring out of sea-green portholes as you might well describe them as, I uses goggles reading. Sand in the Red Sea done that. One time I could read a book in the dark, manner of speaking.

A 'malarial fever' contracted in Rome and the 'rheumatic fever' which occurred in Trieste have been cited as causes of Joyce's uveitis, but is either diagnosis much more convincing than Red Sea sand? Malaria occurred formerly in Southern Italy but there is no evidence that Joyce was infected by a *Plasmodium*. Rheumatic fever, a disease not infrequently confused with other forms of polyarthritis, is more common in children than in adults and tends to affect the heart especially when there are repeated attacks. Moreover, uveitis is rare in rheumatic fever, occurring with greater frequency in certain other rheumatic diseases.

Tuberculosis, an important cause of uveitis, might be suspected in a young Irishman whose race appears to have an increased susceptibility to tuberculosis but, in view of the associated severe rheumatism, it is improbable. Syphilis was responsible for fifty per cent of cases of acute primary iritis in the first quarter of the present century but can be confidently excluded: syphilitic iritis usually occurs in the secondary stage of syphilis when other diagnostic signs abound; the Wasserman reaction (positive in syphilis) would have been a routine test in any eye clinic; pain tends to be slight and after two to eight weeks the iritis subsides and does not recur; it is often accompanied by neuro-retinitis and choroiditis and is a sign of virulent lues—Trousseau, the great physician of the Hôtel Dieu, found that out of forty patients with syphilitic iritis, thirty-four developed grave complications including carditis and G.P.I.

There is nothing to suggest that Joyce had syphilis, but from the evidence of Gogarty's letters, quoted in an earlier chapter, it appears that he acquired gonorrhea, another cause of uveitis, in Dublin.

> Buck Mulligan stood up from his laughing scribbling, laughing: and then gravely said, honeying malice:
> —I called upon the bard Kinch at his summer residence in upper Mecklenburgh street and found him deep in study of the *Summa contra Gentiles* in the company of two gonorrheal ladies. Fresh Nelly and Rosalie, the coalquay whore.

To be the direct cause, however, gonorrhea should have led to iritis earlier than 1907, the date of the first frank attack. It is possible that the neuralgic pains which troubled Joyce in Paris in 1903-04 were due to low-grade iritis, but this antedates the venereal infection to which Gogarty referred in 1904 and brings decayed teeth harbouring streptococcal infection to the forefront of the differential diagnosis.

If, on the other hand, the iritis commenced in 1907 it may have stemmed from the same cause as the disorder diagnosed, probably incorrectly, as rheumatic fever. The elucidation of Joyce's eye disease would depend, then, on the accurate identification of a rheumatic disorder which relapsed now and then without causing permanent incapacity and without affecting his heart. The likelihood of rheumatic fever and rheumatoid arthritis recede when we consider the high incidence of endocarditis and the rarity of uveitis in the former; the almost invariable involvement of permanent joint damage in the hands in the latter.

Having exculpated these common disorders two other possibilities must be considered—ankylosing spondylitis and Reiter's disease. Not described until 1916 the latter did not become generally known for many years; the former in its less severe forms is often overlooked; neither is mentioned in ophthalmology textbooks published early in the century. L. Webster Fox of Philadelphia (1904) referred to 'rheumatism' without further qualification; Parsons of London, a little less vague, added gout and rheumatoid arthritis (1923); *Swanzey's Diseases of the Eye* (1925) edited by Werner ('Cashel Boyle O'Connor Fitzmaurice Tisdal Farrell walked as far as Mr Lewis Werner's cheerful windows, then turned and strode back along Merrion Square, his stickumbrelladustcoat dangling'—*Ulysses*) mentioned subacute articular rheumatism. Later editions of *Parsons' Diseases of the Eye* by Sir Stewart Duke Elder include Reiter's disease and spondylitis.

Some recent research into the cause of 'rheumatic' iritis is germane. Two hundred and nine patients with uveitis attending the out-patient clinic of the Manchester University Department of Ophthalmology were examined for rheumatic diseases (Stanworth and Sharp, 1956); uveitis was specifically associated with Reiter's disease and ankylosing spondylitis, the latter being sometimes mild and apparently inactive. Another large group of male patients studied at the Institute of Ophthalmology in London (Catterall, 1960) showed a high instance of Reiter's disease and ankylosing spondylitis, and in these cases there was a significantly high incidence of chronic infection of the prostate and bladder.

One or other of these disorders seems a likely cause for Joyce's chronic ill-health. He had iritis, arthritis, one or two episodes of urethritis, at least one attack of sciatica, and possibly an episode of colitis.

In ankylosing spondylitis the permanent joint changes may be confined to the spine; Joyce in some photographs, seems a little stooped and according to Dr Louis Berman he had spinal arthritis. Spondylitis of this type, as we have seen, has a high incidence of iritis. Sciatica is a common manifestation and frequently there is an associated urogenital infection. Reiter's disease (a tentative diagnosis which would have intrigued the punster Joyce) is characterised by arthritis, urethritis, and ocular involvement. Colitis, latent or active, may be a predisposing factor.

The differentiation of mild non-progressive ankylosing spondylitis from Reiter's disease is not always easy in life even when full diagnostic facilities are available. Retrospectively it is impossible, all that can be said is that either would explain Joyce's illness; the acute onset, the colitis, and the visual deterioration favour a diagnosis of Reiter's disease. Studying the prognosis of acute uveitis, Stanworth (1960) found that uveitis associated with spondylitis, despite a liability to multiple recurrences, has a good prognosis whereas in Reiter's disease he encountered changes suggestive of granulomatous uveitis, an equal tendency to multiple recurrences and a worse prognosis regarding ultimate visual acuity.

The symptom-complex of Reiter's disease is a curious one requiring further elucidation. The urethritis is commonly, but not invariably, due to a non-specific venereal infection, not necessarily acquired during extra-marital sexual intercourse. A variety of germs including viruses and pleuropneumonia-like organisms has been thought to be responsible, but none has been consistently isolated. The iritis is unlikely to result from direct infection of the eye. Allergy or tissue sensitivity may explain it or, according to a current theory, it may be an auto-immune phenomenon.

It is, of course, possible that Joyce's rheumatism and uveitis although initially coincidental were due to unrelated causes. In the majority of cases of uveitis, indeed, the cause remains undetermined. A series of five hundred patients studied by Stanworth included 384 cases with no causally associated disease.

The treatment of uveitis has been improved by corticosteroid drugs (cortisone analogues). Had Joyce been born forty years later, his sufferings might have been negligible. But Bloomsday would have been 16 June 1944, and *Work in Progress* still in progress.

*   *   *   *

Joyce's letters give a clear idea of his internal reaction to the ocular disorder which plagued him so. Protesting occasionally, despairing at times, at least once questioning the correctness of his treatment and sending for a medical textbook to see if he was not being poisoned by scopolamine, his over-all response seems to have been good-humoured[3] and courageous acceptance. His friends and acquaintances have provided a series of penpictures which reveal the increasing helplessness of the almost-blind Joyce as he appeared to the world at large.

Even in youth and in good health his eyes had attracted attention. Gerald Griffin remarked how Joyce while he anathematized the Abbey Theatre in the National Library 'stared fixedly with his steely grey-blue eyes into space' and Padraic Colum found Joyce aloof, 'and his blue eyes, perhaps because of defective vision seemed intolerant of approach.'

Frank Budgen recalled their first meeting in 1918 with a painter's visual perception.

> Following Taylor's look I saw a tall slender man come into the garden through the restaurant. Swinging a thin cane he walked deliberately down the steps to the gravelled garden path. He was a dark mass against the orange light of the restaurant glass door, but he carried his head with the chin uptilted so that his face collected cool light from the sky. His walk as he came slowly across to us suggested that of a wading heron. The studied deliberateness of a latecomer, I thought at first. But then as he came nearer I saw his heavily glassed eyes and realised that the transition from light interior to darkening garden had made him unsure of a space beset with iron chairs and tables and other obstacles.

Budgen observed that 'Behind the powerful lenses of his spectacles his eyes are a clear, strong blue, but uncertain in shape and masked in expression.' Later Budgen noticed that

> Joyce's eyesight made his manner of looking at pictures strange and peculiar. I have seen him take pictures when their size allowed him to do so and look at them close up near a window like a myope reading small print.

Augustus John, too, was struck by Joyce's odd way with pictures: 'Although almost blind [he] took a great interest in my drawings, examining them microscopically through his powerful double lenses.'

Diseased eyes lose their lustre and perhaps some details of Sylvia Beach's recollections of Joyce in the early 1920s should be accepted with reserve: 'His eyes, a deep blue, with the light of genius in them, were extremely beautiful. I noticed, however, that the right eye had a slightly abnormal look and that the right lens of his glasses was thicker than the left.'

Arthur Power visited Joyce frequently at the time when *Ulysses* was being printed.

At that time he was living in a flat near the Eiffel Tower, and it was a common thing to walk in and find him lying on his bed stuping his eye in the darkened room. This terrible and aggravating misfortune he regarded, as far as he was able, with the detachment of a writer, noting every symptom and phase of these attacks. And it was a constant practice of his, as he drove across the Place de la Concorde on his way to visit the oculist in the evening, to test the strength of his vision by counting the total number of lights in the square, which he knew, though for me, I had always regarded them as countless; like those of a constellation.

One of the early subscribers to *Ulysses* was Ernest Hemingway who, in *A Moveable Feast*, recollected dining beyond his means in Michaud's and seeing the Joyce family there, 'Joyce peering at the menu through his thick glasses, holding the menu up in one hand.'

Mary Colum recalled a walk with Joyce in Paris.

I remember as we went along I read an advertisement that was across the street. 'Can you really read what is over there?' Joyce asked me in surprise. Then I realised how poor his eyesight was. His eyes often had the lonely, patient look of the blind.

She remembered, too, Joyce writing *Work in Progress* on long strips of paper or cardboard with different coloured crayons.

Not having seen him for twentyfive years John Eglinton called on Joyce.

I waited for him in the lounge of his hotel and presently a slim tallish man advanced into the room, gazed helplessly about him through large round glasses and then stood for a few moments with bent head. He was moving away again, when I touched him on the shoulder and looked into a face which I clearly recognised. It had grown unexpectedly massive, through toil, no doubt, and suffering, and the handsome brow beetled in a manner I had forgotten, but the Dublin brogue and the musical intonation remained unaltered. The liquid-burning eyes were now, alas, hidden behind large dark glasses, and as we turned towards an unoccupied corner of the room I felt a surge of pity for his Miltonic affliction.

Lucie Noël whose philosopher husband Paul Léon, a Russian exile, was Joyce's amanuensis, 'manager' and close friend from 1928 on, remembered Joyce 'groping for a tumbler of water on the table and not finding it' and how after he visited their appartment in the rue Casimir-Périer someone would always guide him downstairs and see him safely into a taxi.

Sometime after Vogt's operation:

> . . . when we were all sitting in our livingroom he suddenly exclaimed: 'Mrs Léon are you not wearing a white blouse? I believe I can see something white.' This seemed to all of us an event of tremendous importance, and we were all moved by the hope that Joyce's eyes were getting better. He claimed he saw better with the artificial pupil than with the 'well eye.'

When Joyce and Paul Léon went walking arm in arm in the Paris streets they made such an arresting sight—Joyce looking skywards his hat at an angle on his head, Léon shuffling with a scholar's stoop—that someone called them *'l'aveugle et le paralytique.'*

Louis Gillet, the French Academician, who came to know Joyce more intimately than most, recalled Joyce speaking about a passage from *Work in Progress*: 'this is the merriest thing I ever wrote and I was in despair.' Gillet's *Claybook for James Joyce* from which the following passages are taken should be read by everyone interested in the enigma of Joyce.

> I can still see the spectre of the author of *Ulysses*—gaunt as if discarnated, his profile like a crescent under his thick lenses, eye vexed and obstructed by a black felt patch—slide gropingly, with a step at the same time hesitant and lordly, among respectful people ready to make room for him.
>
> . . . For twenty years, the great poet was half-blind; the left eye was lost and in the other remained only a flap of retina. Reading and writing was a torture . . . I still see him, in order to decipher a text, placing the paper sideways and bringing it into the narrow angle where a ray of his ruined sight still subsisted. To wend his way in the street, he went along tapping the iron point of his white cane on the pavement, with a gesture groping and self-assertive. In fact, this unusual walker was not of this world.

He was a stranger, a phantom whose shadow only was among us and who wandered with sureness in the universe of his thoughts and memories.

Harold Nicholson called on Joyce in February 1934 in his appartment at 42 rue Galilée. Joyce entered the room quietly moving cautiously and feeling the furniture.

> . . . his sockless feet slipped tentatively along the parquet in carpet slippers of blue and white check . . . From time to time his hand would finger and adjust the loose lenses in his heavy steel spectacles. His half-blindness was so oppressive that one had the impression of speaking to someone who was very ill indeed.

Patricia Hutchins spoke to those who remembered Joyce in S. Gérand-du-Puy where he had settled at the beginning of the war. 'He was almost blind and used to feel for the pavement with his white stick . . .' And an ironmonger recalled that Joyce had come to him to get his stick mended and that one day it was the talk of the place that Joyce had narrowly escaped being run down by a car near the hairdresser's.

CHAPTER 17

A STOMACH DISORDER

'Eh bien, il était bien rusé, Monsieur Joyce!' the hairdresser's husband remarked to Patricia Hutchins who was also told how in S. Gérand-du-Puy in 1940 Joyce would slip into the Café de Paris through the backdoor—'So that his wife or Madame Jolas wouldn't see him have a Pernod there! It wasn't supposed to be good for him, some kind of pain he had at times.'

For years, off and on, he had been bothered by abdominal symptoms of one kind or another, the earliest being the unpleasant hunger pangs which he had experienced in Paris.

> Your order for 3s/4d of Tuesday last [he wrote to his mother in 1903] was very welcome as I had been without food for 42 hours (forty-two). Today I am twenty hours without food. But these spells of fasting are common with me now and when I get money I am so damnably hungry that I eat a fortune (1s/-) before you could say knife. I hope this new system of living won't injure my digestion.

A week later he informed his father: 'I am sorry to say that after my dinner on Tuesday I became very ill and at night I had a fit of vomiting.' But the pain by which he was afflicted in Pola in December 1904, and which he mentioned in a letter to Stanislaus, appears to have been more alarming and severe: 'One night I had a severe cramp in my stomach and Nora prayed, "O my God, take away Jim's pain."'

Because of its rich endowment of autonomic nerves the stomach is at the mercy of the emotions and reacts to tension, anxiety, and disappointment. The interplay may occur subconsciously but aware of the psychosomatic relationship, Joyce acknowledged it when writing to his brother from Trieste in October 1905: 'I received your letter today after two days' severe gastrical disarrangement consequent on your silence.' And from Rome two years later: 'I must break off this letter now as I am not very well. All this trouble and bustle always finds its way into the bosom of my stomach.'

While in Rome he seems to have fasted and feasted alternatively. At times the feasting was Gargantuan.

Yesterday being the anniversary of the day of my espousal and of the day of the gladness of my heart, we went out into the country and ate and drank the greater part of many larders. Here is the full and exact list of what we ate yesterday.

10.30 a.m.	Ham, bread and butter, coffee.
1.30 p.m.	Soup, roast lamb, potatoes, bread and wine.
4.00 p.m.	Beef-stew, bread and wine.
6.00 p.m.	Roast veal, bread, gorgonzola cheese and wine.
8.30 p.m.	Roast veal, bread and grapes and vermouth.
9.30 p.m.	Veal cutlets, bread, salad, grapes and wine.

There is literally no end to our appetite. I don't believe I ever was in better health. . . .

In later years he ate sparingly, merely toying with the fine fare of the best restaurants in Paris. And his health, of course, was wretched then, dominated by the tedious and incapacitating eye-illness beside which the abdominal symptoms may have been something of a minor annoyance, erupting every now and then into a more acute crisis.

He liked to compare notes with other sufferers and he often discussed his symptoms with Mrs Stuart Gilbert who had a stomach ulcer. More struck by the similarity of their pains than by the dissimilarity of their personalities they inclined to argue that Joyce, too, must have an ulcer. The doctors whom he consulted had a different interpretation.

Certainly that diagnosis could not have explained all of Joyce's alimentary symptoms and he referred to a particularly unpleasant indisposition when writing to Frank Budgen in 1928.

As for me the worst Xmas and New Year I can remember. I have been and am painfully ill—Inflammation of the intestines—caused by overwork and worry . . . I shall really have to go away and rest or I shall have a worse nervous breakdown.

He continued to be troubled by 'tiredness and intermittent pains' of which Paul Léon remarked in a letter to Harriet Shaw Weaver, 'as with every exceptional personality his pains cut deeper into his system than with us—but his recovery—as he often does recover—is the more admirable.'

Lucia's mental illness was a constant worry to her father whose disquiet concerning his own problems was increased when a misguided person told him in March 1933 that his eyes were ruined, and that Vogt would never agree to operate on him again. Having slept badly for several nights Joyce experienced occipital headache and immediately jumped to the conclusion that he was developing meningitis. A 'collapse' ensued but Dr Debray expressed an optimistic prognosis. According to Paul Léon the doctor examined Joyce 'very minutely'; the blood-pressure was normal for his age, 140/80. 'He examined his liver and digestive tube and he emphatically says that they are in perfect order. . . .'

But Léon's account to Miss Weaver leaves us in no doubt that however well the *soma* was functioning the *psyche* was rebelling.

> And as regards himself though I repeat I find him much stronger he still perhaps as a reaction varies from states of great irritation and impotent fury to sudden lachrimose fits. These happily are very rare now. I prefer him furious to the state of dejection he was in last week.

A month later Léon described a further crisis.

> On Friday night Mr Joyce suffered from a very acute attack of colitis and could not sleep at all with the result that in the morning he could not move from tiredness and from the continuing soreness of all his inside and muscles. I saw him in the morning . . . and he was in a rather desperate condition. After I had gone in the afternoon the attack came back this time it was so extremely acute that Mrs Joyce and Miss Joyce got alarmed. You cannot imagine how strong these pains can be and how utterly helpless and strengthless they leave Mr Joyce. His son was called up and eventually, in the absence of Dr Debray, Dr Fontaine was asked to come. She came only by six o'clock when the spasmodic attack had passed. She thoroughly examined Mr Joyce and to our general relief found that there was nothing the matter with him at all. She does not think that he suffers from colitis but on the other hand attributes the dreadful spasms to a disequilibrium of the system of the sympathetic nerve with the focus of the dislocation in the epigastric part of his stomach provoking the terrible pains. She did not think it necessary to prescribe any particular diet and on the contrary declared that the state of his intestines was infinitely better than they were when she last saw them i.e. 3 or 4 years ago. In this part of her diagnosis she in fact confirms what Dr Debray told me. But she insisted perhaps even more emphatically than he did that absolute

and complete calm was necessary in fact a rest cure was not only advisable but thoroughly needed. Since this visit Mr Joyce seems to be physically better. . . .

He was sufficiently well to visit Zürich, Evian-les-Bains, and Geneva during the spring and summer of 1933 but soon after returning to Paris he was laid up for a week with abdominal pain. Paul Léon kept Miss Weaver informed: 'Dr Debray who was alone in Paris came to see him and relieved the pains which were sometimes continuous for seven or eight hours by laudanum compresses. Mr Joyce had lost seven kilo during the summer. His diagnosis was decidedly that the causes of the pains were due to nerves and as you know the hell which Mr Joyce has been going through all the summer and which was however he says but a culmination of continuous worry in the last four or five years there is little reason to be surprised that his nerves gave way at last.'

Debray complained that his patient's family and over-officious friends put *'une interpretation trop facile'* on the case. The doctor disagreed with their diagnosis and protested that any doctor who had seen Joyce for more than fortyeight hours would not agree with their interpretation.

What was the facile suggestion offered by the amateur diagnosticians which so offended Dr Debray? We can only guess, but they may have insisted that Joyce had a peptic ulcer; and since a calamitous complication led to an unequivocal diagnosis of ulcer eight years later we may be tempted, inspired by hindsight, to give the palm to the amateurs.

Anyone with experience of the differential diagnosis of 'stomach pains' will resist that temptation. Peptic ulcer often presents so typically that a student in his first clinical year can recognise it, but it can be mimicked, too, by a dozen disorders. One of these is 'functional pain', nervous dyspepsia due to intestinal spasm in tense, anxious individuals. The clinical picture of the psychogenic ailment is usually not difficult to recognise but, in turn, it can be simulated by an atypical ulcer. The diagnostic puzzle may be solved by X-rays but an ulcer is not always visualized even by the most searching radiological examination. Furthermore, identical symptoms in a particular person may be caused by nervous spasm at one period and later by an ulcer: the diagnosis is beset by pitfalls.

The pain of peptic ulcer—a deep gnawing ache varying in intensity from mild to very severe—is abdominal, situated centrally, or a little

214

to one or other side of the midline between the breastbone and the navel; typically it occurs either before or after meals (being relieved by food in the former instance) and at nighttime; ant-acids ease it whereas certain foods are aggravating; vomiting is not uncommon and relieves the pain temporarily. In the early stages it is episodic, persisting for weeks then disappearing but returning eventually; as time passes the symptom-free intervals shorten and pain become intractable. Reasonably stoical individuals manage, nevertheless, to remain at work despite active ulceration unless compelled to rest by their doctors.

Looking at Joyce's gastric history a pattern of episodic pain is discernible but this alone is insufficient to point infallibly to an ulcer. The crucial evidence—the pattern of symptoms during those episodes —bore little resemblance, apparently, to the symptom-pattern of ulceration. And besides, there was the incontrovertible evidence of an affective disorder, the irritability, irascibility, and weeping fits mentioned by Paul Léon.

A bedside diagnosis in any particular case is arrived at by weighing the sifted evidence of signs and symptoms against all the possible causes—the most probable being the diagnosis. In Joyce's case the evidence favoured a 'functional' nervous complaint in 1933. An X-ray might have disclosed over-riding evidence and prudence would demand that it be done. Joyce or his friends do not mention a barium X-ray in their extensive correspondence where matters concerning his health occupy an important place but we have Dr Fontaine's assurance that it was done and with a negative result.

That the diagnostic process is fallible any experienced clinician will concede without demur. Every diagnosis needs re-scrutiny from time to time. The emergence of a new sign or some subtle alteration of symptoms may afford fresh insights.

Continuity of observation is important, too, and Joyce's peregrinations rendered that impossible. What doctor could follow him through a half dozen countries, or even in Paris to a dozen different addresses?

His favourite physician was Dr Thérèse Bertrand-Fontaine who had a number of expatriate authors among her patients. She attended Samuel Beckett when he was stabbed in the chest, and she also treated Hemingway, Stuart Gilbert, and Mary Colum whose expression of gratitude directed to the profession generally—'I think that doctors are the nearest approach to saints on earth, they devote themselves so wholeheartedly and disinterestedly to their patients'—was doubtless intended for Dr Bertrand-Fontaine in particular.

The Ecole de Médecine is not far from rue Dupuytren where Sylvia Beach first opened her book-shop and library. Thérèse Bertrand while still a student became a member of the library and Miss Beach marvelled at the young Frenchwoman's ability to read all the new books and still pass her examinations with distinction. In due course she became *Médecin des Hôpitaux* an unusual honour for a lady doctor.

Mrs Joyce—introduced by Sylvia Beach—was one of Dr Bertrand's earliest patients and examination revealed cancer of the womb. She was dismayed, as any young doctor would be, to find herself dealing with a celebrity's wife suffering from an unpromising condition. But the operation she advised was 'miraculously' successful. Later Joyce consulted her about his own complaints.

From a doctor's viewpoint she found him a charming, interesting patient with a good sense of humour, his only fault being a lack of co-operation for he thought he knew more than his medical advisers. He obviously did have some medical knowledge of an unscientific type.

By 1939 Joyce's health had declined notably.[1] When Gisèle Freund came to photograph him for *Time* (having used her married name 'Bloom' when seeking his consent) she observed that his lips were dry and bloodless and his face had lost its ruddy glow and was abnormally pale.

She handled him tactfully as his apprehension at the thought of being photographed in colour was apparent; but his nervousness communicated itself to her and she began to drop things and stumble over the wires. The atmosphere became tense and Joyce glared at the photographic apparatus as if it were a predatory beast menacing him. Then to make matters worse he hit his head on the lamp. With a cry, as if stabbed, he clutched his forehead.

'I'm bleeding. Your damned photos will be the death of me.'

'Nora, have you got some scissors?' With admirable presence of mind Gisèle Freund recalled a household cure for bruises.

The ladies pressed the cold steel against an almost imperceptible scratch to prevent swelling and soothed Joyce as they might have soothed a child. Then Miss Freund got on with the job.

He told her that he felt ill and was troubled constantly by stomach cramps and indigestion. While she photographed him he predicted gloomily. '*Finnegans Wake* will be my last book. There is nothing left for me to do but die.'

*   *   *   *

The melancholy mood evoked by his daughter's illness was not inappropriate to the times. Even then jack-booted men were goosestepping on the frontiers. Joyce and his friends were soon to experience an utter upheaval of their lives, their personal problems rendered insignificant by the general tragedy.

From the windows of a hospital where they had lunched together, Sylvia Beach and Thérèse Bertrand-Fontaine watched the refugees pouring into Paris in 1940. And behind them the German armour and the arrogant grey-clad soldiers. Dr Bertrand-Fontaine, who was active in the Resistance, survived the war and still practises in rue de Poitiers. Her twenty-year-old son died in Mauthausen prison camp.

The Joyces joined their friend Maria Jolas in S. Gérand-du-Puy in the Allier. Following later, the Léons were separated on the way; Mrs Léon arrived first, her husband came along next day in a donkey cart.

Towards the end of that summer Mrs Jolas and her daughters went to the United States. The Léons unwisely returned to Paris where on 21 August 1941 the Gestapo arrested Paul. He was imprisoned in Drancy and was shot when he collapsed during a march to an extermination camp.

Eventually the Joyces obtained Swiss entry-permits. Shocked by their undernourished appearance, the friend who met their train in Zurich on 13 December 1940 thought they looked 'like some of the angular figures in a Picasso drawing, huddled together on the platform. Their clothes had grown too large for them and hung loosely about their thin forms.'

But in the relaxed atmosphere of a neutral country Joyce's spirits rose. Christmas day was spent in the comfortable home of old friends. In party mood Joyce sang and performed his famous high-kicking dance.

On Thursday, 9 January 1941 he took his grandson for an afternoon walk and came home laughing and joking with the child. The evening was spent at Paul Ruggiero's birthday dinner at the Restaurant Kronenhalle. Joyce drank a considerable amount of Neuchâtel white wine and had a stomach-ache after returning home. He retired at his usual hour but at four a.m. on Friday 10th he was awakened by sudden intense abdominal pain.

The events of the next twelve hours, understandably, have not been recorded in detail and we are left to re-create that crucial period as best we can: the sudden agony and the vain hope that it would pass; the remembrance of similar crises which had resolved; the lights turned on, the household disturbed, the scene of panic, the need to do something to relieve the dreadful pain; the feeling of helplessness, waiting for the doctor to arrive, each minute dragging endlessly.

By an added misfortune Joyce's usual doctor was away. Another practitioner, a Dr Wehrlii, came eventually, more accustomed no doubt to such nocturnal alarms than the family who welcomed him. The procedure from the doctor's viewpoint was straight-forward, but easier said than done: first to diagnose the cause of the pain; then to take appropriate steps to treat the cause. And it is axiomatic in all medical schools that until the cause has been diagnosed nothing can be given to dull the pain despite the patient's urgent pleas. To neglect this rule is to invite disaster.

Lord Moynihan has said that the clinical picture of a perforated ulcer—a diagnosis necessitating urgent operation—is so characteristic that error is hardly possible.

> . . . the agony suffered by the patient is almost beyond belief, and is written on every line of a face that speaks of torture. The face is pale, haggard, anxious and appealing, the eyes wide and watchful, the brow and temples bathed in sweat, the hair soaked. The patient struggles for breath in short, panting respirations which are wholly costal, for the diaphragm, being an abdominal muscle, is fixed. Words are jerked out in expiration only; every syllable is part of a deep moan. What strikes every onlooker is that the patient's body is rigid and motionless, no slightest movement dare be attempted. If an endeavour is made to touch the abdomen, the patient's hands are at once lifted in protest and in protection, but the chest and abdomen stay motionless. When examination is made, it is realised at once that the patient is cold; and the temperature will rarely be found more than 95° or 96°F. The abdomen is immobile and the muscles are taut and rigid; 'hard as a board' it is said, but if there is anything harder it is the abdomen in this time of catastrophe.

In recalling that night of crisis in Zurich we cannot say if the signs were less typical than usual. Perhaps the history of previous episodes which had settled uneventfully misled the doctor. Perhaps the patient would not brook further delay in the administration of a pain-killing drug. Whatever the explanation an injection of morphine was given, which in retrospect must be seen as a therapeutic error.

His pain eased, Joyce slept. When the doctor returned later in the day he was dissatisfied with his patient's progress and asked for a consultation. In the evening he came back with a surgeon, von

Heinrich Freysz,[2] a man with more than thirty years' experience, a former pupil of Kocher and Sauerbruch.

Freysz found Joyce in a state of great nervousness, his pulse rapid, his belly distended and tender to pressure but lacking the rebound tenderness of peritonitis. The signs which an experienced surgeon would have interpreted without difficulty prior to the morphine injection were by then equivocal. Quite certain, nevertheless, that there was something seriously amiss Freysz insisted that Joyce be taken without delay to the Schwesterhaus Vom Roten Kreuz.

Little Stephen Joyce watched his grandfather being carried out by ambulance men, his sunken eyes wide-open, his body 'writhing like a fish' beneath the restraining straps of the stretcher.

Next morning Joyce was worse. A stomach tube was passed and the discoloured washings gave a positive reaction to the benzidine test for blood. An X-ray showed air below the diaphragm confirming beyond doubt that an ulcer had perforated. But thirty hours had elapsed since the moment of perforation. Peritonitis had inevitably set in, diminishing the likelihood of a successful operation. The mortality rate rises steeply if operation has been delayed: recovery is the rule when cases are dealt with within six hours of perforation; 5 to 10 per cent die when there is a delay of six to twelve hours; more than 25 per cent die if the delay is twelve to twenty-four hours and operations performed in the course of the third day after perforation are seldom successful. And yet, for Joyce, an operation presented the only hope of survival.

The appalling pain convinced him that he had a malignant growth. 'Is it cancer?' he asked Giorgio.

'No.'

'You've never lied to me. Tell me the truth now.'

'It's not cancer,' his son assured him.

'All right, then. But how are you going to pay for this?'

Joyce was taken to the operating-theatre at midday on Saturday, 11 January. Freysz, a skilled operator, used a local anaesthetic. There was a gush of fluid and air when he opened the abdomen. Then without difficulty he located an indurated duodenal ulcer near the pylorus. The perforation measured three millimetres in diameter. He sutured it easily and covered it with a patch of omentum.

Stimulants and an intravenous saline drip were given. Joyce looked better on the Sunday morning. 'Jim is tough,' said Nora daring to feel hopeful. But in the afternoon he had an internal haemorrhage and collapsed. This was a major setback. The simultaneous occurrence of perforation and bleeding is the most dangerous combination of complications which can befall any ulcer patient.

Blood donors were summoned, one of them a Neuchâtel man which Joyce with his liking for the wine of the area thought a good omen. Dr William Löffler[3] used Becquart's syringe to give the transfusion which went without a hitch. But by this time paralytic ileus had developed and Joyce passed gradually into coma. Later he regained consciousness, briefly, and asked Nora to sleep in his room that night. The hospital staff decided, however, that it would be better if Giorgio took her home, and promised to telephone if there was a change.

James Joyce spoke to the nurses at 1 a.m. on 13 January. He asked for his wife and son but his life was ebbing then. 'Loonely in me loneness. For all their faults. I am passing out. O bitter ending! I'll slip away before they're up.' And slip away he did, dying before they could come to him on that bleak January morning.

CHAPTER 18

POST-MORTEM

They'll never see. Nor know. Nor miss me. Nor did they see the
living man again, but missing him they mourned him desolately. He
was buried on 15 January, a dismal day with sleet falling from a bitter
sky. As petrol was rationed taxis were unavailable and almost all the
funeral party, which included Dr Vogt, went up to the cemetery by
tram.[1] 'In the church by the hearseyard. Pax Goodmens will.' They
were shown into a mortuary chapel but there was no priest to direct
the ceremony and they stood about awkwardly, looking at one another
in an almost embarrassed way. There were no prayers; instead of the
usual murmur of human voices the roaring of animals in the nearby
Zoo was faintly audible.

At the graveside the cold was intense, the pale and spectral winter
sun shrouded in mist. Nora,[2] bird-like and swooping, bent forward to
cast a last glance through the glass lid of the coffin as it was lowered
into the clay.

*   *   *   *

Before Joyce's body was removed from the hospital Dr Zollinger had
performed a post-mortem examination in the presence of Dr Freysz
and Dr Löffler. Later M. Paul Speck, a sculptor, took a casting for a
death-mask.

The autopsy was a restricted one, section of the head not being
permitted. In the re-opened abdomen the pathologist encountered
enormously dilated loops of intestine daubed with the fibrinous exudate
of peritonitis. Freysz's patch-work on the perforated ulcer was intact
but when the stomach was opened a second shallow ulcer containing
blood clots was visible in the duodenum. The liver and spleen were
normal, the bile ducts unobstructed but the pancreas had a rag-like
consistency. The heart was normal. The lining of the thoracic aorta
(the principal artery of the body) showed areas of hardening that might
be expected in any elderly man; this degenerative change was extensive
in the abdominal aorta.

The congested lungs were large and when Zollinger drew his knife
across them dark blood oozed from the cut surfaces. The pathologist's

diagnoses were: paralytic ileus and peritonitis; extensive bleeding from a second duodenal ulcer; oedema of the lungs and hypostatic pneumonia; atheroma of the aorta.

*   *   *   *

When Louis Gillet arrived in Zurich on the Sunday following the interment Giorgio showed him the death-mask. To Gillet who had never before seen Joyce's face without the thick lenses which had seemed almost a part of him the mask was bare and revealing.

It was indeed the prominent forehead, the slender cheeks and sharply-etched bones, the determined chin, the long phiz—that is the word—of a Don Quixote just lifting his vizor. I still saw defiance in it. This was not the look of someone vanquished, of someone defunct—as termed by the beautiful language in which the Church embalms its dead, *defunctos,* those that have resigned, relieved themselves from existence—there was never so much hautiness, so much inflexibility, never a look of pride more abrupt!

He discerned in the strangely unrelaxed and disdainfully pouting death-mask an attitude of combat and yet

the mask's lower part stood in contrast with the upper part—as in the mountains where some earth on the slopes is overhung by a bare rock. Joyce was smiling—a smile mischievous and somewhat waggish, the gaiety of an escaped prisoner, of a mystifier who had just played a hoax. This smile seemed to say: 'Good evening! The farce is over, I am out of the trap. Where I am, you will never catch me. You will never know if I made fun of you. Hands off! Your politics, your fights, your tragedies, your playthings, just as you like, much good may they do you. I slip away, unseen, unknown. Disentangle it yourselves, my friends!' It was a smile from beyond all there is, from beyond the grave, the smile of a survivor certain to have come through the venture without loss and, as they say, to have found salvation.

We can picture the elderly critic standing in the parlour of the Pension Delphin with his dead friend's son, gazing at the mask, his mind grappling with shadows. Today a desire to call forth the essence of James Joyce, the man, encounters the almost impenetrable mass of biographical and exegetical material (not a little of the former being

222

discreditable, the latter quite often factually ill-founded) which has accumulated since his death. A daunting task not to be lightly essayed and beyond the scope of the present study, the author of which must be content to regard Joyce as he might regard a patient whose case he has watched with interest, amusement, and irritation for more than a quarter of a century. When such a man dies and the autopsy is over, the doctor, no longer obsessed by diagnosis, suffers a sense of loss. Looking the record over before closing the file he tries to read between the lines to discover finally the nature of his patient's quirks and foibles, the source of his virtues, the depth of his humour, the explanation of his weaknesses.

Few patients leave so well-documented a dossier as Joyce's. Skimming it again we see the toddler in Bray and Dublin and Sunny Jim so receptive to beauty ranging the streets, exploring the suburbs of a city which remained in his mind all the days of his life.

> . . . the cornflowers have been staying at Ballymun, the dusk rose has choosed out Goatstown's hedges, twolips togatherthem by sweet Rush, townland of twinedlights, the whitethorn and the redthorn have fairygeyed the mayvalleys of Knockmaroon. . . .

From Clongowes to Belvedere, narrowly missing C.B.S. North Richmond Street—'Excuse theyre christianbrothers irish?'—and to the university. 'We've had our day at triv and quad and writ our bit as inter-midgets. Art, literature, politics, economy, chemistry, humanity, Etc.'

Meanwhile the once deeply religious youth had lost his faith. 'You were bred, fed, fostered and fattened from holy childhood up in this two easter island on the piejaw of hilarious heaven and roaring the other place.' Drunken, disaffected, and practically penniless he decided 'he would far sooner muddle through the hash of lentils in Europe than meddle with Ireland's split little pea.' With his companion[3]—'eloping for that holm in Finn's Hotel Fiord, Nova Norening' —the aspirant author fled to the meagre living of a language teacher. 'And trieste, at trieste ate I my liver!'

Tormented by poor health and by vacillating publishers, his hand-to-mouth existence was such that Ezra Pound wrote:

> My dear Job: you will establish an immortal record. At what period the shift of terminal sound in your family name occurred I am unable to state, but the —yce at the end is an obvious error. The arumaic —b is obviously the correct spelling. Possibly an

intermediate form Jobce can be unearthed, but the line of your descent from the patriarch is indisputable.

His poverty was eventually relieved by a Civil List grant of £100 annually from the British Government and more munificently by Mrs Harold McCormick (daughter of John D. Rockefeller) and by Miss Harriet Shaw Weaver. His growing literary reputation was crowned by the success of *Ulysses* but in the public eye he became a figure of notoriety. Paul Léon said that when Lady Wright was introduced to Joyce in Paris she seemed taken aback that he was not nude and wearing roses in his hair.

Even at the present day the Irish as a whole show little warmth for Joyce and are slow to participate in the international acclaim which their fellow-countryman has earned. 'He is still, as far as may be possible, blasted by the sneers of minor Irish writers,' declared Seán O'Casey and Basil Payne protests against the general slighting:

> Which is the traitor, then?—the artist, self-consumed
> By silence, exile, cunning; haunted by
> Creation's chimera? or the multitude,
> Eating the gaudy lotus in the land
> Whose hammocks are suspended in the past;
> Where heroes are the order of the day,
> And artists public nuisances or fools?

Mahaffy,[4] one of the earliest scoffers, said, 'It's an ill bird that fouls its own nest. James Joyce is a living argument in defence of my contention that it was a mistake to establish a separate University for the aborigines of this island—for corner-boys who spit into the Liffey.'[5] It can hardly be denied that there was something of the cad in Joyce's character as a young man but he is rejected less for this, or for obscenity, by his co-religionists than for his abjuration of Catholicism. To combine blasphemy and laughter, as he did, is an unforgivable sin!

This revulsion of pious souls[6] is as understandable as the fact that non-Catholic writers have found Joyce's defection laudable. But the former should realize that loss of faith is not a voluntary process and the latter must remember that, to so devout a Catholic as Joyce, the event was traumatic to an incalculable degree. Those who have been raised in agnosticism can view the cosmos with a degree of equanimity that the lapsed-Catholic who has been a fervent believer cannot attain. Pervading the desolate immensity of their new freedom is the echo of St Augustine's great cry, *'Inquietum est cor nostrum donec requiescat in Te.'*

Lying on the deck of the cross-channel steamer in Calais harbour the twenty-year-old Joyce listened to the sound of young voices lifted above the splash of the waves. 'The sea moves with the sound of many scales . . . Beyond the misty walls in the dark cathedral church of Our Lady, I hear the bright, even voices of boys singing before the altar there.' Hearing them he must have known a void in his unbelieving soul.

In *Epiphanies* he expresses a sense of loss and yearning for Mother Church.

> She comes at night when the city is still; invisible, inaudible, all unsummoned. She comes from her ancient seat to visit the least of her children, mother most venerable, as though he had never been alien to her. She knows the inmost heart; therefore she is gentle; nothing exacting; saying, I am susceptible of change, an imaginative influence in the hearts of my children. Who has pity for you when you are sad among strangers? Years and years I loved you when you lay in my womb.

And he expresses beautifully in *Ulysses* the Irish devotion to the Blessed Virgin:

> . . . the quiet church whence there streamed forth at times upon the stillness the voice of prayer to her who is in her pure radiance a beacon ever to the storm-tossed heart of man, Mary, star of the sea.

The clergy refer to 'the gift of faith' but in the Maudsley Lecture for 1968 Dr William Sargent discoursed on 'The Physiology of Faith' illustrating how faith can be suddenly acquired or lost through alterations of brain function. If Sargent's arguments are valid it must be accepted that the conflicts of religious belief so common in adolescence may be influenced by physiological reactions beyond the control of the individual. To whatever organic stresses Joyce, an unusually pious and devout boy, succumbed must be added the disedifying example of his father.

> —O, he'll remember all this when he grows up, said Dante hotly—the language he heard against God and religion and priests in his own home.

His pastors, too, may have unwittingly contributed to his fall from grace. A member of the Capuchin Order has recently referred to the deficiencies of Irish Catholic attitudes to religion, justified by the historical situation, earlier in the century: 'Religion in Ireland . . . has been a strong, assertive Catholicism, aggressive even, with little occasion or energy for reflective self-justification.' This priest saw it as a 'predominantly rural, even "peasant" Catholicism, crude but strong'; he remarked that even today 'there is too much emphasis on sin, too much talk about the sixth commandment and not half enough about the seventh or eighth.' A mind so intelligent, so subtle, so sceptical as Joyce's was inevitably repelled by the crude exposition of the eternal verities to which he listened in the Dublin churches at the turn of the century.

Sargent reminds us that 'without a supportive faith of some sort or another few people can hope to live constructive or happy lives' and we may be sure that in his maturity Joyce cast some regretful backward glances to the City of Zion where he could abide no more. Henry Morton Robinson would have it, indeed, that the two hundred and sixteen 'h.c.e.'s of *Finnegans Wake* derive from the most sacred moment of the Mass symbolising the priest's words at the consecration: *Hoc est enim corpus meum; Hic est enim calix sanguinis mei.*

A consequence of his failure to conform was the quarrel with his mother, a quarrel which seared his soul and from which emanates the appalling vision in 'Circe':

> *Stephen's mother, emaciated, rises stark through the floor in leper grey with a wreath of faded orange blossoms and a torn bridal veil, her face worn and noseless, green with grave mould. Her hair is scant and lank. She fixes her bluecircled hollow eyesockets on Stephen and opens her toothless mouth uttering a silent word. A choir of virgins and confessors sing voicelessly.*

The wound did not heal. Stanislaus Joyce, referring to his last meeting with his brother, said, 'I knew that the idea of conflict between the mother, who lives in fear of God, and the outcast son, wandering upon the hostile earth, was still milling about in his mind, and it saddened me.'

For religion Joyce substituted art—'O, you were excruciated, in honour bound to the cross of your own cruel fiction!'—thereby accepting a bondage to poverty.

His refusal to use his pen in a workaday way to support his family may belong to an admirable tradition which tells literary men never to make

> . . . *a poorer song*
> *That you may have a heavier purse,*

but even the unworldly Ezra Pound did not think that Joyce would have demeaned himself by earning a living.[7]

> Your 'having nothing to offer Dial and Ath' is not really the point. Wot t'ell do I offer the Ath. save a general dislike of the modern English theatre? However it is a question of how much this sort of work wd. bore you, and how much it wd. put you off your real work. I cling to the rock of Gautier, deluding myself perhaps with the idea that he did journalism for years without becoming an absolute shit.

The notion that a man should support his family by his own endeavours may be based on bourgeois values lacking sympathy for the compulsions of a creative temperament. But Lytton Strachey, not by any means a bourgeois, remarked while reading Dostoievsky's letters, 'His life was perfect hell till six years before he died; and his letters are almost entirely occupied with begging for money—always "pour l'amour du Christ." At last whenever you see Christ on a page you skip it because you know that an appeal for 125 roubles will follow. It's deplorable and it's impossible not to have rather a lower opinion of the man.'

Harking back to Joyce's student days Mary Colum said, 'What maturity he had then!' but his dependence on others throughout his life suggests immaturity[8] of character an impression strengthened by additional flaws—a strongly obsessional temperament; a nature highly susceptible to feelings of persecution; a personality which became increasingly rigid and reserved as he grew older.

Those whose acquaintance with Joyce was superficial were often left with an unfavourable impression. His handshake was limp and boneless. 'When he holds out his hand for you to shake,' a lady recalled, 'you feel nothing but five little raw, cold sausages.' He sighed a good deal (a common feature of an anxiety neurosis) and used to exclaim so frequently that his daughter called him 'l'Esclammadore.'

Harold Nicholson has described an occasion in London when the Joyces were invited to luncheon by Constant Huntington, Chairman of Putnam, the publishers.

Mrs Joyce enters followed by her husband. A young-looking woman with the remains of beauty and an Irish accent so marked that she might have been a Belgian. Well dressed in the clothes of a young French bourgeoise: an art-nouveau brooch. Joyce himself, aloof and blind, follows her. My first impression is of a slightly bearded spinster: my second is of Willie King made up like Philip II: my third of some thin little bird, peeking, crooked, reserved, violent and timid. Little claw hands. So blind that he stares away from one at a tangent, like a very thin owl.

The chorus girls in the Stadttheater in Zurich nicknamed him 'Herr Satan;' Hemingway said '. . . he was nice but nasty,' and according to Gisèle Freund, 'No one outside his own family seemed really at home with Joyce. His friendships, even the most intimate, were darkened by friction and misunderstanding.'

But in his relations with his family and with the close friends of his later years the fine qualities of the man emerge. Joyce's letters reveal an extraordinary warmth of affection and irrepressible humour disposing of the charge that he was a cold fish.

An accumulation of events wounded him in mind and body; creation took its toll and through sorrow he eventually matured. 'It was life but was it fair?' The bibulous, libidinous young man grew into the shy celebrity who disliked smutty stories.[9] Given the right company, however, he shed his cares. He once described himself as the 'escaped continentalized Dubliner afflicted with the incurable levity of youth.'

Through the eyes of friends we see a different picture of Joyce. Constantine Curran who knew him better than most said that he was naturally rather a silent person but capable of play-acting, often verging on the grotesque which may have led to his being misinterpreted. His derisory comments in his letters to Stannie regarding so many people are poking fun rather than genuinely intended. Curran lent him small sums of money in his youth: 'for these small endowments in Bewley's or elsewhere he rewarded me by sending me signed copies of his books.' And during the 'twenties and 'thirties: 'Joyce was so generous that he would take possession of you, make all arrangements for your movements in Paris, take you to expensive restaurants and insist on paying the bills.'

Padraic Colum's portrait of the artist on his fortyninth birthday runs as follows:

Slender, well-made, he holds himself very upright; he is tastefully dressed, and wears a ring in which there is a large stone.

The pupils of his eyes are enlarged because of successive operations, but his gaze is attentive and steady. There is a small tuft of beard on his chin. The flesh of his face has softness and colour and the glow that a child's face has. A detail: his hands have now the softness, the sensitivity, of a man who has to depend a good deal on touch. All the lines of his face are fine; indeed his appearance is not only distinguished but winning.

Kay Boyle, too, recalled Joyce as 'a figure of gentlemanly distinction . . . a British diplomat, you might have decided if you didn't know otherwise, in his well-cut grey suit and his felt hat imported from Italy.' Others have described him setting out for the Opera wearing a flowing satin-lined opera cloak, a silk hat set a little on the side of the head, and carrying a monogrammed ivory-tipped cane.

At parties he loved to repeat to Mary Colum rhymes he had learned from grammars as a schoolboy:

> Common are to either sex
> *Artifex* and *opifex*,
> *Convivia, vates, advena,*
> *Testes, civis, incola*

and she remembered his hilarity as he declaimed

> With *nemo* never let me see
> *Neminis* or *nemine*

and how he choked with laughter and cried, 'Oh, the imperiousness of it! "Never let me see!"'

Some of his happiest evenings were spent at the Jolas's home in Neuilly. Maria Jolas a fine musician with a beautiful contralto voice, Joyce a fine tenor, and Giorgio a deep baritone sang solos, duets and trios. In the early hours Paul Léon would sit at the piano to play Chopin, winding up with his repetoire of Gypsy music. And looking 'like a Polichinelli practising high jinks' Joyce brought the festivities to a close with his famous high-kicking dance.

He had a charming way with children who, like dogs, are good judges of people. They loved him because he talked to them simply and seriously as if they were grown-ups.

A devoted father, he was grieved beyond telling by the tragedy of his daughter's illness. What wealth he had attained was gladly disbursed among the mental specialists of Europe in an unavailing quest for a cure. Time and again he confided his distress to Louis Gillet who referred to it movingly:

> During his last years it gave him no peace. The image of his suffering daughter tortured him. This was almost the only topic of our conversations. Sometimes I fancied hearing the complaint of King Lear carrying Cordelia in his arms. *Stabat Mater* was written. The Middle Ages have multiplied the group of the *Pietà*. Few artists except Shakespeare and Balzac knew how to depict the Passion of the Father. Joyce did not write his passion; he lived it.

But despite this, or probably because of it, he prayed with indomitable courage, 'Loud, heap miseries upon us yet entwine our arts with laughters low!' We are left marvelling at his resilience and so it is that glancing back through the chapters of Joyce's life the less commendable features become obscured; his innate kindness, his inextinguishable good-humour, and his captivating moments of extravagance capture the imagination. We remember, for instance, the sad evening in Dublin when he sat on the stairs with his arms about his little sister, comforting her; the occasion at the Paris Opera when he stood up and shouted, to the delight of the crowd, '*Bravo! Sullivan, et merde pour Lauri Volpi*'; the wartime night in La Baule when the soldiers, enchanted by his singing, stood him on a café table and made him lead them in the Marseillaise. Add to these human things his genius and we have no option but to echo Ezra Pound's toast: 'May his spirit meet with Rabelais' ghost at Chinon and may the glasses never be empty.'

NOTES: CHAPTER 1

1. The 'Square' as Basil Payne points out had only three sides; Joyce was
   > Begotten on the humble, terraced base
   > Of this green-parked, isosceles triangle,
   > Miscalled, by public arrogance, a 'Square.'

2. Baron Guillaume Dupuytren (1777-1835) the son of a French provincial attorney was the most celebrated surgeon of his day. His prowess won him a title and great wealth but he brooked no rivals and he had no friends. He was known as 'the brigand of the Hôtel Dieu' and was described as 'the first of surgeons and the least of men'.

3. The ordeal of confession was also mentioned by Thomas Moore in *Travels of an Irish Gentleman*: 'I used to set off early in the morning to — street chapel, trembling all over with awe at the task that was before me, but finally resolved to tell the worst without disguise. How vividly do I, even at this moment, remember kneeling down by the Confessional, and feeling my heart beat quicker, as the sliding panel in the side opened, and I saw the meek and venerable head of the kind Father O'H—stooping down to hear my whispered list of sins. The paternal look of the old man,—the gentleness of his voice, even in rebuke,—the encouraging hopes he gave me of mercy as the sure reward of contrition and reformation,—all these recollections come freshly over my mind, as I now read the touching language employed by some of the Fathers on this subject . . .'

4. Kafka and Gertrude Stein also considered a medical career. The former's period as a medical student was brief; Miss Stein spent some years at the Johns Hopkins Hospital but did not take her final examination.

NOTES: CHAPTER 2

1. James Nahor Meenan (1879-1950) a classical scholar at Clongowes was physician to St Vincent's Hospital.

2. One of Ireland's most distinguished anatomists he was born in Ballinrobe, Co. Mayo in 1864 and educated at Castleknock College and the Catholic University. He died on 23 January 1905.

3. Patrick Joseph Fagan, F.R.C.S.I., a former pupil of Castleknock College, had intended to study for the priesthood. He was surgeon to St Vincent's Hospital and died suddenly at his own fireside on 10 October 1910 at the age of forty-six.

4. Alexander Joseph McAuley Blayney, F.R.C.S.I., professor of surgery at U.C.D. and surgeon to the Mater Hospital, died suddenly on 12 July 1925 while strolling with his wife and young children across Portmarnock golf links.

5. T. J. Maclagan, M.D., M.R.C.P., of 9 Cadogan Place, Belgrave Square, was Physician in Ordinary to their Royal Highnesses Prince and Princess Christian of Schleswig-Holstein.

NOTES: CHAPTER 3

1. 'By the stench of her fizzle and the glib of her gab know the drunken draggletail Dublin drab. You'll pay for each bally sorraday night every billing sumday morning.' (*F.W.* 436. 25)

2. Not to be confused with 'the Citizen' in *Ulysses*.

3. A celebrated handball contest between the students and the police held in Mountjoy Police Station was described by Byrne in mock-Hiawathan stanzas:

Sickly green, and still more sickly,
Till he staggered from the ball-court
To his friends who gathered round him
And he spoke to them in thus wise:
'Weak and sick I am, my comrades,
Sick and weak, I am as Panguk
Much I fear I've got the wigwumps
In my insides, for I cannot
Play until I rest a little.'
Then we helped him to the fireside
In the mess-room of the Poleese,
Where we placed him on the hearthstone,
Just beside the burnt-out embers,
And the Medas stood about him
As he lay in sleep Nepakwim.

4. This would have won notoriety rather than esteem but there are many of his ilk in Dublin as in any city. The present author recalls a cadger of the 1940's who, planning his evening, said, 'If I've money I'll go to the cinema but if I'm broke I'll have to go drinking.'

5. One of Broderick's verses was printed in *St. Stephen's*:

Plumer tried the Boers to foil
With alcohol and castor oil,
And when they still his men defied
He tried sulph. hist. and –ous Chloride,
Guaiacum resin that was all;
And out of Cronje took a fall.

6. *St. Stephen's* reporting the Mater 'smoker' on Shrove Tuesday, 1904: 'Mr. S. P. Kerrigan, with darkened visage, dancing with wonderful agility, that most intricate of all dances—"The Cake Walk"—in an inimitable manner. His short, crisp, curly locks quite suited the character which he so well personated.'

NOTES: CHAPTER 4

1. How interesting that the well-off Dr. Henry Gogarty recognised the worth of an institution which the Joyces' spendthrift father disparaged! ('Christian Brothers be damned! said Mr. Dedalus. Is it with Paddy Stink and Mickey Mud?') Joycean commentators, who sometimes lack objectivity, might keep this point in mind.

2. One wonders what the British ENT surgeons thought of the ebullient Irishman who refers to this meeting in later years. 'I remember a cross section of the skull which I drew on a blackboard to demonstrate something to the members of my section. Someone asked me what the *crista galli* was. I told him that it represented "The Cock of the North;" nobody laughed but the Scotsmen.' He also remarked: 'I learned much in Aberdeen, though not necessarily from the medical conference I was summoned to attend. I learned that every Scotsman is potentially a poet.'

3. An example is the shaft directed at a surgeon involved in a divorce case.

'There's a man who made his reputation with his knife and lost it with his fork.' And in a somewhat less malevolent vein his utterance in the Royal College of Physicians when looking about him he saw that he was standing near the portrait of a former President, Dr. John Magee Finny:

John Magee Finny
My fee is a guinea
The branchial cleft closes late
In the finny tribe—
That's why that fellow
Always talked through his neck.

4. His wit was sometimes coarse. Anna Livia, adulterated by sewage, is not the purest of rivers and after taking part in the Liffey swim Gogarty said: 'I wasn't really swimming, just going through the motions.'

5. Gogarty was referring to the *Primary* examination for Fellowship.

NOTES: CHAPTER 5

1. A former Assistant Master of the Coombe Hospital Dr. Wm. Roe, M.D., F.R.C.S.I., lived at 13 Fitzwilliam Street. He was professor of midwifery at the R.C.S.I. 1877–93.

2. Despite (or possibly because of) his daily contact with so many women Sir Andrew opposed a resolution to admit females to the Fellowship of the College and in doing so perpetrated an Irish bull. 'This is a dreadful resolution,' he said. 'I hope that the College will throw out this resolution and will throw it out not only unanimously but unanimously by a large majority.'

3. The late Dr. D. Macnamara of Corofin, Co. Clare.

4. The composition of his library does not, of course, give us even an approximate idea of the extent and range of Joyce's reading. Stuart Gilbert told T. E. Connolly, author of *The Personal Library of James Joyce* that, 'Even before he weeded it out . . . his library was remarkably small. He rarely read modern books and kept few of the many that were given to him.' 468 items were acquired by the Lockwood Memorial Library of the University of Buffalo. Among the periodicals listed (including *The Baker and Confectioner*, August 9, 1929, *The Hairdressers' Weekly Journal*, August 10, 1929, *Poppy's Paper*, *Television Magazine*) are *The Optician and Scientific Instrument Maker*, August 9, 1929 and *La Psychologie et la Vie* II No. 10, October 1928. Items 67 and 165 are Jacques Descroix's *La gynecocratie ou la domination de la femme . . . précéde d'une etude sur le masochisme dans l'histoire et les traditions* par Laurent Tailhade, Paris 1902, and Allan Kardec's *La genèse les miracles et les prédictions selon le spiritisme* Paris 1883.

5. These have been closely examined by R. J. Janusko and P. F. Herring to whose publications readers are referred for detailed information.

6. The gestation chart in the British Museum note-sheets starts at the first month: 'corion; amnion; yolk; punctus; solitary; worm.' There are no notations for the fourth month in either chart.

7. For Joyce the hall through which Bloom enters represents the fallopian tube, which is topsy turvy anatomy; the hall should be the 'vestibule' and one inevitably recalls the words of Tom Garry, a famous Dublin anatomy grinder: 'the vestibule, a place of pleasure.'

NOTES: CHAPTER 6

1. Patrick Boyle points out in his essay in *A Bash in the Tunnel* (ed. Ryan) that these are technical terms used in distilleries and do not refer to 'swoons and endoparisitic helminths'.

2. And also the passage in *Finnegans Wake* p. 540: 'This seat of our city it is of all sides pleasant, comfortable and wholesome. If you would traverse hills, they are not far off. If champain land, it lieth of all parts. If you would be delited with fresh water, the famous river, called of Ptolemy the Libnia Labia, runneth fast by. If you will take the view of the sea, it is at hand. Give heed!'

3. Extract from a letter to Thomas Bodkin from James Stephens, August 2nd, 1914: 'I have dipped into Joyce's book. It is interesting but unpleasant and must be counted among his many wild oats, that man's crop seems interminable. I wonder what he would do now if he were to write, having got rid of these illnesses he might do good work for he knows how to write, or he may be one of those whose youth is his sole energy and who grow old and barren in a flash.'

NOTE: CHAPTER 7

1. James Little (1837-1916) lived at 14 St. Stephen's Green, N. He was physician to the Adelaide Hospital and held the chair of physic at T.C.D. For some years he was editor of the *Dublin Journal of Medical Science*.

NOTES: CHAPTER 8

1. George Francis Macnamara, L.R.C.S.I., L.A.H., formerly a surgeon in the Irish Transvaal Ambulance Corps was Resident Medical Officer to the South Dublin Union Workhouse.

2. Constantine Curran visited him and found him edentulous, physically decayed, and mentally confused.

NOTES: CHAPTER 9

1. We find, however, from the 'suppressed letters' in the Cornell Joyce Collection that she was sometimes prepared to take the initiative.

2. After the elopement Francis Sheehy-Skeffington referred to Nora as Joyce's 'companion'.

3. 'In my letter to Giorgio I mention that I had simply sent on F's opinion. Nobody knows anything about rheumatism except that young people are liable to get it. As for the splendour of American hospitals close your eyes for a moment and try to imagine what the Dublin one (sic) must be like after 12 sweepstakes. Can you see those golden staircases, the diamond studded doors, the bedspreads of solid African ivory, the curtains of silk from Samarcand? What a wonderful animal is the horse!' (J.J. to Giorgio and Helen.)

NOTES: CHAPTER 10

1. Robert Menzies McAlmon b. Clifton, Kansas 9 March 1896 son of a Presbyterian minister, d. 2 Feb. 1956.

2. R. E. Knoll gives the following summary of McAlmon's later years: 'By 1935 McAlmon's literary life was nearly complete. Aside from a few poems

printed in a few little magazines, he wrote nothing more. Wandering and living hard, he was of considerable concern to his old friends. The war found him still in France. He did not return finally to the United States until 1946 when he went to El Paso. There he worked for his brothers in a surgical supply house. Having contracted tuberculosis as early as 1940, in the Fifties he went to the deserts of the Southwest. He died there, in the desert, in February 1956. It is said that he was discouraged and embittered at the last.'

3. Vaziri has studied the incidence of oligophrenia, psychopathy, and alcoholism in the families of 219 schizophrenic patients. The occurrence of feeblemindedness and psychopathy did not exceed that in the general population. Alcoholism, however, was surprisingly high (13.3 per cent) and occurred in 26 per cent of the parents of schizophrenics (46 per cent of the fathers).

NOTES: Chapter 11

1. His predecessor at the Hospital for Stone was another Irishman, Sir Peter Freyer (Dermot Freyer, his son, the author of *Rhymes and Vanities*, *Not All Joy* etc. was a friend of Oliver St. John Gogarty), an expert at prostatectomy. Swift Joly lacked Freyer's panache. A slow-moving man, never in a hurry, his letters were invariably signed 'In haste' to the amusement of his colleagues, one of whom said that he was neither swift nor jolly.

2. By an odd coincidence that would have charmed Joyce a beach club at Pornichet, a short distance from *l'Hôtel des Charmettes*, is called 'Nausicaa.'

NOTES: CHAPTER 12

1. *One Doctor in His Time*, the autobiography of Bethel Solomons (1885–1965) tells of his various achievements; Irish rugby International, Master of the Rotunda Hospital 1926–33, President of the R.C.P.I. Estella Solomons, his artist sister, married Seumas O'Sullivan.

2. Green-painted public urinals.

3. How very unfair to Sir William Osler, steeped in the best traditions of medicine, Greek, European, and American!

4. The fountain bore an inscription composed by the Earl of Carlisle, the Lord Lieutenant: 'This fountain has been placed here—a type of health and usefulness—by the friends and admirers of Sir Philip Crampton, Bart., Surgeon-General to her Majesty's Forces. It but feebly represents the sparkle of his genial feeling, the depth of his calm sagacity, the clearness of his spotless honour, the flow of his boundless benevolence.'

5. His son, Dr. L. E. Werner, recalls a coloured inset in the consulting-room which may explain 'cheerful window'.

6. Louis Aloysius Byrne, F.R.C.S.I., who lived at 79 Harcourt Street, was surgeon to Jervis Street Hospital.

7. It was said of Sir Charles Cameron (1830–1921) that 'he appeared to be a permanent feature of Dublin life'. He was Public Analyst and M.O.H. for the city retaining the latter post (though he had relinquished the duties a few years previously) at the time of his death. Commenting caustically on his career someone said, 'there is little doubt that he would have taken a higher rank as a sanitarian had he retired from office a generation ago'.

8. John Stephen McArdle (1859–1928) had a boyhood ambition to be a jockey and was briefly apprenticed to a trainer before studying medicine. His

fabulous success in surgery places him among the 'surgeon princes'.

9. Sir William Thornley Stoker, Bart. (1845–1912) held appointments as a surgeon to Baggot Street and the Richmond Hospitals and was President of the R.C.S.I. in 1894–96. A governor of the Irish National Gallery, an art collector, he was Hon. Professor of Anatomy to the Royal Hibernian Academy of Art.

10. Dr Sigerson lived at 3 Clare Street close to Finn's Hotel. Joyce advised Nora to consult him in September 1904: 'I hope you haven't got that horrible pain this morning. Go out and see old Sigerson and get him to prescribe for you.' Her complaint may have been a female equivalent of a minor malady which Gogarty called 'engaged man's gonad' a dull ache following prolonged and unrelieved genital tumescence.

11. There was, however, a Dr. Thomas Dawson Finucane (c. 1823–1920) in Blackrock, some miles from Paddy Dignam's residence.

12. Bohemian football club for amateur soccer players.

13. A prize-winner at T.C.D. Dr. Collins took the M.R.C.P., Lond., in 1913 and was elected F.R.C.P. in 1931. He held appointment as Honorary Clinical Pathologist and Honorary Physician to the General Hospital, Cheltenham. D. 1966.

14. The son of a crofter and dealer in farm implements Corrigan (1802–1880) was educated in the Lay College attached to the seminary at Maynooth, Sir Patrick Dun's Hospital, and Edinburgh University. He held appointments at Jervis Street and the Richmond Hospitals and from the former published a famous paper 'On the Permanent Patency of the Mouth of the Aorta, or inadequacy of the Aortic Valves'. He was well known abroad; aortic incompetence was called *maladie de Corrigan* and in Arcachon there is an 'Avenue de Corrigan'. In addition to professional publications he wrote a book entitled *Ten Days in Athens*. From 1870 to 1874 he was a Member of Parliament.

NOTE: CHAPTER 13

1. Marcel Brion, who with a perception straining credulity, could discern in Joyce's pages 'a strange vibration of cells, a swarming of the lowest Brownian movements under the lens of the microscope,' suggested (*Our Exag.*) that Joyce 'could write an unprecedented book composed of the simple interior physical existence, of a man . . .' but was not, apparently, aware that something of the sort was already incorporated in *Ulysses*.

NOTES: CHAPTER 14

1. 'Made a hottentot of dulpeners crawsick with your crumbs' (*F.W.*).

2. Born Brookfield, Conn. 22 Sept. 1866, Joseph Collins studied at the University of the City of New York. He was founder of the Neurological Institute of N.Y. and professor of nervous and mental diseases at N.Y. Postgraduate Medical School. He was the author of a series, *The Doctor Looks at Biography . . . at Literature . . . at Love and Life . . . at Marriage and Medicine*. In view of his comments on *Ulysses* it is interesting to learn from Ernest Jones that Collins was 'notorious for his proclivity to indecent jokes.' He died from cirrhosis of the liver on 11 June 1950.

3. 'After all obscenity is of divine origin. It began when God united the highest function of the body, and all its incalculable physical, emotional, and

intellectual reactions, with the lowest eliminatory functions in one organ. This was God's dirty little joke, and all the others since speech began . . . have only been variations on that theme.' (Stanislaus Joyce, *Open Letter to Dr Oliver Gogarty*.)

4. The issues involved are discussed in George Steiner's well-balanced essay, 'Night Words.'

5. 'As a matter of fact I know very little about women and you, probably, know less and I think you ought to submit this part of the case to Aunt Josephine who knows more than either of us.' (James Joyce to Stanislaus Joyce, 12 July 1905, *Letters* vol II.)

6. Morse, and Molly's other hostile critics, R. M. Adams, Mary Colum, S. L. Goldberg, H. Kenner, H. Levin, and Darcy O'Brien are cited by Phillip F. Herring ('The Bedsteadfastness of Molly Bloom') who admonishes them in rather immoderate terms.

7. Budgen mentioned a very unusual lady who lived in Locarno; she gave Joyce a valise of books dealing with erotic perversion 'remarking that he might find the contents useful as documentation for his writing.'

NOTES: CHAPTER 15

1. To which Joyce riposted in *F.W.* '*A New Cure for an Old Clap*' (104.23).

2. Paul Léon an intimate during the period that Joyce was writing the *Wake* said, 'Sir, this may be genius, maybe this is art, I grant you all that, but please don't ask me to understand it.'

3. Louis Gillet referred to his extraordinary philological memory and his astounding gift for playing with words in any language.

4. According to Lord Brain this theory was advocated by L. Bloomfield (1914) and by W. Wundt (1928).

5. The Irish, an island race, are not noted for the gift of tongues but Ireland, nevertheless, has produced some remarkable linguists. Father J. J. O'Carroll, S.J. spoke German, French, Italian, and Spanish not only fluently but without a trace of a foreign accent. Applying for a post at the Royal University this very modest man wrote that in addition to those languages, 'I am perfectly at home in *Portuguese*, and I know well the *Dutch, Swedish*, and *Danish* languages. Morover, I have studied *Icelandic* and *Anglo-Saxon*; and to some extent *Roumanian* and the dialect of the Grisons.

'In regard to languages not included in the "Modern Language" Department of the Royal University, I am well acquainted with important languages of the *Turanian, Slavonic*, and *Celtic* Stocks. I have lived in Hungary and made myself acquainted with the *Magyar* Language and Literature.

'I know *Polish, Bohemian*, and *Russian*; as also the leading dialect of the Southern Slavs in its *Servian, Dalmatian*, and *Croatian* forms. I made some study of *Carmiolese* with a native, and have an elementary knowledge of Bulgarian.

'I am an enthusiastic Gaelic student and have contributed original composition to the *Gaelic Journal*, and critical articles on our older literature. I speak the language fluently.

'I have studied *Romaic* and can read *Modern* as well as *Ancient Greek* with fluency.

'I take peculiar interest in the older forms of our Modern European Languages and Mediaeval literature.'

NOTES: CHAPTER 16

1. Arthur Henry Benson, M.B. Dubl., F.R.C.S.I. was Ophthalmologist and Aural Surgeon to the Royal City of Dublin Hospital, Baggot Street and Surgeon and Lecturer in Clinical Ophthalmology at the Royal Victoria Eye and Ear Hospital.

2. Born in Aargan, Switzerland on 31 October 1879 Vogt studied at the local Gymnasium and the Universities of Basel and Zürich and took a medical degree in 1902. He was appointed chief resident physician at the Aargan Hospital in 1909 and in 1920 became Professor of Ophthalmic Surgery at Basel. Three years later he was Sidler Huguenin's successor in the chair of Ophthalmology at Zurich. Meanwhile he had published *The Handbook and Atlas of Slit-lamp Microscopy of the Living Eye.*

An authority on furnace-worker's cataract and retinal detachment he was the pioneer in the use of the electrocautery and of electrolysis in the treatment of the latter. His practice was enormous and his reputation attracted many foreign notabilities. He began his visits to the nursing-homes at 6 a.m. and then operated and lectured at the University Clinic until midday when he had his first meal of the day. In the afternoon and until late in the evening he saw private patients. His manner was gruff and taciturn but he was extraordinarily patient and persistent and had an excellent operative technique. He died on 10 December 1943 after a long illness.

3. He called himself 'the Negus of Amblyopia.'

NOTES: CHAPTER 17

1. Kay Boyle has referred to a health food restaurant in Zurich which the Joyces patronized in 1938. 'It was a depressing place: cold oatmeal was moulded into the shape of pork chops, and then sprinkled with bread crumbs and fried; and beefsteaks were fashioned out of some other substance, and tinted red. Cranberry juice was served in wine glasses, but no alcohol could be purchased there.

2. Von Heinrich Freysz, b. Winterthur, Switzerland, studied medicine in Lausanne, Munich, and Zurich graduating in 1908. His teachers included Kocher, Kronlein, and the redoubtable Sauerbruch. He quarrelled with Sauerbruch who treated his assistants dictatorially and was dismissed from a post at the Kantonspital of Zurich. He worked in Strasburg, Berne, Geneva, and Vallence before returning to Zurich where in 1916 he set up in private practice.

In his early years Freysz was gay but the problems of practice added to an unhappy marriage and the regrettable consequence of his defiance of Sauerbruch evoked a change; he became reticent and introverted. An accomplished general surgeon he later specialized in abdominal surgery. After his death in 1963 a younger colleague described him as, 'A modest unassuming man, respectful of his colleagues, blessed with sound commonsense, methodical in action and consistent in performance; a man of impeccable character and deeply concerned for his patients.'

3. William Löffler has retired from practice. B. 1887, ed. Geneva, Basle, and Vienna Universities he was Director of the Medical Clinic (1921-37) and Medical Policlinic (1937-56) of Zurich University. He has published scientific papers on a variety of subjects and has achieved eponymous fame for discovering 'Löffler's syndrome'.

1. 'Yes, Mr Bloom said, and another thing I often thought is to have munici-pal funeral trams . . . Run the line out to the cemetery gates. . . .' (*U*)

2. Visiting Zurich in 1949 Kees Van Hoek, *Irish Independent* columnist, stayed in the same *pension* as Mrs Joyce: 'She is in her sixties now, medium of height, somewhat plumpish. The auburn tresses have long since turned to carefully coiffed grey curls . . . Of late, arthritis is crippling her. She goes about slowly, at times painfully, with the help of a stick.' He added that 'she would good-naturedly upbraid me if I left the house too late on a Sunday morning to be in time for the beginning of Mass, for she herself is a practising Catholic.' Nora Joyce died on 10 April 1951.

3. 'those hornmade ivory dreams you reved of the Ruth you called your companionate.' (*F.W.*)

4. 'That stern chuckler Mayhappy Mayhapnot.' (*F.W.*)

5. Mahaffy's biographers challenge the authenticity of this comment.

6. 'Those crawthumpers, now that's a good name for them, there's always something shiftylooking about them.' (*U*)

7. Loyal to Joyce, Pound wrote to John Quinn: 'He is also dead right in refusing to interrupt his stuff by writing stray articles for cash.'

8. Cyril Connolly (*Previous Convictions*) referred to Joyce's 'absolute refusal to let himself mature through the spiritual struggles and intellectual discoveries of his time.'

9. Bawdy songs were permissible as Kay Boyle recalls: 'There were to be times in the thirties when he sang for an entire evening with Giorgio and Laurence Vail, French and Italian ribald drinking songs, and one "naughty" Cockney number that went: "I've a little pink petty from Tommy, and a little blue petty from John, but the point that I'm at is that underneath *that*, I haven't got anything on!"'

BIBLIOGRAPHY

A Century of Service. Dublin, 1934.
ADAMS, R. M. *Surface and Symbol*. New York, 1967.
A Page of Irish History. Dublin, 1930.
ATHERTON, J. S. *The Books at the Wake*. London, 1959.
BEACH, S. *Shakespeare and Company*. London, 1960.
de BEAUVOIR, S. *The Second Sex*. New York, 1963.
BENNETT, A. James Joyce's *Ulysses*, *Outlook* (London) 29 April 1922.
BRAIN, Lord. *Speech Disorders*. 2nd ed. London, 1965.
British Medical Journal. A Poet's Anatomy, 9 May 1925.
BROWNE, I. W. and KIERNAN, T. J. The Dilemma of the Human Family.
　J. Irish Med. Assn., LX, 1, 1967.
BUDGEN, F. *James Joyce and the Making of Ulysses*. London, 1934.
—— Joyce and Martha Fleischmann, *Tri-Quarterly*, 189, Winter 1967.
—— *Myselves When Young*. London, 1970.
BYRNE, J. F. *Silent Years*. New York, 1953.
CATTERALL, R. D. Uveitis, Arthritis, and non-specific Genital Infection.
　Brit. J. Vener. Dis., 36, 27, 1960.
—— and PERKINS, E. S. Uveitis and Urogenital Disease in the Male. *Brit.*
　J. Ophthalmology, 45, 109, 1961.
COLLINS, J. *The Doctor Looks at Literature*. New York, 1923.
COLUM, M. *Life and the Dream*. 1947.
—— and P. *Our Friend James Joyce*. London, 1959.
CONNOLLY, T. E. The Personal Library of James Joyce. 2nd ed. Buffalo,
　1957.
CRITCHLEY, MACDONALD. The Neurology of Psychotic Speech. *Brit.*
　J. Psychiat., 110, 353, 1964.
CURRAN, C. P. *James Joyce Remembered*. London, 1968.
—— *Irish Times*. 14 January 1941.
CUSHING, H. *The Life of Sir William Osler*. Vol. I. Oxford, 1925.
DEUTSCH, H. *Psychology of Women*. Vol. I. London, 1946.
DOOLIN, W. *Dublin's Medical Schools—A Retrospect*. London, 1952.
DRABBLE, M. *Jerusalem the Golden*. London, 1969.
EDEL, L. *James Joyce—The Last Journey*. New York, 1947.
EGLINGTON, J. *Irish Literary Portraits*. London, 1935.
ELLMANN, R. *James Joyce*. New York, 1959.
—— *Letters of James Joyce*. Vols. 2 and 3. London, 1966.
—— *Ulysses on the Liffey*. London, 1972.
FABRICANT, N. D. *Thirteen Famous Patients*. Philadelphia, 1960.
FLEETWOOD, J. *History of Medicine in Ireland*. Dublin, 1951.
FORD, W. J. James Joyce An Artist in Adversity. *Quart. Bull. Northwest.*
　Univ. Med. School., 23, 495, 1949.
FREUND, G. and CARLETON, V. P. *James Joyce in Paris: His Final Years*.
　London, 1965.
GANDON, Y. Examen de conscience litteraire de James Joyce irlandais,
　Hippocrate. Paris, 1, 995, 1933.
GARRISON, F. H. *History of Medicine*. Philadelphia, 1929.
GILBERT, S. *James Joyce's Ulysses*. London, 1965.
GILLET, L. Preface to *A Chaucer A.B.C.* by Lucia Joyce. Paris, 1936.

—— *Claybook for James Joyce*. London, 1958.
GLASHEEN, A. *A Second Census of Finnegans Wake*. Chicago, 1963.
GOGARTY, O. St. J. *As I Was Going Down Sackville Street*. London, 1937.
—— *Tumbling in the Hay*. London, 1939.
—— They Think They Know Joyce. *Saturday Review of Literature*. 18 March 1950.
—— *Mourning Became Mrs. Spendlove*. New York, 1948.
—— *It Isn't This Time of Year at All!* New York, 1954.
—— *Collected Poems*. New York, 1954.
GORMAN, H. *James Joyce*. London, 1941.
GOULD, G. *The New Statesman*. 27 June 1914.
GRIFFIN, G. *The Wild Geese*. London, 1938.
HEMINGWAY, E. *A Moveable Feast*. London, 1964.
HERRING, P. E. The Bedsteadfastness of Molly Bloom. *Modern Fiction Studies*, xv, 49, 1969.
—— *The Ulysses Notesheets in the British Museum*. University of Virginia Press, 1972.
HOLROYD, M. *Lytton Strachey*. Vol. 2. London, 1968.
HORIA, V. Viaje a Los Centros de la Tierra. *Tribuna Medica*. 5 December 1969.
HOTCHNER, A. E. *Papa Hemingway*. London, 1968.
HUTCHINS, P. *James Joyce's Dublin*. London, 1950.
—— *James Joyce's World*. London, 1957.
HYDE, D. Preface to *Bards of the Gael and Gall* by George Sigerson. 2nd ed. Dublin, n.d.
JOHN, A. *Chiaroscuro*. London, 1952.
JOHNSTON, D. A Short View of the Progress of Joyceanity. *Envoy*, 5, 13, 1951.
JOLAS, M., Ed. Interview with Mr. John Stanislaus Joyce. *A James Joyce Yearbook*. 1949.
JONES, E. *The Life and Work of Sigmund Freud*, abridged ed. Harmondsworth, 1964.
JOYCE, S. *My Brother's Keeper*. (ed. Ellmann, R.). London, 1958.
—— *Recollections of James Joyce*. New York, 1950.
—— The Background to *Dubliners*. The Listener, 51, 526, 1954.
—— *The Dublin Diary*. ed. Healy, G. H. London, 1962.
JUNG, C. G. *Ulysses*: A Monologue. *Nimbus*, 2, 7, 1953.
KANDEL, L., in *The Hippie Papers*. ed. Hopkins, J. New York, 1968.
KAVANAGH, P. Who Killed James Joyce? *Envoy*, 5, 12, 1951.
KATZMAN, M. B. and HIGGINS, J. W. Determinants in the Judgement of Obscenity. *Amer. J. Psychiat.*, 125: 12, 1969.
KIRKPATRICK, T. P. C. The Schools of Medicine in Dublin in the Nineteenth Century. *Brit. Med. J.* 15 July 1953.
KLEIN, A. M. The Oxen of the Sun, *Here and Now*. 1, 28, 1949.
KNOLL, R. E. *Robert McAlmon*. Nebraska, 1959.
LANGDALE, A. B. *Phineas Fletcher*. New York, 1937.
LIDDENDALE, J. and NICHOLSON, M. *Dear Miss Weaver*. London, 1970.
LIDDY, J. *Esau My Kingdom for a Drink*. Dublin, 1962.
McALMON, R. *Being Geniuses Together*. London, 1938.
—— and BOYLE, K. *Being Geniuses Together*. London, 1970.

MACNAMARA, D. W. Doing the Coombe in 1916. *J. Irish Med. Assn.*, L vii, 102, 1966.
MALLENSON, N. *A Handbook on British Student Health Services.* London, 1965.
MITCHELL MORSE, J. Molly Bloom Revisited. *A James Joyce Miscellany.* 2nd series. 1959.
MONTGOMERY, N. Joyeux Quicum Ulysse. *Envoy*, 5, 31, 1951.
NICOLSON, H. *Diaries and Letters 1930–39.* London, 1966.
NOEL, L. *James Joyce and Paul L. Léon.* New York, 1950.
OBITUARY NOTICE. Riviere: Scientist and Humanitarian. *Arch. Phys. Med.*, 27, 231-3, 1946.
O'BRIEN, D. *The Conscience of James Joyce.* Princeton, 1968.
O'BRIEN, E. *Girls in their Married Bliss.* London.
O'CONNOR, U. *Oliver St. John Gogarty.* London, 1964.
O'MAHONY, B. E. Religion in Modern Ireland. *The Irish Times*, 12 December 1967.
PARSONS, J. H. *Diseases of the Eye.* London, 1923.
POHLMAN, A. G. The Purple Island of Phenias (sic) Fletcher. *Johns Hopkins Hospital Bulletin*, 18, 317, 1907.
POWER, A. *From the Old Waterford House.* Waterford, 1940.
PRESCOTT, J. The Characterization of Molly Bloom. *James Joyce Miscellany*, 3rd series, ed. Marvin Magalanen, Cartondale, 1962.
READ, F. ed. *The Letters of Ezra Pound to James Joyce.* New York, 1967.
REYNOLDS, M. T. Joyce and Nora. *Sewanee Review*, lxxii 29, 1964.
RODGERS, W. R. Joyce's Funeral. *Irish Times*, 20 June 1964.
RUSSELL, J. and RUSSELL, V. Death in Zürich. *The Sunday Times*, 17 January 1965.
RYAN, J. ed. *A Bash in the Tunnel.* London, 1970.
ST. JOHN-STEVAS, N. *Obscenity and the Law.* London, 1956.
ST. STEPHENS. 1902–1904.
SAMILOWITZ, H. *Psychiat. Commun.*, 10, 21, 1968.
SARGANT, W. The Physiology of Faith. *Brit. J. Psychiat.*, 115, 505, 1969.
SASSE, C. Dichter kämpfen um ihr Augenlicht. *Cesra*, Oct.-Dec., 1962.
SCHOLES, R. E. *The Cornell Joyce Collection.* Ithaca, 1961.
SHEEHY, E. *May It Please the Court.* Dublin, 1951.
SOLOMONS, B. *One Doctor In His Time.* London, 1956.
STANFORD, W. B. and McDOWELL, R. B. *Mahaffy.* London, 1971.
STANWORTH, A. and SHARP, J. *Ann. rheumatic dis.*, 15, 140, 1956.
STEINER, G. *Language and Silence.* London, 1967.
SULLIVAN, K. *Joyce Among the Jesuits.* New York, 1958.
THE LANCET, 1, 870, 1969.
THE STORY OF THE NATIONAL MATERNITY HOSPITAL (by a Governor). Dublin, 1929.
THORNTON, W. *Allusions in Ulysses.* North Carolina, 1968.
TURNBULL, A. *Scott Fitzgerald.* London, 1962.
VAN HOEK, K. I Met James Joyce's Wife. *Irish Digest*, xxxv, 23, 1950.
VAZIRI, H. Frequence de l'oligophrenie, de la psychopathie et de l'alcoolisme dans 79 familles de schizophrenes. *Schweiz. Arch. Neurol. Psychiat.*, 87, 160, 1961.
WEBSTER FOX, L. *Diseases of the Eye.* New York, 1904.

WERNER, L. ed. *Swanzey's Diseases of the Eye.* London, 1925.
WHITEHORN, K. *The Observer.* 12 May 1968.
WIDDESS, J. D. H. *The Charitable Infirmary, Jervis Street, Dublin.* Dublin, 1968.
WILSON, E. *The Wound and the Bow.* London, 1952.

ACKNOWLEDGEMENTS

Permission to quote from Joyce's writings was granted by the Society of Authors, representing the James Joyce Estate (*Giacomo Joyce, Letters, Finnegans Wake, Critical Writings, Pomes Penyeach*); by The Bodley Head and Random House, Inc. (*Ulysses*); by Jonathan Cape (*Dubliners, A Portrait of the Artist as a Young Man, Stephen Hero, Chamber Music*); by the Viking Press, Inc. (*Giacomo Joyce, Letters, Dubliners, Finnegans Wake, A Portrait of the Artist as a Young Man, Critical Writings, Collected Poems*); and by New Directions (*Stephen Hero*).

Material from the following books is used with the consent of their respective authors and publishers: *Shakespeare & Co.* by Sylvia Beach, Faber and Faber; *My Brother's Keeper* by Stanislaus Joyce, Faber and Faber; *Pound/Joyce* ed. Forrest Read, Faber and Faber and New Directions; *James Joyce* by Richard Ellmann, Oxford University Press, London and New York; *James Joyce in Paris: the Final Years*, by G. Freund and V. B. Carleton, Cassell and Co.; *Obscenity and the Law* by Norman St. John Stevas, Secker and Warburg; *May it Please the Court* by Eugene Sheehy, C. J. Fallon Ltd.; *Esau My Kingdom for a Drink* by James Liddy, Dolmen Press; *Life and the Dream* by Mary Colum, Dolmen Press; *Our Friend James Joyce* by Mary and Padraic Colum, Gollancz; *Being Geniuses Together* by Robert McAlmon and Kay Boyle, Michael Joseph; *The Complete Dublin Diary of Stanislaus Joyce* ed. George H. Healy, Cornell University Press; *Jerusalem the Golden* by Margaret Drabble, Weidenfeld and Nicholson; *The Second Sex*, by Simone de Beauvoir, Jonathan Cape and Alfred Knopf Inc.; *Girls in their Married Bliss* by Edna O'Brien, Jonathan Cape; Harold Nicolson's *Diaries & Letters 1930–39* ed. Nigel Nicolson, Collins; *Oliver St John Gogarty* by Ulick O'Connor, Jonathan Cape; *From the Old Waterford House* by Arthur Power, Mellifont Press; *Many Lines to Thee* ed. James Carens, Dolmen Press.

Mr. Oliver D. Gogarty, S.C. has graciously allowed me to quote from his father's unpublished letters and from *Tumbling in the Hay*.

It has been my good fortune to experience cordial assistance from the Librarians and staffs of the Library of the Royal Dublin Society and the National Library in Dublin, the Library of the Wellcome Historical Institute, London, the Cornell University Library, Ithaca, New York, the Lockwood Memorial Library, Buffalo, New York, and the Yale University Library, New Haven, Connecticut.

I have been helped in ways too various to mention by the late Mr Frank Budgen, Dr John Clancy of Iowa City, Dr Macdonald Critchley of London, the late Mr Constantine Curran, Mr Jack Dalton, Dr J. F. Meloni of Zürich, Dr Thérèse Bertrand Fontaine of Paris, the late Mr Stuart Gilbert, Mr P. Herriman, Mr Robert Janusko, Dr W. Löffler of Zürich, Miss Jane Lyons of Dalkey, Mr Breon Mitchell, Mr Darcy O'Brien, Mrs Mary T. Reynolds, Mr Paul Ruggiero, Mr Fritz Senn, Dr Pierre Mérigot de Treigny of Paris; if others remain unnamed I ask their indulgence for the oversight. A particular word of thanks is due to Mr Richard Ellmann not only for replying to certain queries but because his scholarly editing of Joyce's letters has provided so much vital information. Finally, my wife and Miss Rita Kearney, my secretary, each in her own endearing way, have been enormously helpful.

15, FITZWILLIAM SQUARE,
DUBLIN.

J. B. LYONS
M.D., F.R.C.P.I.

INDEX

Richmond Asylum, 145
Richmond Hospital, 51-2, 146, 236
Rivière, Dr A. J., 31, 33
Robinson, H. Morton, 226
Rockefeller, John D., 224
Roe, Dr William, 70, 233
Rome, 117, 186, 211
Röntgen, Wilhelm K., 148
Rotunda Hospital, 51, 70-1, 147, 151
Royal College of Physicians, 158
Royal Hospital, 145
Royal University, 55-6
Ruggiero, Paul, 217
Russell, George (AE), 16
Rutherford, Lord, 177, 184
Rutty, Dr John, 153-4
Ryan, John, 234
Salerno, 79
Sargent, Dr William, 225-6
Sasse, Carl, Preface
Sax, Mr and Mrs V. A., 142
Schaurek, Mrs F., 107, 112
Schofield, M., 14
Sensation, 79, 80
Sex, determination of, 73
Shannon, Dr J. R., 189
Sharpe, Dr J., 205
Shaw, G. B. S., 14, 68, 126, 133, 174
Sheehan, Dan, 42
Sheehy, Eugene, 14, 95, 97
Sheehy-Skeffington, Francis, 14, 234
Sigerson, Dr George, 27-8, 151, 153, 236
Sinigaglia, Dr Gilberto, 117, 121
Sir Patrick Dun's Hospital, 145, 148, 236
Skeffington, Mrs, 47
Solomons, Dr Bethel, 147, 235
Solomons, Estella, 235
Sorbonne, 30, 34
Spallanzani, Lazaro, 149
Speech, Physiology of, 176
Sponge, forgotten, 73
Spurzheim, Johann Caspar, 79
Speck, Paul, 221
Stanworth, Dr A., 205-6
Starkie, J. S., 64
St Brendan's (Grangegorman) Hospital, 145

Steevens, Mme Grisel, 145, 147
Stein, Gertrude, 176, 231
Steiner, George, 176, 237
Stephen Hero, 14, 28, 39, 40, 44, 46, 48, 98
Stephens, James, 234
Sterility, 72
Stephens, St., 24, 70-1, 232
Stevas, Norman St John, 165
Stoker, Sir Thornley, 52, 151, 235
Stonyhurst College, 50, 55
Story, G. E., 54
Strachey, Lytton, 165, 227
St. Vincent's Asylum, 145
St. Vincent's Hospital, 146-7
Sullivan, John, 133, 199, 220
Sullivan, Kevin, 21
Swinburne, Algernon, 165
Symonds, Arthur, 33
Synge, John Millington, 31
Taylor, Blanche, 32
Thomas, Dylan, 98
Thompson, Francis, 28
Thornton, Richard, 90
Tibbles, Dr Sidney Granville, 151
deTreginy, Dr Pierre Mérigot, 191
Trench, Samuel Chenevix, 63
Trieste, 65-6, 104-7, 109, 110, 115, 125, 171-2, 185-7, 211
Trinity College, 18, 25, 26, 50, 56
Trollope, Antony, 154
Tuberculosis, 33
Twilight sleep, 73
Tyndall, J., 20
Ulysses, Preface, 22, 27, 35, 49, 56, 63, 70, 72, 90, 109, 124, 146-8, 151, 153, 156, 162-5, 173-4, 185, 199, 203, 208, 224-5, 236
University College, 14-5, 22-3, 29, 38, 44
University College, London, 17
Vail, Laurence, 239
Vallenti, G., 149, 150
Vance, Eileen, 170
Venice, 133
Verlaine, Paul, 33, 35
Vesalius, Andreas, 149
Vienna, 65-7, 70-7
Vincent, Elizabeth, 157
Villon, François, 35